FATHER INVOLVEMENT IN THE EARLY YEARS

An international comparison of policy and practice

Edited by Marina A. Adler and Karl Lenz

D1452446

First published in Great Britain in 2017 by

Policy Press
University of Bristol
1-9 Old Park Hill
Bristol
BS2 8BB
UK
t: +44 (0)117 954 5940
pp-info@bristol.ac.uk
www.policypress.co.uk

North America office:
Policy Press
c/o The University of Chicago Press
1427 East 60th Street
Chicago, IL 60637, USA
t: +1 773 702 7700
f: +1 773-702-9756
sales@press.uchicago.edu
www.press.uchicago.edu

© Policy Press 2017

British Library Cataloguing in Publication Data
A catalogue record for this book is available from the British Library

Library of Congress Cataloging-in-Publication Data
A catalog record for this book has been requested

ISBN 978-1-4473-1899-6 hardcover
ISBN 978-1-4473-1900-9 paperback
ISBN 978-1-4473-1903-0 ePub
ISBN 978-1-4473-1904-7 Mobi
ISBN 978-1-4473-1902-3 ePdf

The right of Marina A. Adler and Karl Lenz to be identified as editors of this work has been asserted by them in accordance with the Copyright, Designs and Patents Act 1988.

Cover design by Dave Rodgers
Front cover image: istock
Printed and bound in Great Britain by by CPI Group (UK) Ltd, Croydon, CR0 4YY
Policy Press uses environmentally responsible print partners

Contents

List of tables and figures

Conclusion

Figure

Notes on contributors

Marina A. Adler (USA) is Professor of Sociology in the Department of Sociology and Anthropology at the University of Maryland, Baltimore County, USA. Her research involves cross-national gender, work and family intersections, inequality (race, class, gender), social policy, and social change.

Matthew Aldrich (UK) is a Lecturer in Economics at the University of East Anglia (UEA), and the Associate Dean for Employability at the Faculty of Social Sciences. His interests are in microeconomics, labour economics and the economics of the public sector. His research includes the relationship between human capital, soft skills and the labour market, the changing nature of work roles in families, and the decline of the male-breadwinner model.

Sara Connolly (UK) is a Professor in Personnel Economics at the Norwich Business School, University of East Anglia (UEA) and the UEA lead for the Eastern Academic Research Consortium (between UEA and the Universities of Essex and Kent) in the Quantitative Social Sciences. Her research interests are in gender and the labour market and current projects include fatherhood in the 21st century, gender differences in the professions, and careers and management in international public administrations.

Petteri Eerola (Finland) is Postdoctoral Researcher and Lecturer of Education and Family Studies at the University of Tampere, Finland. His research focuses on men's parental practices and gendered parenting.

Živa Humer (Slovenia) is Research Fellow at the Peace Institute, Institute for Contemporary Social and Political Studies, Ljubljana, Slovenia. Her current research areas cover topics related to gender, care, families, fatherhood and gender-equality politics.

Jouko Huttunen (Finland) is a Senior Lecturer (Emeritus) of Family Studies in the Department of Education at the University of Jyväskylä, Finland, where he previously served as Professor of Education and Chair. His research focuses on gendered parenting practices in different family contexts and fathering experiences in the narratives of Finnish fathers.

Karl Lenz (Germany) is Professor and Chair of Micro-Sociology, as well a Vice-Rector for University Planning, at the TU Dresden, Germany. His research focuses on the sociology of personal relationships, sociology of gender and the life course.

Margaret O'Brien (UK) is Professor of Child and Family Policy at University College London where she directs the Thomas Coram Research Unit. Her research interests are in fathers, work and family life, comparative studies of parental leave systems, gender, care and work through the life course, and fathers and family support.

Eloise Poole (UK) is a Policy and Research Officer at Arts Council England. She was previously a Senior Researcher in the Children, Family and Work Team at NatCen Social Research. Her research interests include family relationships, the parental role and arts and cultural engagement.

Elisabetta Ruspini (Italy) is Senior Associate Professor of Sociology in the Department of Sociology and Social Research at the University of Milano-Bicocca, Italy. Her research interests include the social construction of gender identities, gender role convergences, and transformations of motherhood and fatherhood.

Svetlana Speight (UK) is a Research Director at NatCen Social Research. Her research interests are in gender, fatherhood and early childhood education and care. Her current projects include fatherhood in the 21st century and an evaluation of early years education in England.

Yve Stöbel-Richter (Germany) is Professor of Health Sciences at the University of Applied Sciences Zittau/Görlitz, Germany. Her research in medical sociology focuses on fertility and gendered aspects of health, and the relationship between inequalities at work and health.

Nada Stropnik (Slovenia) is Senior Researcher at the Institute for Economic Research, Ljubljana, Slovenia. Her main research areas are family policy, social policy, work–life balance, poverty and social inclusion.

Maria Letizia Tanturri (Italy) is Associate Professor of Demography in the Department of Statistical Sciences at the University of Padua, Italy. Her research focuses on the determinants of childlessness and on the relationship between gender arrangements, time use and reproductive behaviour.

Introduction

Marina A. Adler and Karl Lenz

The social context of parenting, care work and paid work, as well as the gender division of labour, has been affected by large-scale societal trends relating to gender values, family structures and workplaces over the last few decades (Kamerman and Moss, 2009; Oláh et al, 2014). As part of the changing landscape of parenting in Western advanced countries since the 1970s, women have increasingly become earners in addition to still being the main providers of childcare, and the dominance of male-breadwinner households continues to erode (Lewis, 2002). However, due to cultural perceptions of masculinity and fatherhood, in daily practice, men's provider position in the family has remained more relevant than their participation in childcare. Specifically, despite increased cultural expectations that men should be active and involved fathers, men have changed much less than women with regard to the amount of care and paid work they perform (OECD, 2012). Fatherhood is clearly in transition and being challenged by often contradictory forces: societal expectations to be both an active father and provider; men's own wish to be more involved with their children; and the institutional context in which fathers work and live. There is a gap between cultural ideals, personal aspirations and the structures that would encourage and facilitate new, more inclusive male identities and active fatherhood (Lewis, 2002; Hobson and Fahlén, 2009, 2012). Hence, in terms of combining work and care responsibilities, mothers have almost closed the gender gap in employment, but fathers continue to show a 'care deficit' (Hochschild, 2002), and increasingly feel work–family conflict (Aumann et al, 2011). This book explores these phenomena in the context of cross-national variation in governmental and workplace policies and their relation to the daily childcare practice of fathers.

Another hallmark of changing gender relations in Western societies is a de-standardisation of the family life course, an increased diversification of the forms of living together and related changes in the gender division of labour (Oláh et al, 2014). The definitions of what constitutes families, 'good' mothers or 'good' fathers have become more inclusive, and everyday parenting practices and experiences vary according to social class, ethnicity, age and sexual orientation. Cross-national research shows that, just as for the case of marriage and parenthood, biological father status and social father involvement are increasingly decoupled (Hobson and Morgan, 2002). Although studies of men's fertility behaviour remain rare, trends over the last few decades show that fewer men are becoming fathers (Eggebeen, 2002) and more men have left fatherhood (Oláh et al, 2002, 2014). Just as women's life course is less determined by maternity and more characterised by 'child-free' time (Presser, 2003; Adler, 2004), paternity-free manhood is on the rise (Marks and Palkovitz, 2004). According to Ehrenreich (1987), men's retreat from marriage and fatherhood as key life goals had already begun right after the Second World War. It appears reasonable to assume that in the current climate of voluntary paternity, those men who want to have children will likely be more involved fathers (Marks and Palkovitz, 2004).

Today, fathers are expected to be more engaged in everyday childcare activities and routine care for children than ever before. Yet, dominant constructions of masculinity, institutional barriers to fathers' increased participation in care work and 'new circumstances' (time pressures, the need for two incomes in increasingly precarious employment situations) may prevent men from spending more time with their children (see Holter, 2007; Hobson and Fahlén, 2009, 2012). Hence, while gender values are shifting towards egalitarianism and societal ideology demands more father involvement, institutional arrangements at work and in the family can prohibit fathers from being active carers in practice (Wall and Arnold, 2007). For example, workplace performance expectations continue to be based on the ideal of the 'unencumbered worker' or 'disembodied worker' (Hobson and Fahlén, 2012), who is available to the workplace 24/7 and free of family obligations. Thus, workplaces do not generally welcome substantial shifts towards shared parental caring in terms of encouraging the use of paternity leave and reduced or flexible hours (Hobson and Fahlén, 2009, 2012).

Until recently, policy measures related to childbearing and child-rearing have targeted mothers rather than fathers because cultural ideals related to masculinity did not include the expectation that fathers are carers for small children. Before the advent of the notion that masculinity can include a nurturing component, fathers were not expected to actively engage in significant amounts of routine care for their children: 'The idea of hegemonic masculinity suggests that, despite the apparent range of ways of "doing masculinity," there remain deeply embedded and subtly coercive notions of what it really means to be a man' (Morgan, 2002: 280). However, recently, competing ideas about masculinity as related to fathering and 'a plurality of competing linkages between fatherhood and masculinities' (Morgan, 2002: 281) have emerged within and among countries. While the specifics of how to be a 'good father' may vary cross-culturally, among advanced countries, the contemporary image of 'active fathers' generally includes a de-emphasis on being economic providers and increased expectations for fathers to significantly participate in childcare (see Ranson, 2012).

It appears that, today, both women and men are increasingly responsible for 'doing it all': good fathers are expected to be providers and carers (Settersten and Cancel-Tirado, 2010; Aumann et al, 2011). In cultural terms, the image of the 'good mother' has moved increasingly away from a stay-at-home mother towards a 'working mother' and that of a 'good father' has moved from an economic provider to a 'working father'. According to Aumann, Galinsky and Matos (2011: 5), there is a 'new male mystique', which means that 'men are experiencing what women experienced when they first entered the workforce in record numbers – the pressure to "do it all in order to have it all"'. The authors found that while societal values have shifted towards gender egalitarianism and women now contribute significantly to family income, men continue to feel 'the pressure to be the primary financial providers for their families' (Aumann et al, 2011: 5). As a consequence, new research demonstrates that not only mothers, but also fathers, struggle to combine employment with parenting activities in the current workplace culture (for a meta-analysis, see Byron, 2005). Hence, the issue of 'boundary management' between work and family (Jurczyk et al, 2009) is now an everyday challenge for both genders. While dominant gender norms expect both women and men to be 'embodied workers', that is, workers who strive to combine child-rearing with employment (Hobson and Fahlén, 2009, 2012), policies in many countries continue to measure good fathering mainly by the economic contributions of fathers rather than by their ability to nurture and provide care.

A growing number of anthologies address cross-national variations in the social construction of fathering (what is expected of good fathers in different cultures), active fatherhood and paternity leave policies (Hobson, 2002, 2014; Shwalb et al, 2013; Eydal and Rostgaard, 2014). New journals, such as *Fathering: A Journal of Theory, Research, and Practice about Men as Fathers*, and special issues in the major family and men's studies journals have been dedicated to studies on various aspects of fatherhood in different countries. In 2011, the United Nations (UN) published a comprehensive report on *Men in families and family policy in a changing world*, which addresses several key topics related to men and fatherhood in families, care work, and gender equality, and includes case studies presenting specific interventions, legal approaches and social policies from numerous countries and cultural contexts across the world.

There is an abundance of recent cross-national research on the effects of 'family-friendly' or 'woman-friendly' policies on gender equality, work–family reconciliation and mothers' or children's well-being (see, eg, Pettit and Hook, 2009; Kamerman and Moss, 2009; Hobson, 2014). Historically, most research in this area has examined how national family policies and benefit levels affect the *work–life balance* [1] of working mothers or the well-being of children in various countries. Fathers' care work and 'father-friendly policies', however, have only recently moved to the centre of sociological questions about the intersection of gendered families, labour markets and welfare states (see, eg, Hobson, 2002, 2014; O'Brien et al, 2007; Gregory and Milner, 2008; Seward and Richter, 2008; Hobson and Fahlén, 2012; Hook and Wolfe, 2012). Despite decades of feminist calls for men's increased participation in care work, comparative policy scholars have – until recently – considered fathers mainly as wage-earners and family providers (Silverstein, 1996). However, according to Kimmel (1987), the development of new ideas about masculinity was inevitable because of the tensions between the prevailing male-breadwinner and involved father ideals. A new cultural construction of masculinity and fathering includes emotional expression, caring and empathy, which are also part of involved parenting, disregarding gender. Dowd (2000) refers to 'nurturing' fatherhood as physical, emotional, intellectual and spiritual care based on the needs of children. This definition not only de-genders childcare, but also separates the idea of fatherhood from mere legal, biological or economic consideration (Marsiglio and Roy, 2012).

The idea that involved parenting is neither sex-specific nor gender-related has entered the debate only relatively recently. Contrary to popular ideas about mothering, Silverstein (1996) points to a lack of research documenting that women are more competent parents or have more capacity to nurture than men. Any observed gender differences in parenting styles appear to be socially constructed based on cultural ideas about appropriate gender-specific behaviours. In fact, Lamb (1987) found that neither men nor women are 'natural' carers – both genders have to learn how to be parents. Nevertheless, essentialist views of mothering, which consider mothers the best carers for children, particularly in the early years, still predominate. According to Oláh, Richter and Kotowska (2014: 24): 'intensive mothering means being child-centred and committed to spending considerable time, money and energy to benefit the child while sacrificing one's own individual needs'. Thus, research shows that unlike in the case of housework, for which women have reduced their time involvement over time, mothers often insist on their time commitment to childcare by reducing their own sleep and leisure time rather than relying on fathers to get involved (Craig, 2007). This may reflect *maternal gatekeeping*, the practice of mothers actively discouraging fathers to more actively participate in childcare (Bianchi and Milkie, 2010; Craig and Mullen, 2011). These ideas are based on an *essentialist maternalist* view that considers women to be the natural and only appropriate carers of children, a view often reflected in national policies encouraging mothers to take extensive leave. Consequently, because mothers tend to spend more time with infants, their skill set increases more rapidly than that of fathers. This lower opportunity for fathers to learn can, over time, change the potentially equal capability to nurture into a competence discrepancy and lead to a lack of confidence among fathers to nurture.

At each contextual level of contemporary societies – gender regime (gendered normative expectations), family policies and culture of care (gendered entitlements and social rights to care), resistant workplace culture (time and policies), and daily individual agency – contradictory forces create a particular constellation of factors that build the context of fatherhood in a society, including fathering practice. The egalitarian cultural mandate for fathers to be both providers and nurturers is misaligned with lingering gendered maternalist ideas and state policies, and workplace practices that prohibit fathers' full participation in childcare. Governments can reinforce or challenge the traditional gender order (male breadwinner and female childcare provider) explicitly or implicitly. This occurs via 'familialist' (Leitner, 2003)[2] policies, such as long paid maternity leave, short paid paternity leave and a lack of affordable day care provision, or 'de-familialist' policies that encourage dual-earner families with publicly funded day care. Nevertheless, even if men are entitled to paid paternity leave, gendered workplace cultures demanding high levels of work commitment may discourage the use of these entitlements. In reference to the mismatch between fathers' aspirations to be involved fathers and their actual daily childcare practice, Hobson and Fahlén (2009) speak of an agency gap, by which they mean that fathers' rights to care for their children are constrained by gendered workplace cultures and lingering maternalist cultural ideas.

This book intends to reduce the gap in international research relating family policy to daily father involvement. It is mainly interested in the fathers themselves: their activities and well-being and the outcomes for them based on father involvement in different policy contexts.

The chapters present the current state of knowledge on how different kinds of father involvement with young children, defined as children aged from birth to mandatory school age, are related to various 'father-friendly' policies. The book covers six countries from different welfare state regimes with unique policies related to parenting in general and fathers in particular: Finland, Germany, Italy, Slovenia, the UK and the US.

Fatherhood, fathering and types of fathers

First, a clarification of the terminology in the area of fatherhood research is necessary in order to distinguish among various terms used to describe fatherhood, types of fathers, their activities and levels of father engagement. The most basic distinction occurs among *fatherhood*, *fathering* and *types of fathers*. *Fatherhood*, according to Hobson and Morgan (2002: 11), is defined by the 'cultural coding of men as fathers', which includes societal ideals of 'good fathers' based on the culture-specific social expectations about fathers' responsibilities, obligations and duties. By extension, Coltrane (2004) considers fatherhood as a normative set of institutionalised practices within a cultural, religious and political framework. Country-specific notions of fatherhood thus emerge within a cultural, political and institutional context and are defined by legal structures and policies. The term 'active fatherhood' is used to describe the current normative expectation in Western countries that good fathers are actively engaged with their children, both as providers and as nurturers. The distinction between *social fatherhood* and *biological fatherhood* is based on the legally recognised relationship between a child and a man. This has become more important in the context of reproductive technologies. Sheldon (2005) refers to a 'fragmentation of fatherhood' involving the separation of fatherhood from active fathering practices via reproductive technologies, patchwork families and the legal status of paternity. Hence, a man may be a biological father but may never engage in fathering because he is either anonymous (artificial heterologic insemination) or removed geographically or emotionally from the child (after the relationship with the mother breaks up). Conversely, a man may not have biological children but may be very active in socially fathering adopted children. The research presented in this book does not make such a distinction and includes all co-residential father figures.

In contrast to fatherhood, *fathering* can be thought of as the direct parenting activities and practices that are carried out by fathers with children in the context of families and familial relationships. Morgan

(2002: 278) aptly notes that *fathering* involves 'a recognition of a growing plurality of fathering practices rather than the unified normative model of fatherhood' and 'a recognition of "competing narratives of fatherhood"'. In other words, fatherhood can be expressed in numerous ways through 'doing fathering' (Lammi-Taskula, 2008), similar to West and Zimmerman's (1987: 125) 'doing gender', which means gender or fathering is 'a routine accomplishment embedded in everyday interaction'. Similarly Jurczyk et al (2009) also refer to 'doing family', which describes daily routines and rituals involving activities with children, household tasks and the organisation of family-related time. Thus, 'doing fathering' involves activities and behaviours in everyday direct interactions with children. The level of *father involvement* is part of doing fathering and, here, it is important to distinguish between the quality and quantity of activities. For example, how much time per day does a father routinely spend in various direct care activities, such as bathing, feeding and changing the nappies of the child, or on other activities, such as playing with and reading to the child. In practice, one can distinguish 'active time with children' (primary activity) from 'passive childcare' (secondary activity), where the former refers to activities where the child is in the direct care of the parent (eg physical care of the child and reading to the child) and the latter describes situations where parents and children are mainly physically proximate (at mealtime or while watching TV) (Bygren et al, 2011). While active childcare may be more central to what is meant by father involvement, passive childcare also requires parental presence and accessibility and, thus, is also necessary for the father–child relationship (Bygren et al, 2011).

Based on the amount and quality of father involvement, a number of *father* typologies have been developed in the literature (Palkovitz, 2002). Scholars distinguish among father types on a continuum of the level of involvement from generative to nurturing fatherhood. Various father types (eg traditional fathers, new fathers, involved fathers, active fathers or absent fathers) and fathers' parental styles (hands-on, distant, authoritarian, egalitarian or permissive) have been identified, measured and combined (Hobson, 2002; Palkovitz, 2002; Marsiglio and Roy, 2012; Marsiglio, Lohan and Culley, 2013). Ranson (2012) explains that these can shift intergenerationally towards more involvement, so that: among the older generation, a 'work-focused father' prevails; in the middle generation, there are mainly 'family men'; and the youngest men follow a more 'hands-on' father model. As part of the current model of involved fatherhood, the literature has introduced a new category, referred to interchangeably as 'responsible fathers', 'active fathers' or 'new fathers', to describe fathers who are more engaged with their children than the traditional fathers of the past. Specifically, what is 'new' about this model is that men are expected to be both providers and nurturers. Whether and how fathers translate these aspirations into daily action in terms of hands-on childcare is one of the empirical questions pursued here.

Of particular interest to this book is Sullivan's (2004), Holter's (2007), Ranson's (2012) and Hobson and Fahlén's (2009, 2012) work related to changing fatherhood. These authors point to a split between general ideological support for de-gendering care work and the practical limits placed on fathers' capacities to equalise gender relations at home. For example, Sullivan's (2004) theoretical framework connects changes in gender egalitarian attitudes, prevalent images of masculinity and fatherhood, and daily interactions in personal relationships. Her model places doing gender into the context of very slowly changing institutional structures, such as workplaces and families, and more rapidly changing ideological frameworks, including public policies and attitudes about egalitarianism. She presents 'a conception of change that is slow and uneven, in which daily practices and interactions are linked to attitudes and discourse, perhaps over generations' (Sullivan, 2004: 207).

Similarly, Holter (2007) examines the slow ideological change from 'breadwinner masculinities' towards 'caring masculinities' in European public discourse about fathers. Despite shifting gender ideals from gendered work–family separation towards the de-gendered parental sharing of work and family responsibilities, workplaces remain structured by ideas about organisational masculinity and traditional breadwinner norms. The 'hidden rules' of these 'greedy institutions' (Oechsle, 2014), which demand complete dedication to work (Coser, 1974) in a context of increased job insecurity, tend to devalue and sanction the caring efforts of men. These workplace cultures can discourage men from taking family leave or from working reduced hours in order to accommodate their family obligations. Thus, fathers may face an *agency gap* between their rights and obligations to care for their children and their actual ability to claim these rights: fathers do not feel entitled to, are uncomfortable asking for and, hence, often do not claim their rights (Hobson, 2014). According to Holter's model, both ideological factors and practical reasons account for the slow pace of change in fathers' agency in childcare. Most men change only moderately towards more father involvement, mainly because of the new circumstances surrounding precarious working conditions and time pressures associated with both parents having to be employed to make ends meet. Some 'new men' shift more dramatically from being breadwinners to carers because they are committed to the ideals of gender equality. They are akin to Ranson's (2012) conceptualisation of the 'working father', who equitably shares in direct childcare provision and the responsibility to maintain family well-being, and who rearranges his work life to meet family demands. Ranson suggests that the current research discourse should focus more on these involved fathers as 'forerunners of change', albeit slow change, rather than as exotic anomalies.

An extreme version of the working father is a new group of men, referred to by Kaufman (2013) as 'superdads', who consciously reduce their work lives to have more time with their families. Superdads see themselves more as carers than as breadwinners and are engaged in activities that are usually associated with mothers. They take extended leaves, cut back to part-time work or become stay-at-home fathers. Holter's new men and Kaufman's superdads would be involved in Dowd's (2000) 'nurturing fatherhood'. The key question is how caring for children is combined with employment: is fatherhood fitted into the life of a worker or is employment fitted into the life of a father? If most fathers are in the first category, they will make minor adjustment to their work lives when they become fathers. Those in the second category appear to be empowered to act upon their aspirations to be active fathers (Marsiglio and Roy, 2012).

Theoretical framework of this book

From the discussion about changes in fatherhood from breadwinning towards caring masculinities, it becomes clear that both gendered institutional arrangements and gender ideology affect the daily actions of fathers. Father involvement occurs in a structural context, which includes a number of state–family–market intersections. According to Hobson and Morgan (2002: 9–10), the extent to which states govern the economy will determine to what degree workers are dependent on the labour market:

> policy regimes reflect differences in the degree to which the state provides benefits and services or relies on the family as a form of welfare ... and the extent to which the market is the source of benefits and services for families.

The resulting policies vary quite dramatically in different countries based on prevailing ideas about gender relations and competing masculinities.

The term 'policy' is used here very broadly to include a range of social initiatives by federal, state and local entities that deal with parents and children. Until quite recently, these policies were mainly aimed at supporting mothers' time with children rather than at increasing fathers' opportunities to be involved in their children's lives. A glance at policy developments in various countries reveals that policies specifically promoting father involvement evolved first in Scandinavian countries. Recent father-centred policies in various nations have been framed in terms of: (1) benefiting gender equality (de-gendering care work) and reducing women's work–life conflict; (2) increasing opportunities for fathers to interact with children (empowering involved fathers); (3) improving father–child and parental relationships (family stability and well-being); or (4) improving child outcomes (child well-being).

There are numerous policy instruments at the state and employer level to help parents take care of young children: they can commodify care via affordable and convenient day-care centres; they can provide parental leave policies for fathers and mothers; and they can offer flexitime and reduced hours to workers. These policies are motivated by different priorities in the various countries. For example, some policies are attempts to increase fertility rates (pro-natalist policies), to lower unemployment rates (long maternal leave policies), to increase gender equality in care work within families (affordable, easily accessible childcare coverage) and to increase opportunities for fathers' time with children (paternal leave and flexitime) (Haas and Rostgaard, 2011). However, the justifications for policy development rarely include consequences for fathers' well-being and work–life conflict, such as effects on men's occupational, earnings and career outcomes, the stress in combining work and family, and health outcomes (United Nations, 2011). Previous research on the consequences of father involvement has primarily concentrated on child outcomes, the gender division at home and relationship quality rather than on the fathers themselves (Pleck, 2012).

It is important to examine whether policy is the main influence on the behaviour of fathers, or whether economic considerations and gender norms play an independent role in affecting father involvement. In order to take the dynamic interplay of various institutional domains as they affect fathers' agency into account, this book integrates and develops further a number of concepts and analytical levels used by previous authors. Contemporary fathers' capability to care for children is affected by gendered cultural, policy and workplace assumptions about fathers at the structural level, as well as motivation, skill level and commitment at the individual level. As a sociological approach that includes the structural and individual levels of analysis, Hobson and Fahlén (2009: 216; 2012) and Hobson (2014) present a capabilities and agency framework. In their analysis of fathers' agency to care for children, the authors argue that 'the disjuncture between norms/values and practices and between policies and fathers' capabilities to exercise them' (Hobson and Fahlén, 2009: 214) leads to 'agency inequalities', preventing fathers from claiming their rights to care for their children. 'For fathers, inequalities are seen in work pressures and working times that do not permit active fathering, involvement in family life, and knowledge about and care for their children' (Hobson and Fahlén, 2009: 219). Although fathers have increased obligations (normative expectations to be active fathers) and enjoy increased legal rights to be carers (paternity leave and flexitime), research shows a continued lag in men's claims of their entitlements (Hobson and Fahlén, 2009, 2012) and their involvement in routine childcare. It appears that not only would a growing number of fathers like to have more time to engage in childcare activities, but that they are also experiencing pressures from partners, friends and government advertisement campaigns to do so (Hobson and Fahlén, 2009). While the majority of European fathers in Hobson and Fahlén's study wanted to reduce their work hours and considered the reconciliation of work and family a high priority, they faced the conflicting claims of intensive and insecure employment and higher expectations regarding family involvement. Explanations for this agency gap focus mainly on prevailing gender norms and current neoliberal workplace expectations that: (1) ideal workers are unencumbered by family responsibilities; (2) work commitment is measured by time spent at work; (3) pay is the incentive for high performance; and (4) fear of job loss motivates workers (Hobson and Fahlén, 2009, 2012). Depending on how prevalent these patterns are and to what extent policy intervenes in ameliorating them, the agency gap for fathers is expected to be wider or narrower in the countries presented here. Thus, the focus now turns to the question of how family- or father-friendly the policies in these nations are.

The structural level: welfare states and policy regimes

There is quite a bit of variation among advanced countries with respect to policy support for working parents. Scholars typically assign advanced Western nations to a number of different welfare state clusters and policy regimes in order to compare the generosity of their social safety net, their family support and the gendered nature of their policies (Esping-Andersen, 1999; Korpi, 2000; Hobson and Morgan, 2002; Orloff and Monson, 2002; Gregory and Milner, 2008). Esping-Andersen's initial typology of welfare regimes, which uses the principle of decommodification, that is, to what extent workers (usually men) are dependent on the labour market for survival, has been extended to also examine the degree to which families are supported by policies (familism) (Esping-Andersen, 1990, 1999). A familist welfare state and its policies assume that families themselves assume most responsibility for their own welfare, while de-familising policies reduce individuals' dependence on family support. Here, Esping-Andersen (1999) distinguishes between de-familisation via public social policies (eg widely available public childcare) and de-familisation via service provision through the market (eg widely available private childcare providers). Leitner (2003) refines this scheme in her 'varieties in familialism' approach, which includes four 'ideal types' of familialism: in the case of *explicit familialism*, policies support families in caring for children with long leave, but public or market-driven alternatives to family care are limited; in the case of *optional familialism*, public childcare is provided so that family care is optional and 'the family's right to care [is] not equated with the family's obligation to care' (Leitner, 2003: 359); in the *implicit familialism* case, there is no policy support for de-familialisation or for the caring function of families and, thus, the family remains the primary carer because of a lack of alternatives; the *de-familialism* case can be supported either through the state or market provision of care services (or both) and while this relieves families' responsibilities to care, it also does not honour families' right to care.

In addition, differing 'gender arrangements' (Pfau-Effinger, 1998, 2004) or 'gender regimes' (O'Connor, 1993; Lewis, 1997; Sainsbury, 1999) have been conceptualised. These schemes involve patterns in a number of measures of the degree of 'family-friendliness', 'gender egalitarian policies' and 'work–family reconciliation policies', and are mainly focused on policy effects on the status of women or employed mothers, rather than on fathers. For example, Crompton (1999) used 'breadwinner regimes' to arrive at classifications of how work and family responsibilities are divided among women, men, the state and the market. This is similar to Pfau-Effinger's (2004) typology, which classifies countries as: dual-earner/female part-time carer; female primary carer (familist); dual-earner/collective childcare; or dual-earner/state carer. Specifically, 'cultures of care' (Von Wahl, 2005; Adler and Brayfield, 2006) are considered part of a country's gender culture and refer to what extent childcare falls into the domain of state support (public childcare centres), market competition (private childcare centres) or the family (women at home). Thus, Haas (2005) arrives at the following five types: the traditional breadwinner model (male breadwinner and female full-time carer); the modified breadwinner model (male breadwinner with female part-time worker); the egalitarian employment model (two full-time earners and women doing most of the care work); the universal carer model (dual earners and both sharing care equally); and the role reversal model (female breadwinner with male full-time carer or part-time worker). The last two models would be most conducive to high levels of father involvement.

For the analysis of fathers' agency in terms of father involvement and everyday practice, it is relevant to examine to what extent states and workplaces use their policies to decommodify fathers and support fathers' capability to care for their children. Hence, Esping-Andersen's (1999) typology of welfare state regimes (liberal, social-democratic and conservative) is combined here with Leitner's (2003) 'varieties in familialism' approach and Haas's (2005) gender regimes. This strategy results in several gender regime clusters (see also Von Wahl, 2005): (1) the liberal and market-oriented countries (the English-speaking countries) that leave families to their own devices and rely on the market for childcare, which may reinforce traditional breadwinner or modified breadwinner (dual-earner families); (2) the Nordic, social-democratic countries where the state provides support for the egalitarian model (dual-earner and dual-carer families); (3) the social-conservative, coordinated market economies with general family support, which includes countries in continental Europe that have traditional familist policies and a modified breadwinner model (a one-and-a-half-earner model (Lewis et al, 2008); (4) the conservative Mediterranean countries that combine a strong familist orientation with male-breadwinner norms to encourage a traditional breadwinner model; and (5) the post-socialist countries with a strong dual-earner tradition, but that may, today, orient themselves on any of the other clusters – from egalitarian dual-earner/dual-carer, to familism, to market-oriented models.

According to Bygren, Duvander and Ferrarini (2011), these multidimensional schemes are superior to one-dimensional conceptualisations of 'family-friendliness' because they are sensitive to the potentially contradictory and gendered features of policies regarding paid and unpaid work. Specifically, policies can either maintain the traditional division of labour in families (male breadwinners and female carers) or support families with egalitarian carers and dual earners (Bygren et al, 2011). Hobson and Morgan (2002: 8) argue that these gender regime typologies typically reflect 'different policy logics around women's access to the labour market', but:

> [i]f we turn the lens toward men as fathers and the construction of fatherhood, we find the meaning and content of what a strong, moderate and weak breadwinner society is may have to be reconceived, since men as fathers are embedded in family law and social policy, with different economic responsibilities for their fatherhood.

Hence, one would expect countries with different gender regimes to also vary by their fatherhood regimes (Hobson and Morgan, 2002; Gregory and Milner, 2008), that is, in terms of their fatherhood obligations, fatherhood rights, institutional support for father involvement and, most importantly, in everyday fathering practices. Similar to ideas about 'good mothers' and employed mothers, correspondent conceptualisations of men as parents and workers take on differing forms in specific national contexts and policies. As an extension of the idea of the gender regime, the fatherhood regime (Hobson and Morgan, 2002) incorporates the rights and obligations of fathers as embedded in domestic power relations, national institutions and policies of the state, family and economy. Hobson and Morgan's (2002: 12) fatherhood regime model is constructed along two dimensions: 'rights to custody and care and obligations (economic responsibilities for child support and alimony)'. By extension, Gregory and Milner (2011) added Mutari and Figart's (2001) concept of the national 'working time regime' as another dimension to the model. This conceptualisation uses the degree of working time flexibility (regulated, standardised work week versus contractual, low-paid, part-time and overtime full-time) and the degree of gender equity (gendered part-time/full-time work, gender segregation of the labour market, gender wage gap). Thus, countries can be classified along the equitability of the working time regime, which, in turn, affects the capabilities of fathers to be involved with their young children.

Fatherhood obligations are also anchored in societal gender norms associated with being an active father, and fatherhood rights include statutory rights to care leave with adequate compensation, flexible work hours and reduced work hours. Institutional support includes workplace encouragement and partner support to take leave, to spend time with children and to engage in numerous direct and indirect childcare activities. The degree to which organisations empower parents to integrate work and family has been measured by Den Dulk, Groeneveld and Peper (2014). The authors examined the workplace policies of 21 nations along various dimensions and arrived at a ranking of organisations into low, medium and high capabilities provided to parents. Based on this scheme, for each country, the percentage of organisations in the high capabilities cluster is reported. The ability to combine providing and caring also assumes a certain degree of 'de-familialism' in society – meaning that the state supports the dual-earner model by providing publicly funded childcare, or that there are private childcare providers, which lets parents chose their preferred options (Leitner, 2003; Javornik, 2014).

The countries presented in this book were chosen because of their membership in these different clusters and their unique policy features related to fathers. Finland is part of the Nordic social-democratic welfare states, has a very generous social policy regime and is a dual-earner (egalitarian employment) regime with high state support (Lammi-Taskula and Takala, 2011). It is also in the 'optional familialism' category because there is widespread use of publically financed childcare in addition to relatively long parental leave. Germany is an interesting case because German unification in 1990 combined the West German classic example of the continental/conservative/corporate welfare state and traditional breadwinner system with the East German post-socialist, egalitarian, dual-earner system (Ostner, 2002; Adler and Brayfield, 2006). The merger resulted in a combined modified breadwinner system with major regional variation (one-and-a-half earners and dual earners), which only recently began efforts to include fathers more actively in its leave policies (Erler, 2011). Overall, Germany is characterised by 'explicit familialism' because public childcare for children under age two is not widely used and parental leaves are long.

Italy is a Southern Mediterranean or 'familialistic' (Hobson and Morgan, 2002) welfare state with little state support and a traditional breadwinner regime (Magaraggia, 2013). Leitner (2003) also classifies Italy as 'explicit familialism' because formal childcare is not widely used and not well-financed as maternal childcare is assumed. Slovenia is part of the post-socialist cluster of welfare states and has a dual-earner (egalitarian) gender regime (Korintus and Stropnik, 2011). According to Javornik (2014: 251), Slovenia features 'supported de-familialism' on her *index of state de-familialism* for post-socialist countries because 'public responsibility for childcare has been a long-standing principle and parents' right to family time has received limited recognition'.

While the UK and the US are typically identified as part of the liberal welfare state cluster, they occupy different positions in terms of policy and gender regimes, with the UK being more generous in terms of family policy than the US. The UK has a 'one-and-a-half-breadwinner' (modified breadwinner) gender regime (Pascall and Lewis, 2004; Lewis et al, 2008) and, according to Leitner (2003), is a part of the 'de-familialism' cluster because there is widespread use of formal childcare but little public financial support for it. The US is considered a dual-earner system (egalitarian employment) and while it appears to fall into the 'implicit familialism' category because there is no public policy support for families, private childcare is widely used as there are no publically financed alternatives.

The individual level: father involvement

After presenting the structural context in which parenting occurs, and basic theoretical concepts used in this book, the focus now turns to the literature on how father involvement plays out in everyday life in various settings. The conceptualisations of father involvement vary over time and culture; yet, fathers generally fulfil various normative social, economic and instrumental obligations.

Pleck (2012: 252) observes that 'in the coming decade, the parenting discipline can make progress ... by exploring how the concepts and approaches distinctive in paternal involvement research can contribute to greater understanding of ... parenting in a truly gender-inclusive perspective'. While his approach is mainly centred on child outcomes and needs, Pleck's 'paternal involvement perspective' can provide an agenda for developing a cross-cultural 'best practices' blueprint for examining father involvement. The original 'engagement, accessibility and responsibility' conceptualisation of father involvement (Lamb et al, 1985; Lamb, 1987) has inspired a large body of research dealing with fathers' time use in interaction with children, their activities when 'on duty' with children and general activities that ensure children's needs are met. According to this model of father involvement, engagement (or positive engagement) refers to direct interaction with the child in terms of undivided attention. Accessibility (or availability) means that the father is in the proximity of the child but does not actively engage with the child. Responsibility refers to the even more remote aspects of taking care of a child's needs. This may include buying items for the child, planning activities and other aspects of the economic provider role. Father involvement tends to be conceptualised as the type and quantity of time of fathers' activities with their children.

Lamb (1987, 2000) and Pleck (2010, 2012) identify four sources of father involvement: social support; absence of institutional barriers; motivation; and skills and self-confidence. As part of social support, a varied amount of paid paternity leave, the so-called 'daddy months', have become the norm in most advanced countries. At the same time, a common concern has been the relatively low level of uptake of paternal leave, which prompted experimentation with optimal incentives for fathers, such as universal coverage, flexibility, father bonuses, father quotas, high compensation during leave, parental leave sharing and mandatory or longer leave (O'Brien et al, 2007; Haas and Rostgaard, 2011). Research, especially in the Nordic countries, shows mixed effects of the various provision schemes; however, it appears that making fathers' leave mandatory and including high levels of compensation increase the odds of uptake (Haas and Rostgaard, 2011; Eydal and Rostgaard, 2014). Nevertheless, while the effects of taking paternal leave on subsequent levels of father involvement appear positive (O'Brien et al, 2007; O'Brien, 2009; Boll et al, 2014), other factors, such as being present at the child's delivery and taking infant care courses, also have positive consequences for future paternal engagement (Plantin et al, 2011). This leads some scholars to conclude that it is not just social support or time availability per se, but fathers' perceived parenting skills or parental self-efficacy, that increase father interaction with infants (Ehrenberg et al, 2001; Sanderson and Thompson, 2002).

Outline of the book

This book presents the current state of knowledge on father involvement in the context of the existing work–life options for parents that are limited by demanding workplaces, available family policies and a culture demanding more father involvement in advanced Western countries. It focuses on fathering practices with young children (birth to entry into primary school) in six unique countries with vastly different support for active fatherhood. In this book, the contributors describe the extent to which policy and practice are congruent with the ideals of the active father, who is both provider and nurturer of children, in the various countries.

This review is limited to fathers of young children for several reasons. First, in order to understand how the policy context affects father behaviour in terms of uptake of paternal leave, the time period from birth to compulsory school age is the most important. Second, in terms of the length of family leave and the generosity of childcare policies, the care of young children is particularly relevant in the context of whether mothers typically stay at home with young children for a relatively long period of time or whether they re-enter the labour market very quickly. Third, research shows that father involvement is particularly important for child development at an early age. Finally, studies also show that fathers are most involved with their children before they reach compulsory school age.

The chapters do not intend to provide a comprehensive historical account of the development of fatherhood images, related policies and research in each country; rather, the focus is on recent trends. This is based on the idea that, according to Hearn (2002), the 1970s ushered in an 'ideology of change' with respect to fatherhood-related policies in Western countries. Social science research began investigating men's nurturing behaviour and participation in care work and the psychological effects of the interactions of fathers with children on their well-being in the 1970s (Lamb, 1987). In the 1980s, research about 'new' fathers and men began to prepare the way for intense debates about the meaning of masculinity for men's identity formation and the predominance of hegemonic masculinity in work–family arrangements (see Connell, 2005). The goal is to contextualise the current status of father involvement in the description of the recent history of social change in each country. The literature and research reviewed will emphasise statistics, trends, themes and developments over the last 10 years.

Although fathers are by no means a homogeneous group, the focus is on residential fathers. The exclusion of non-residential fathers means that the important topics of absent and incarcerated fathers will not be dealt with. However, information on single fathers, full-time fathers, gay fathers, disadvantaged fathers and relevant patterns by social class, education, race and ethnicity are included where available.

The book is organised around the individual countries. Each chapter begins with a presentation of the unique cultural and policy context for father involvement in the country and includes a discussion of available family leave provisions. This is followed by a discussion of current contextual information on country-specific demographic and family-related trends related to fatherhood. Next, fathers' use of parental leave and their provision of childcare are presented. Then, the authors report the most recently available time-use and survey data regarding father involvement with young children in order to show the amount of time spent with children and in what types of fathering activities. In the next section, any available multivariate research results on father involvement and its effect on the well-being of fathers themselves are discussed, followed by a review of available fatherhood programmes.

In order to examine what fatherhood regime prevails in the country, the authors present dominant father types in the context of dominant masculinities and related policies. This includes cultural-specific work–life policy regime information in terms of gender regimes and the gender division of labour. Each chapter concludes with a summary that shows important gaps in research, promising initiatives and recommendations for researchers and policymakers.

In Chapter One, Jouko Huttunen and Petteri Eerola show how Finland, as an exemplar of a social-democratic welfare state with a generous social policy regime, has recently very intentionally targeted the inclusion of fathers (Huttunen and Eerola, 2011). One question is whether the recent introduction of a 'fathers' quota' increases fathers' participation in the childcare of young children (quantity of time), and what this means in terms of their practices regarding engagement, accessibility and responsibility.

In Chapter Two on Germany, the example of the conservative/continental welfare state, Marina Adler, Karl Lenz and Yve Stöbel-Richter introduce the context of current policies, with special emphasis on remaining regional differences since unification in 1990. West Germany's legacy of the strong male-breadwinner system continues to have a different gendered 'culture of care' than the East, where the socialist dual-earner system has left its mark (Ostner, 2002; Adler and Brayfield, 2006). While there is a common public discourse on the desirability of the 'active father' for young men, data on the engagement, accessibility and responsibility of fathers with young children reflect a mixed picture of father involvement in general and by region.

In Chapter Three, Elisabetta Ruspini and Maria Letizia Tanturri present Italy as a Southern or familistic welfare state with a traditional breadwinner regime that is changing into a dual-earner regime among the younger generation. They investigate how the tensions among cultural norms of familism, changing laws expanding paternal rights and obligations, and narratives of active fathers and 'good fathers' (Magaraggia, 2013) affect father involvement with young children.

Chapter Four, by Nada Stropnik and Živa Humer, introduces Slovenia as an example of a post-socialist welfare state with a dual-earner gender regime (Korintus and Stropnik, 2011; Švab and Humer, 2013). While the division of care and paid work continues to be gendered, recent policies encouraging fathers to be more involved with young children may have helped support an increase in active fathers.

In Chapter Five, Margaret O'Brien, Sara Connolly, Svetlana Speight, Matthew Aldrich and Eloise Poole present information on contemporary fathering practices in the UK liberal welfare state context, where recent legislation has expanded fathers' rights (O'Brien, 2005, 2009). Data are provided to show whether the new cultural mandate for active fathers holds for the quantity and the quality of time fathers spend with young children in the context of long working hours and a modified breadwinner model.

In Chapter Six, Marina Adler shows that the US, the classic liberal welfare state with a dual-earner regime, is unique in being the only advanced country and one of only four nations in the world that has no statutory right to paid maternity leave (or paternity or parental leave) for employees (Hara and Hegewisch, 2013). While the cultural mandate of the father as good provider still predominates, the 'working father' model may be gaining support (Harrington et al, 2013).

In the conclusion, Marina Adler and Karl Lenz provide an analytic comparison of the countries, synthesise the lessons learned for the patterns found, propose an elaborated conceptual model of father involvement and provide some recommendations for policy and practice. Based on the evidence from the six countries, the editors examine to what extent the integration of the concepts of 'capability to care' and 'agency gap' into the fatherhood regime model is useful in understanding the intersections of gender regime, family policy and related cultures of care, workplace culture and fathers' individual agency and practice (claiming entitlements, time spent with children, care activities). What are the commonalities and differences in how cultural norms regarding masculinity and maternalism, degrees of gender egalitarianism, and related policy constellations translate into specific fathering practices in terms of engagement, accessibility and responsibility? What can be learned from the different attempts to increase father involvement with young children in order to promote gender egalitarianism and family well-being that includes empowered fathers?

Notes

[1] The term 'work–life balance' has gained popularity over the last decades to describe employees' attempts to coordinate the distribution of time between employment and family/leisure activities. As there are multiple definitions and measures of the concept in the literature, and the notion of 'balance' depends on context, we do not consider it very useful to describe parents' decision-making regarding boundary management between work and family time. Instead, we will refer to work–family conflict or attempts to reconcile the demands of work and family.

[2] The terms 'familialism' or 'familism' and their derivatives are used interchangeably in the literature. Leitner (2003) refers to 'familialism' and when referencing her work, this chapter (and the rest of the book) will use her terminology. Otherwise, the term 'familism' will be used.

References

Adler, M.A. (2004) '"Child-free" and unmarried: changes in the life planning of young East German women', *Journal of Marriage and Family*, 66: 1167–76.

Adler, M.A. and Brayfield, A. (2006) 'Gender regimes & cultures of care: public support for maternal employment in Germany and the United States', *Marriage & Family Review*, 39: 229–53.

Aumann, K., Galinsky, E. and Matos, K. (2011) *The new male mystique. National study of the changing workforce*, New York, NY: Families and Work Institute.

Bianchi, S. and Milkie, M. (2010) 'Work and family research in the first decade of the 21st century', *Journal of Marriage and Family*, 73(3): 705–25.

Boll, C., Leppin, J. and Reich, N. (2014) 'Paternal childcare and parental leave policies: evidence from industrial countries', *Review of Economic Households*, 12: 129–58.

Bygren, M., Duvander, A.-Z. and Ferrarini, T. (2011) 'Moulding parents' childcare? A comparative analysis of paid work and time with children in different family policy contexts', in S. Drobnič and A.M. Guikken (eds) *Work–life balance in Europe. The role of job quality*, London: Palgrave Macmillan, pp 207–30.

Byron, K. (2005) 'A meta-analytic review of work–family conflict and its antecedents', *Journal of Vocational Behavior*, 67(2): 169–98.

Coltrane, S. (2004) 'Fathering: Paradoxes, contradictions, and dilemmas', in M. Coleman and L. Ganong (eds) *Handbook of contemporary families: considering the past, contemplating the future*, Thousand Oaks, CA: Sage.

Connell, R. (2005) *Masculinities*, Cambridge: Polity Press.

Coser, L.A. (1974) *Greedy institutions: patterns of undivided commitment*, New York, NY: The Free Press.

Craig, L. (2007) *Contemporary motherhood: the impact of children on adult time*, Aldershot: Ashgate Publishing.

Craig, L. and Mullen, K. (2011) 'How mothers and fathers share childcare: a cross-national time-use comparison', *American Sociological Review*, 76(6): 834–61.

Crompton, R. (1999) *Restructuring gender relations and employment: the decline of the male breadwinner*, Oxford: Oxford University Press.

Den Dulk, L., Groeneveld, S., Peper, B. (2014) 'Workplace work–life balance support from a capabilities perspective', in B. Hobson (ed) *Work–life balance: the agency and capabilities gap*, Oxford: Oxford University Press, pp 153–73.

Dowd, N.E. (2000) *Redefining fatherhood*, New York, NY: NYU Press.

Eggebeen, D.J. (2002) 'The changing course of fatherhood: men's experience with children in demographic perspective', *Journal of Family Issues*, 23: 486–506.

Ehrenberg, M.F., Gearing-Small, M., Haunter, M.A. and Small, B.J. (2001) 'Childcare task division and shared parenting attitudes in dual-earner families with young children', *Family Relations: Interdisciplinary Journal of Applied Family Studies*, 50: 143–53.

Ehrenreich, B. (1987) *The hearts of men: American dreams and the flight from commitment*, Garden City, NY: Anchor Press/Doubleday.

Erler, D. (2011) 'Germany: taking a Nordic turn?', in S.B. Kamerman and P. Moss (eds) *The politics of parental leave policies. Children, parenting, gender and the labour market*, Bristol: The Policy Press, pp 119–34.

Esping-Andersen, G. (1990) *The three worlds of welfare capitalism*, Princeton, NJ: Princeton University Press.

Esping-Andersen, G. (1999) *Social foundations of postindustrial economies*, New York, NY: Oxford University Press.

Eydal, G. and Rostgaard, T. (eds) (2014) *Fatherhood in the Nordic welfare states: comparing care policies and practice*, Bristol: The Policy Press.

Gregory, A. and Milner, S. (2008) 'Fatherhood regimes and father involvement in France and the UK', *Community, Work and Family*, 11(1): 61–84.

Gregory, A. and Milner, S. (2011) 'What is "new" about fatherhood? The social construction of fatherhood in France and the UK', *Men and Masculinities*, 14: 588–606.

Haas, B. (2005) 'The work-care balance: Is it possible to identify typologies for cross-national comparisons?' *Current Sociology*, 53: 487–508.

Haas, L. and Rostgaard, T. (2011) 'Fathers' rights to paid parental leave in the Nordic countries: consequences for the gendered division of leave', *Community, Work & Family*, 14(2): 177–95.

Hara, Y. and Hegewisch, A. (2013) 'Maternity, paternity, and adoption leave in the United States', IWPR Briefing Paper #A143 Update (May), Institute for Women's Policy Research. Available at: http://IWPR.org

Harrington, B., Van Deusen, F. and Fraone, J.S. (2013) *The new dad: a work (and life) in progress*, Boston, MA: Boston College Center for Work & Family.

Hearn, J. (2002) 'Men, fathers and the state: national and global relations', in B. Hobson (ed) *Making men into fathers. Men, masculinities and the social politics of fatherhood*, Cambridge: Cambridge University Press, pp 245–71.

Hobson, B. (ed) (2002) *Making men into fathers. Men, masculinities and the social politics of fatherhood*, Cambridge: Cambridge University Press.

Hobson, B. (2014) 'Introduction: capabilities and agency for work–life balance – a multidimensional framework', in B. Hobson (ed) *Work–life balance. The agency and capabilities gap*, Oxford: Oxford University Press, pp 1–31.

Hobson, B. and Fahlén, S. (2009) 'Competing scenarios for European fathers: applying Sen's capabilities and agency framework to work–family balance', *The Annals of the American Academy of Political and Social Sciences*, 624: 214–33.

Hobson, B. and Fahlén, S. (2012) 'Father's capabilities for care: a European perspective. Family, ties and care', in H. Bertram and N. Ehlert (eds) *Family transformation in a plural modernity; the Freiburger survey about family transformation in an international comparison*, Obladen: Budrich, pp 99–116.

Hobson, B. and Morgan, D. (2002) 'Introduction', in B. Hobson (ed) *Making men into fathers. Men, masculinities and the social politics of fatherhood*, Cambridge: Cambridge University Press, pp 1–21.

Hochschild, A.R. (2002) 'Love and gold', in B. Ehrenreich and A.R. Hochschild (eds) *Global woman: nannies, maids, and sex workers in the new economy*, New York, NY: Owl Books, pp 15–30.

Holter, Ø.G. (2007) 'Men's work and family reconciliation in Europe', *Men & Masculinities*, 9(4): 425–56.

Hook, J.L. and Wolfe, C.M. (2012) 'New fathers? Residential fathers' time with children in four countries', *Journal of Family Issues*, 33(4): 415–50.

Huttunen, J. and Eerola, P. (2011) 'Metanarrative of the "new father" and narratives of young Finnish first-time fathers', *Fathering: A Journal of Theory, Research, & Practice about Men as Fathers*, 9: 211–31.

Javornik, J. (2014) 'Measuring state de-familialism: contesting post-socialist exceptionalism', *Journal of European Social Policy*, 24(3): 240–57.

Jurczyk, K., Schier, M., Szymenderski, P., Lange, A., and Voss, G.G. (2009) *Entgrenzte Arbeit – Entgrenzte Familie. Grenzmanagement im Alltag als neue Herausforderung* [*Blurring boundaries between work and family*], Berlin: edition sigma.

Kamerman, S.B. and Moss, P. (2009) *The politics of parental leave policies: children, parenting, gender and the labour market*, Portland, OR: Policy Press.

Kaufman, G. (2013) *Superdads. How fathers balance work and family in the 21st century*, New York, NY: NYU Press.

Kimmel, M.S. (1987) *Changing men: new directions in research on men and masculinity*, New York: Sage Publications, Inc.

Korintus, M. and Stropnik, N. (2011) 'Hungary and Slovenia: long leave or short?', in S.B. Kamerman and P. Moss (eds) *The politics of parental leave policies. Children, parenting, gender and the labour market*, Bristol: The Policy Press, pp 135–57.

Korpi, W. (2000) 'Faces of inequality: gender, class, and patterns of inequalities in different types of welfare states', *Social Politics: International Studies in Gender, State and Society*, 7(2): 127–91.

Lamb, M.E. (1987) 'Introduction: the emergent American father', in M.E. Lamb (ed) *The father's role: cross-cultural perspectives*, Hillsdale, NJ: Erlbaum, pp 3–25.

Lamb, M.E. (2000) 'The history of research on father involvement: an overview', *Marriage and Family Review*, 29(2/3): 23–42.

Lamb, M.E., Pleck, J.H., Charnov, E.I. and Levine, J.A. (1985) 'Paternal behavior in humans', *American Zoologist*, 25: 883–94.

Lammi-Taskula, J. (2008) 'Doing fatherhood: understanding the gendered use of parental leave in Finland', *Fathering: A Journal of Theory, Research, & Practice about Men as Fathers*, 6(2): 133–48.

Lammi-Taskula, J. and Takala, P. (2011) 'Finland: negotiating tripartite compromises', in S.B. Kamerman and P. Moss (eds) *The politics of parental leave policies. Children, parenting, gender and the labour market*, Bristol: The Policy Press, pp 87–102.

Leitner, S. (2003) 'Varieties of familialism. The caring function of the family in comparative perspective', *European Societies*, 5(4): 353–75.

Lewis, J. (1997) 'Gender and welfare state regimes: further thoughts', *Social Politics: International Studies in Gender, State, and Society*, 4: 160–77.

Lewis, J. (2002) 'Gender and welfare state change', *European Societies*, 4(4): 331–57.

Lewis, J., Campbell, M. and Huerta, C. (2008) 'Patterns of paid and unpaid work in Western Europe: gender, commodification, preferences and the implications for policy', *Journal of European Social Policy*, 18(1): 21–37.

Magaraggia, S. (2013) 'Tensions between fatherhood and the social construction of masculinity in Italy', *Current Sociology*, 61(1): 76–92.

Marks, L. and Palkovitz, R. (2004) 'American fatherhood types: the good, the bad, and the uninterested', *Fathering: A Journal of Theory, Research, & Practice about Men as Fathers*, 2(2): 113–29.

Marsiglio, W. and Roy, K. (2012) *Nurturing dads: social initiatives for contemporary fatherhood*, New York, NY: Russell Sage.

Marsiglio, W., Lohan, M. and Culley, L. (2013) 'Framing men's experience in the procreative realm', *Journal of Family Issues*, 34(8): 1011–36.

Morgan, D. (2002) 'Epilogue', in B. Hobson (ed) *Making men into fathers: men, masculinities and the social politics of fatherhood*, Cambridge: Cambridge University Press, pp 273–86.

Mutari, E. and Figart, D.M. (2001) 'Europe at a crossroads: harmonization, liberalization, and the gender of work time', *Social Politics*, 8(1): 36–64.

O'Brien, M. (2005) *Shared caring; bringing fathers into the frame*, Working Paper Series 18, London: Equal Opportunities Commission. Available at: http://dera.ioe.ac.uk/5299/1/1.73363!shared_caring_wp18.pdf

O'Brien, M. (2009) 'Fathers, parental leave policies and infant quality of life: international perspectives and policy impact', *The Annals of the American Academy of Political and Social Science*, 624: 190–213.

O'Brien, M., Brandth, B. and Kvande, E. (2007) 'Fathers, work and family life', *Community, Work & Family*, 10(4): 375–86.

O'Connor, J.S. (1993) 'Gender, class and citizenship in the comparative analysis of welfare state regimes: theoretical and methodological issues', *British Journal of Sociology*, 44(3): 501–18.

OECD (Organisation for Economic Co-operation and Development) (2012) *Closing the gender gap*, Paris: OECD Publishing.

Oechsle, M. (2014) 'Hidden rules and sense of entitlement – working fathers within organizations', paper presented at the Work and Family Researchers Network Conference, New York City, 21 June.

Oláh, L.S., Bernhardt, E.M. and Goldscheider, F.K. (2002) 'Coresidential paternal roles in industrialized countries: Sweden, Hungary and the United States', in B. Hobson (ed) *Making men into fathers. Men, masculinities and the social politics of fatherhood*, Cambridge: Cambridge University Press, pp 25–57.

Oláh, L.S., Richter, R., Kotowska, I.E. (2014) *State of the art report. The new roles of men and women and implications for families and societies*, Working Paper Series 11: 'Changing families and sustainable societies: policy contexts and diversity over the life course and across generations', European Union: Seventh Framework Programme.

Orloff, A.S. and Monson, R. (2002) 'Citizens, workers or fathers? Men in the history of US social policy', in S.B. Kamerman and P. Moss (eds) *Making men into fathers. Men, masculinities and the social politics of fatherhood*, Cambridge: Cambridge University Press, pp 61–91.

Ostner, I. (2002) 'A new role for fathers? The German case', in B. Hobson (ed) *Making men into fathers. Men, masculinities and the social politics of fatherhood*, Cambridge: Cambridge University Press, pp 150–67.

Palkovitz, R. (2002) *Involved fathering and men's adult development: Provisional balances*, Mahwah, NJ: Erlbaum.

Pascall, G. and Lewis, J. (2004) 'Emerging gender regimes and policies for gender equality in a wider Europe', *Journal of Social Policy*, 33(3): 373–94.

Pettit, B. and Hook, J.L. (2009) *Gendered tradeoffs. Family, social policy, and economic inequality in twenty-one countries*, New York, NY: Russell Sage.

Pfau-Effinger, B. (1998) 'Gender cultures and the gender arrangement – a theoretical framework for cross-national gender research', *Innovation: The European Journal of Social Sciences*, 11(2): 147–66.

Pfau-Effinger, B. (2004) *Development of culture, welfare states and women's employment in Europe*, Aldershot: Ashgate.

Plantin, L., Olukoya, A.A. and Ny, P.N. (2011) 'Positive health outcomes of fathers' involvement in pregnancy and childbirth paternal support: a scope study literature review', *Fathering: A Journal of Theory, Research, & Practice about Men as Fathers*, 9(1): 87–102.

Pleck, J.H. (2010) 'Paternal involvement: revised conceptualization and theoretical linkages with child outcomes', in M.E. Lamb (ed) *The role of the father in child development* (5th edn), New York, NY: Wiley, pp 67–107.

Pleck, J.H. (2012) 'Integrating father involvement in parenting research', *Parenting: Science & Practice*, 12(2/3): 243–53.

Presser, H.B. (2003) *Working in a 24/7 economy: challenges for American families*, New York, NY: Russell Sage Foundation.

Ranson, G. (2012) 'Men, paid employment and family responsibilities: conceptualizing the "working father"', *Gender, Work & Organization*, 19(6): 741–61.

Sainsbury, D. (1999) 'Gender, policy regimes, and politics', in D. Sainsbury (ed) *Gender and welfare state regimes*, Oxford: Oxford University Press, pp 245–75.

Sanderson, S. and Thompson, V.L.S. (2002) 'Factors associated with perceived paternal involvement in childrearing', *Sex Roles*, 46(3/4): 99–111.

Settersten, R.A. and Cancel-Tirado, D. (2010) 'Fatherhood as a hidden variable in men's development and life courses', *Research in Human Development*, 7: 83–102.

Seward, R.R. and Richter, R. (2008) 'International research on fathering: an expanding horizon', *Fathering: A Journal of Theory, Research, & Practice about Men as Fathers*, 6(2): 87–91.

Sheldon, S. (2005) 'Reproductive technologies and the legal determination of fatherhood', *Feminist Legal Studies*, 13(3): 349–62.

Shwalb, D.W., Shwalb, B.J. and Lamb, M.E. (eds) (2013) *Fathers in cultural context*, New York, NY: Routledge.

Silverstein, L.B. (1996) 'Fathering is a feminist issue', *Psychology of Women Quarterly*, 20(1): 3–37.

Sullivan, O. (2004) 'Changing gender practices within the household: a theoretical perspective', *Gender & Society*, 18(2): 207–22.

Švab, A. and Humer, I. (2013) '"I only have to ask him and he does it …": active fatherhood and (perceptions of) division of family labour in Slovenia', *Journal of Comparative Family Studies*, 44(1): 57–78.

United Nations (ed) (2011) 'Introduction', in United Nations (ed) *Men in families and family policy in a changing world*, New York, NY: United Nations, Department of Economic and Social Affairs, Division for Social Policy and Development, pp 1–7.

Von Wahl, A. (2005) 'Liberal, conservative, social democratic, or … European? The European Union as equal employment regime', *Social Politics: International Studies in Gender, State & Society*, 12(1): 67–95.

Wall, G. and Arnold, S. (2007) 'How involved is involved fathering? An exploration of the contemporary culture of fatherhood', *Gender & Society*, 21: 508–27.

West, C. and Zimmerman, D.H. (1987) 'Doing gender', *Gender & Society*, 1(2): 125–51.

ONE

Finland

Jouko Huttunen and Petteri Eerola

The cultural and policy context of fatherhood

As one of the northern social-democratic welfare states, Finland has striven for gender equality since the 1960s and persistent political struggles have borne fruit: in both 2012 and 2013, the World Economic Forum (WEF) placed Finland as the world's second-ranked country in closing its gender gaps in various areas of living, such as educational attainment, health and survival (WEF, 2013). This standing did not affect Finland's economy negatively: according to the WEF's Global Competitiveness Index, in 2013/14, Finland held the third position among 148 countries (Schwab, 2013). Finland also boasts well-functioning and highly transparent public institutions (first place) and private institutions (third place), and is considered to be one of the best-run and most ethical countries in the world. In addition, Finland occupies the top position in 'health and primary education' and in 'higher education and training', which is the result of a strong focus on education over recent decades (Schwab, 2013). This success is based on a culture of struggling for economic, social and educational equality (Välijärvi et al, 2007). Another factor may be the latent contribution of shared parenting, dual-earner parenthood and a relatively high paternal involvement in children's educational development.

The contemporary cultural context of moving towards gender equality appears to bode well for involved fatherhood in Finland, especially because there has been a consensus among politicians to offer coherent egalitarian family policies. The Finnish government has promoted the implementation of the principle of equal pay and the development of more equal and flexible family leaves (Hearn and Lattu, 2002). In fact, the allocation of family leave costs between the mother's and the father's employers and the options for increasing the father's leave-taking quota have been on the governmental agenda since the 2000s. Recently, it was specifically declared that 'the objective is to increase the amount of leave days earmarked for fathers, provide more flexibility to how and when fathers use their family leave, and enable home childcare for longer, supported by the parental allowance' (Programme of the Finnish Government, 2011: 110).

Finland's general spending for family benefits was 3.3% of gross domestic product (GDP) in 2009, which is clearly above the Organisation for Economic Co-operation and Development (OECD) average of 2.6%. Finnish family benefits include: (1) child-related cash transfers to families with children, such as child allowances; (2) public income support payments during periods of parental leave; and (3) public spending on services for families with children, such as the direct financing and subsidising of childcare providers and early education facilities (OECD, 2012). Unlike in some other OECD countries, financial support for families provided through the tax system does not play an important role in Finland. In 2009, the proportion of total social spending on early childhood was 30.2%, which was above the OECD average (25.4%), and was the fifth-largest proportion among OECD countries (OECD, 2012). Spending on maternity and parental leave payments per birth as a percentage of GDP per capita was in third place at 66.6%, compared to the OECD average of 32.3%.

This high public expenditure on services for families with children is typical of the Nordic model and has been quite expensive and challenging to manage. The proportion of GDP that is allocated to release women from family duties is high, and the provision of long and generous parental leaves combined with high-quality public day care are a particular challenge in times of international financial volatility, economic recession and the ageing of the population (see also Datta Gupta et al, 2008).

Leave provisions

In the Finnish context, the term 'family leave' refers to paid maternity, paternity, parental and (child) home-care leaves, as well as leave to care for a sick child. At present, the full family leave 'set', except leave to care for a sick child, starts around one month before the calculated date of delivery and covers the child's first three years (Kela, 2013). The earliest form of family leave – maternity leave – dates back to Finland's independence (1917), and it has been incrementally modified since then into its current format (Salmi and Lammi-Taskula, 1999; Duvander and Lammi-Taskula, 2011). A noteworthy milestone was attained in 1964, when an overall nine weeks of paid maternal leave was introduced (Rønsen, 2004). Paternity leave is 60 years younger; Finland and Norway were the first countries in the world to both introduce it in 1977. Following Sweden's lead (1974), Finland was the second nation to enact parental leave in 1980.

Both maternity and paternity leaves are specifically targeted at mothers and fathers, and unlike parental leave, they cannot be transferred or shared between parents. The length of maternity leave is 18 weeks, which is followed by a shareable 26 weeks of parental leave (Kela, 2013). The length of paternity leave is nine weeks, of which the father can take one to three weeks immediately after the child is born or at the same time as the mother is using the maternity or parental leave. The rest of the paternity leave (or all of it) must be taken after the maternity and parental leaves end, but before the child is two years old. Paternity leave can also be divided into shorter periods. Either parent is allowed to use the temporary childcare leave (currently a maximum of four days at a time) if a child under the age of 10 gets ill (Kela, 2013). Compared to other Nordic countries, the Finnish paternity leave of nine weeks is slightly shorter than the paternity leaves for fathers in Sweden and Norway and is notably less than in Iceland (Lammi-Taskula, 2012).

All these three forms of family leave are wage-related and adjusted to parents' annual income. The approximate average compensation rate is 75% of the monthly income of the recipient (Kela, 2013). These forms of family leave include job security for the parent who is taking the leave. The benefits are resident-based, requiring the parent to live permanently (permanent address) in Finland, and are not dependent on labour-market participation (Salmi and Lammi-Taskula, 2007). After these forms of family leave are taken, either the mother or the father is allowed to stay at home to take advantage of the child home-care leave, during which a modest flat rate benefit is paid to the mother or father. The basic rate is currently €340 per month, but some additional allowances are available according to family conditions and place of residence. In 2012, the average paid monthly amount was €462 (Kela, 2013; OSF, 2013).

The necessary preconditions for women's labour force participation (LFP) have been created by legislation, services and financial support relating to the care of small children and the job security of parents (Ministry of Social Affairs and Health, 2013). Concurrent with the development of family leave arrangements, local authorities have been under pressure to organise day-care opportunities for families with children under school age. The public day-care system has been available since 1973 as a general social service. Since 1996, every child under school age has the right to day care, and local authorities have to offer a day-care placement for each child based on parental request (Salmi and Lammi-Taskula, 2007).

After parental leave, parents have three government-assisted alternatives for their childcare arrangements until the child starts school, usually at the age of seven. These are: (1) public day care – either in a day-care centre or in the home of a family day-care provider; (2) private day care – either in a day-care centre or in the home of a family day-care provider, subsidised through a private day-care allowance; and (3) one of the parents staying at home on child home-care allowance if the child is under the age of three (Ministry of Social Affairs and Health, 2013). The fees in both public and private day care are related to the family's total income; the maximum fee for a family's first child is €264 per month and for subsequent children, it is €238 per month (Ministry of Education and Culture, 2014). Finland's coverage of publicly provided childcare is lower than that in other Nordic countries for all age groups, but less so for children aged three to six.

Overall, Finland has a generous social policy regime with a dual-earner family model and high state support for paternal leave uptake (Lammi-Taskula, 2007; Haataja, 2009). Promoting gender equality in access to both paid work and care work has been the focus of Finnish social and family policy since the 1960s (Forsberg, 2005). The synchronised effort to provide public day-care coverage in order to allow women's participation in the labour market, as well as the family leave system to care for toddlers at home, constitute the context in which 'father-friendly' policies are delivered (Vuori, 2009).

Nevertheless, this governmental enthusiasm regarding egalitarian family policies is not necessarily reflected in the actual everyday practices and family leave usage patterns of parents with small children. Compared to the other Nordic countries, there seems to be a delay in mothers' and fathers' actual use of all the options available to them under Finnish father-friendly family policies. For example, Finnish fathers have not taken paid family leaves, especially the parental leave options, as extensively as they could (Lammi-Taskula, 2006, 2007; Haataja, 2007, 2009). Also, despite some movement towards greater gender equality since the 1990s, mothers still continue to spend more time providing childcare, even in families with two working parents (Ylikännö, 2009).

Family policy experts have recognised that the 'new father' ideology is worth pursuing – both in political decision-making and in family counselling and supervision – because of the many beneficial consequences related to 'new fathers' (Vuori, 2009). Men who spend a lot of time playing, helping, nurturing, monitoring, listening, reading and talking to their children may be more likely to commit to generative social activities that are designed to benefit children (Palkovitz, 2002; Knoester et al, 2007). Unfortunately, Finnish men have not collectively acknowledged and supported the advantages of involved fatherhood, and neither have they expressed considerable political support for 'new father' policies (Holli, 2003). The vast majority of the progress in fathering policies has been the result of activism by feminists – both politicians and publicly engaged mothers – in their individual lives and in the political arena (Leira, 2002).

Despite men's general inaction, fathering has been a popular topic of debate among parental experts and family specialists (Vuori, 2009). Their perspective is that fathers make a difference in children's development and that fathers should participate in childcare from the very onset of parenthood. In addition, the mass media has contributed to promoting a father-friendly culture in Finland. For the last two decades, images of caring fathers with their babies have emerged in mainstream advertisements, magazines and, most recently, social media. Also, support directed towards new fathers via institutional maternity and childcare clinics has become a significant part of Finnish family policies (see Rantalaiho, 2003).

Historically, more efforts have been directed to bringing mothers into paid work than to increasing fathers' share of childcare at home (Anttonen, 1998; Pascall and Lewis, 2004). Yet, according to the Nordic gender regime, and especially in feminist thinking, men's participation in care work at home is as important to achieving gender equality as is women's participation in paid work (Pascall and Lewis, 2004). In this respect, the degree of sharing of childcare responsibilities is a crucial measure of progress towards gender equality. Compared to Sweden, Norway and Iceland, it appears that in Finland, the sharing of childcare is less emphasised than a family's freedom of choice, especially among politicians (Rantalaiho, 2003). In 2003, the implementation of 'bonus days' for fathers who take the last two weeks of parental leave was the first step towards the father's quota, which encourages fathers to share parental leave with mothers (Haataja, 2009). Although the father's quota may increase the proportion of fathers taking parental leave, tentative data analysis indicates that the more clearly certain days or months are the exclusive entitlements of fathers, the more they will use only these specific days rather than the more general entitlements (Duvander and Lammi-Taskula, 2011).

Contextual demographic and family trends related to fatherhood

This section presents key information on demographic trends, features of family structure and LFP patterns that may affect fathers. The statistical sources include the national databases of Official Statistics of Finland (OSF), the OECD and the European Union (EU) (European Commission, Eurostat).

As Table 1.1 shows, per 1,000 population, the current marriage rate is around 5.3 and the divorce rate is around 2.5. Both Finnish marriage and divorce rates are among the highest among the Nordic countries (Haagensen, 2012). While both rates have remained quite stable over the last decade, there has been a slight upturn in marriages, as well as in cohabitation. This phenomenon is one of the causes of the growth of the total number of families. Despite this, the number of families with children continues to decrease.

Recently, increased attention has been paid to reconstituted stepfamilies in Finland, particularly in terms of stepfathering (see Vikat et al, 2004; Broberg, 2010). The number of stepfamilies as a subset of families with children is now approaching 10%. The absolute number of stepfamilies has not increased for seven years; however, because the total number of families with children is decreasing, the proportion shows a slight upturn. Reconstituted families are established equally through marriage or cohabitation, and in both cases, the children in these families are most often the mother's children (60%). Only one third of the children in stepfamilies are shared children, meaning that they were born within the reconstituted family (OSF, 2014b).

As in many other EU countries, family formation has been postponed in Finland. The average age at first birth for women has risen from 27.4 to 28.5. The crude birth rate (CBR) has stayed at around 11.0 over the last decade, and the total fertility rate (TFR) has remained at around 1.8. Since 1969, the number of annual live births has been below the replacement level, at approximately 2.1 children per woman. Births to unmarried women have increased from 39.2% of all births in 2000, to 41.5% in 2012. At the same time, the share of solo mother families has decreased from 11.4% to 10.2%, and the percentage of solo father families has continued to stay at around 2.1%. The data also show that the percentage of husband–wife–children families has been reduced from 36.7% to 30.0%. However, by far, most of the children under age six (87%) are currently living with two parents, and this picture seems to be quite stable.

Table 1.1: Selected indicators related to parenting for Finland, 2000 and 2012

Indicator	2000	2012
Crude marriage rate (per 1,000 population)	5.1	5.3 (2011)
Crude divorce rate	2.7	2.5 (2011)
Total fertility rate	1.7	1.8
Crude birth rate	10.9	11.0
Mothers' mean age at first birth	27.4	28.5
% non-marital births	39.2	41.5
Births per 1,000 men	22.4	22.3
% of family households that are:		
Husband/wife	31.1	35.7
Unmarried couple	11.4	13.9
Husband/wife with children	36.7	30.0
Reconstituted family with children	3.4	3.6
Mother only with children	11.4	10.2
Father only with children	2.1	2.1
% of 0–6 year olds living with:		
Two parents	87.6	87.3
Father only	0.6	0.8
Mother only	11.7	11.9
% of married-couple families that are:		
Dual-earner families	NA	65.7 (2008)
Male-provider families	NA	26.0 (2008)
Labour force participation (LFP)		
LFP rate, men (15–64)	77.6	77.3
Fathers (20–59) of kids under 18	NA	95.0 (2011)
Fathers, youngest child under 3 years	NA	94.4 (2011)
Fathers, youngest child 3–6 years	NA	95.8 (2011)
Men, % full-time	92.9	90.3
Men, % part-time	7.1	9.7
Men, mean number of hours/week	40.2 (2001)	39.1
LFP rate, women (15–64)	72.1	73.4
Mothers (20–59) of kids under 18	NA	80.0
Mothers, youngest child under 3 years	NA	52.6 (2011)
Mothers, youngest child 3–6 years	NA	86.6 (2011)
Women, % full-time	86.1	83.5
Women, % part-time	13.9	16.5
Women, mean number of hours/week	35.7 (2001)	34.9

Sources: http://epp.eurostat.ec.europa.eu/statistics_explained/index.php?title=File:Crude_marriage_rate,_seleted_years,1960-2011_(per_1_000_inhabitants).png&filetimestamp=20130130111229; http://epp.eurostat.ec.europa.eu/statistics_explained/index.php?title=File:Crude_divorce_rate,_selected_years,_1960-2011_(1)_(per_1_000_inhabitants).png&filetimestamp=20130130111212; http://epp.eurostat.ec.europa.eu/tgm/table.do?tab=table&init=1&language=en&pcode=tsdde220&plugin=1; http://epp.eurostat.ec.europa.eu/tgm/table.do?tab=table&init=1&language=en&pcode=tps00112&plugin=1; http://www.stat.fi/til/synt/2013/synt_2013_2014-04-08_tie_001_en.html; http://epp.eurostat.ec.europa.eu/tgm/table.do?tab=table&init=1&language=en&pcode=tps00018&plugin=1; calculated from the population statistics of OSF: http://www.stat.fi/til/vrm_en.html; http://www.stat.fi/til/perh/2012/perh_2012_2013-05-24_tau_001_en.html; http://www.stat.fi/til/perh/2012/02/perh_2012_02_2013-11-22_tie_001_en.html; http://pxweb2.stat.fi/Dialog/varval.asp?ma=030_perh_tau_111&ti=Children+by+age+group+and+type+of+family+1992+%2D+2013&path=../Database/StatFin/vrm/perh/&lang=1&multilang=en; OECD (2011); http://stats.oecd.org/#; http://tilastokeskus.fi/til/tyti/2011/14/tyti_2011_14_2012-09-11_en.pdf

The most typical number of children in a Finnish family is one child and the average number of children in a family with children has been about 1.8 children per family since the 1990s. While the number of families with one child has stayed quite constant, the number of families with two or three children is decreasing (OSF, 2014b).

In 2011, the LFP rate of fathers (aged 20 to 59) of children under age three was considerably high (94.4%) compared to all fathers, as well as to non-fathers. The LFP rate of men in general (aged 15 to 64 years) has been around 77%, and among those aged 18 to 64 years, it is around 80%. The LFP rate of Finnish fathers is higher than the EU-27 average, but the LFP rate of Finnish men in general is close to the EU-27 average. The high LFP rates of Finnish fathers of small children have been explained by the typical male life course: during the first years of his marriage, a Finnish young man usually builds his work career, works on his permanent home and becomes a father (Eerola and Mykkänen, 2013). In many families, it is understood that the man's continuous LFP ensures the optimal family income (Salmi et al, 2009).

Mothers (aged 20 to 59) of three to six year olds have a significantly higher LFP rate (86.6%) than women aged 15 to 64 in general (73.4%). About 84% of employed women (aged 15 to 64) worked full-time compared to 90% of men. These proportions have been declining both in men and in women, possibly because of the increment in the amount of part-time work. The percentage of men working part-time has increased from 7.1% to 9.7%, close to the average of OECD countries. Even though the proportion of women in part-time employment has also increased simultaneously from 13.9 to 16.5%, the share remains below the OECD average of 26.4%.

In families with the youngest child under two years old, the percentage of families where both parents worked full-time was only 38.5% in 2008, but that of families where only one parent (presumably the father) was employed full-time was 45.8%. This male-breadwinner pattern is more common in Finland than in Sweden, where the proportion was only 20.8% (OECD, 2010).

Fathers and parental leave

In 2013, around 83% of fathers took paternity leave after their child was born. Despite the fact that men's share in taking parental leave has risen, fathers still take parental leave significantly less often than do mothers (Kela, 2014). The leave periods that men take are usually relatively short compared to those taken by mothers. The problem is that in cases where leave is not father- or mother-specific, it is more often taken by mothers (Lammi-Taskula, 2012). According to the OSF (2013), in 2012, 18% of parents receiving paid parental leave allowance from the Social Insurance Institution of Finland were fathers (see also Kela, 2014). Of these fathers, 94% used their entitlement for the father's quota, but fathers' share of all the paid days provided was only 4%. Since the father's quota was established in 2003, fathers' proportion of parental leave users has increased annually from around 5% to the current 18%, but fathers' proportion of all paid days has only risen from 1.5% to 4%. Therefore, the impact of the father's quota appears to be twofold: it will encourage fathers to take the father-specific parental leave, but it may change parents', or at least fathers', understanding of the shared parental leave. As Lammi-Taskula (2012) has put it, if a certain portion of parental leave is not particularly identified as father-specific, it is assumed to be mothers' leave. This issue has also been identified in internationally comparative analysis (see O'Brien, 2009).

Overall, while paternity leave in Finland is now taken by the majority of fathers – regardless of their educational or occupational background – parental leave is taken only by a small minority of a more specific group of fathers (Lammi-Taskula, 2003). Fathers with higher education and those working in health-care occupations or doing professional work are more likely to take parental leave, whereas fathers with lower education or those who are self-employed are less likely to take leave (Takala, 2005). In addition, it appears that mothers' education is a remarkable intervening variable: if a well-educated father has a significantly less-educated spouse, the likelihood of him taking leave is significantly lower than in a family situation where both of the parents have higher education (Salmi et al, 2009).

So far, the option for two years' child home-care allowance has been paid to either parent, but in the autumn of 2013, the government proposed that, in the near future, the home-care allowance should be allocated equally to both parents. This proposal is driven by the goal of increasing fathers' share in care work and to facilitate mothers' faster return to the labour force after their parental leave period. The supporters of this reform come mostly from employers with a majority of female employees, and those who oppose are mainly advocates of families with small children, especially mothers living in precarious conditions. Fathers have been relatively silent and invisible in this debate.

Fathers and childcare

In 2011, 63% of Finnish children aged one to six used public or private day-care services (Säkkinen and Kuoppala, 2011). Due to the Finnish home-care allowance system, which makes it possible for one of the parents (usually the mother) to stay at home until the child is three years old, only 41% of children between aged one and two utilised out-of-home day care. Among children aged three to five, the rate was 74%. By far the most frequent arrangement chosen by parents (92%) was the public day-care option, although the private day-care sector is gaining some popularity (Säkkinen and Kuoppala, 2011). Compared to other Nordic countries, Finland has a much lower coverage of out-of-home day care, both for under two year olds and for three to five year olds (Haagensen, 2012). In part, this pattern reflects the fact that Finnish mothers tend to take advantage of all family leave options. Moreover, many mothers are willing to exceed the compensated stay-at-home leave time.

Together with the fact that non-parental childcare is rarely used among parents of birth to three-year-old children, there is also another thought-provoking detail in EU statistics (OECD, 2012): Finnish families do not resort easily to informal childcare arrangements by relatives, friends, neighbours, babysitters or nannies provided either at home or elsewhere. In 2008, only 1.3% of children under the age of two had been in informal childcare, and among three to five year olds, the percentage was only 4.2%. After Denmark, these numbers were the lowest in Europe.

According to Reich's (2012) analysis, Finnish fathers do not appear to provide a significant amount of childcare for young children as the primary carer during the mother's work hours. However, at other times, they are more often the sole or partial provider of childcare. This may happen after the mother's work hours, on weekends or occasionally in circumstances when the children are not (yet) in another care arrangement (Salmi and Lammi-Taskula, 2004).

Research on father involvement

While Finland is part of the Nordic countries in terms of geography, history and culture, linguistically, and to some extent ethnically, it is quite different from its neighbours. Despite increased migration and the arrival of some refugees, Finland remains a relatively homogeneous country ethnically. Consequently, the mainstream of fatherhood research deals almost entirely with the Finnish population;

however, family researchers are increasingly recognising that there are multicultural changes in fatherhood.

In addition to some ethnic diversity, current changes in fatherhood are often referred to as 'new fatherhood', or 'involved' (Forsberg, 2007), 'generative' (Hawkins and Dollahite, 1997) or 'postmodern fatherhood' (Eerola and Huttunen, 2011). In the Finnish context, the 'new father' entails an involved, nurturing and gender-egalitarian father, engaged in the daily care of the child, such as changing nappies and feeding the baby. At times, a full-time commitment to childcare is expected because the new father will take his share of parental leave. In this respect, the new father concept has adopted features that have traditionally been attached to a mother only (Johansson, 2011). However, paternal involvement does not necessarily imply the perfect realisation of gender equality in men's everyday lives. A father may be an exceedingly child-oriented parent, spending a lot of time with his children, while taking on only minor responsibilities for specific childcare and household tasks (Forsberg, 2007).

According to recent studies, men's own accounts of their paternal responsibilities and duties have become more care- and nurture-oriented, probably influenced by changes in overall fathering culture. That is, men's commitment to the nurturing of infants, beginning from birth, has become almost a cultural norm (Paajanen, 2006; Eerola and Mykkänen, 2013; Eerola, 2015). At present, most men interpret nurturing as a key feature of responsible fathering and as a key attribute of a 'good father' (Eerola, 2014). Breadwinning still has an essential role in men's understanding of their parental responsibilities, but, at present, it is considered more as a shared parental responsibility than as a father-specific responsibility. Although there may be a gap between men's accounts of their activities and their actual practices, it appears that contemporary Finnish men's fathering practices are in line with the concept of the new father used in scholarship (Eerola and Huttunen, 2011). However, some studies (Paajanen, 2006; Miettinen and Rotkirch, 2012) show that there are some variations relative to the educational and socio-economic background of fathers: young, highly educated, city-dwelling fathers are in the vanguard of the shifting practices of male parenting.

Nevertheless, the 'new father' concept is still somehow ambivalent, involving some controversy in terms of time and place. Whereas the nurturing norm of 'new fatherhood' pushes fathers to spend more time with their children, the deep-rooted provider ideal leads to their strong commitment to the workplace when they become fathers (McGill, 2014). Thus, the provider requirement draws fathers out of the home because the 'ideal worker' norm demands a high number of work hours from men. Currently, it appears that the provider norm is somewhat more powerful than the 'new father' norm in situations that demand choices between staying at home and going to work.

McGill's (2014) analysis of US data shows that while there is a negative relationship between fathers' work hours and the physical care they provide for their children, there is no correlation between fathers' work hours and their time in play or achievement-related activities with children. A reasonable explanation is that physical care is bound to a certain time and place, and may occur at times when fathers are still at work. This is also the case in Finland as the time-constrained physical childcare activities occur mostly between the first and third year of a child's life. During that time, most Finnish mothers are taking parental or child home-care leave and most fathers work longer hours (OSF, 2014b).

Time engaged with children

The Finnish father-friendly and gender-equality-promoting policies have had several positive outcomes in terms of father engagement. Probably the most interesting – and most important – development that has occurred is that since the late 1980s, men's daily time devoted to caring for their young children has increased by over 60%, and the time gap between fathers and mothers has narrowed substantially from 52 minutes per day in the late 1980s (mothers 104 minutes; fathers 52 minutes) to 35 minutes per day in 2010 (mothers 118 minutes; fathers 83 minutes) (Miettinen and Rotkirch, 2012). Hence, the childcare-related daily activities ratio between fathers and mothers is at present 42% versus 58%.

According to the study of Miettinen and Rotkirch (2012), there are no remarkable variations in men's participation in different forms of care work (hands-on care, monitoring, accompanying, transportation and care work in general). Fathers performed both hands-on care activities and indirect childcare. Nevertheless, men working in professional occupations spent significantly more time in childcare activities than men in blue-collar employment (Miettinen and Rotkirch, 2012).

Recent official Finnish statistics show that from 2000 to 2010, in general, fathers have increased and mothers have decreased their time with their children under age 10 (see Table 1.2). The increment in fathers' time is not remarkable, and it is mostly due to spending more time with children on weekends and holidays. Mothers, however, spend significantly less time with children both on workdays and days off. At present, Finnish working fathers spend similar amounts of time with their under 10-year-old children on days off (6 hours 31 minutes) as the mothers do (6 hours 47 minutes).

Table 1.2: Working fathers' and mothers' daily time with their under 10-year-old children on workdays and days off, 1999–2000 and 2009–2010 (hours:minutes per day)

	Fathers		Mothers	
	1999–2000	2009–10	1999–2000	2009–10
All days	4:09	4:14	6:27	5:55
Workdays	2:52	2:52	4:03	3:41
Days off	7:04	6:31	8:22	6:47

Source: http://www.tilastokeskus.fi/til/akay/2009/06/akay_2009_06_2014-02-06_tau_002_fi.html

According to a recent study by Halme, Åstedt-Kurki and Tarkka (2009), fathers in traditional families spent less time with their young children (three to six years old) and regarded the interaction with their children as less important than did fathers in non-traditional families. For example, fathers in husband–wife families with biological children had less positive attitudes towards father involvement than did cohabiting fathers. In addition, fathers who did not consider father involvement as very important, and who had not discovered much pleasure in fatherhood, spent less active time with their young children and were less accessible to them.

Level of father engagement

In order to understand some of the nuances of Finnish fathers' engagement with children, two key studies by the Family Federation of Finland will be examined in more detail: a family survey on men's parental practices by Paajanen (2006); and a time–use study by Miettinen and Rotkirch (2012). The data of the first study are based on a survey conducted in 2004, which included a representative sample of Finnish fathers with children aged three or under. The second study is based on a representative sample of the time–use diaries of fathers with children aged six or under conducted in 2009/10. These two studies are the most recent and extensive studies available that emphasise paternal practices and give a statistical overview of contemporary Finnish fathers.

As shown in Table 1.3, both 'caring and monitoring' and 'reading and playing' are the most time-consuming care activities performed by working fathers with their under six-year-old children. The average daily time devoted to these activities as a primary activity is about one hour. It seems that Finnish fathers do not spend much time with their children as a secondary activity.

Table 1.3: Working fathers' daily time use for childcare activities when the youngest child is under six years old, 2010 (all days of a year, childcare as a primary or secondary activity)

	Primary activity	Secondary activity
Caring and monitoring	0:35	0:08
Instruction and tutoring	0:01	0:01
Reading and playing	0:25	0:03
Outdoor activities	0:06	0:00
Discussing, talking	0:02	0:07
Other care activities	0:01	0:00
Transportation and accompanying	0:13	0:00
Total childcare	1:23	0:20

Source: Miettinen and Rotkirch (2012: 79).

Over 90% of fathers considered engagement with childcare from the very onset of parenthood as crucially important (Paajanen, 2006). Working fathers participated significantly in childcare when at home, and most of the fathers definitely wanted to spend one-on-one time with their infants, including time without the mother, to increase their parental skills and develop their father–child relationship. However, while fathers found spending time with their children important and satisfying, they also worried whether they were competent and accessible enough as parents (Halme, 2009).

Fathers do engage in many kinds of activities and practices with their children (Paajanen, 2005; Halme, 2009; Miettinen and Rotkirch, 2012). In terms of basic physical care activities, such as feeding, clothing and getting the child to sleep, about half of the fathers participated as much as the mothers, indicating that the activities were equally shared. The remaining fathers also performed those activities but not to the same extent as the mothers (Paajanen, 2006). Only a few fathers stated that they did the majority of – or, alternatively, did none of – the basic care work. Over 60% of the fathers said that playing, reading and doing outdoor activities with their children were either mainly their responsibility or were shared equally with the mother. However, only

40% of the fathers reported that they took time off work when the child was sick (Paajanen, 2006).

According to these studies, fathers' relationships with their children appear relatively close and intense. Almost all fathers reported expressing their love and caring every day by nurturing, cherishing and holding their children. In addition, over 90% demonstrated their involvement by participating in their children's hobbies. Most of the fathers emphasised that an important role in child-rearing relates to their teaching of values and ethics. However, only 50% of the fathers emphasised their parenting responsibilities as gendered or diverging from the mothers' responsibilities (Paajanen, 2006).

In terms of indirect care work, which is done *for*, rather than *with*, the children, father involvement was less pronounced than with basic care activities. For example, over 60% of the fathers stated that the transfer of the children to and from day care was either done mainly by the fathers or shared equally with the mothers. Fewer than 30% stated the same about taking the child to the doctor. Buying new clothes for the children was mainly (over 80%) mothers' responsibility, as was filling out official documents, such as day-care applications or personal data forms of the children (Paajanen, 2006).

Determinants of father engagement with young children

According to Halme (2009), fathers' time spent with their young children is a complex phenomenon affected by numerous factors. Her quantitative analysis shows that the overall stress related to fathers' parenting explained 35% of the variance in the time they spent with children: the less stressful parenting is for fathers, the more time they spend with their children. The second most important explanatory variable for fathers' time involvement was a characteristic of the child: the more a father assessed his child as 'easy' (mostly jovial, behaving according to the father's wishes and not demanding), the more time they spent with the child. The third best predictor was the father's satisfaction with his couple relationship, which also reduced the father's parenting stress level. Interestingly, a father's use of alcohol significantly affected both the father's satisfaction with his couple relationship and his parenting stress, and, consequently, a father's alcohol use reduced his time involvement with his children.

Another important factor in shaping father involvement is the particular way in which parents share childcare and parental leaves. Salmi and Lammi-Taskula (2007) noticed in their national survey that the younger the mother was, the more conventionally she saw childcare as her responsibility. This attitude was strongest among women in lower-paid white-collar positions. Thus, when mothers use all of the gender-neutral leaves, it is very likely that they will continue to do the brunt of childcare work afterwards. However, if both parents share relatively equal stay-at-home periods, fathers will also remain more engaged thereafter. For instance, Duvander and Jans (2009) discovered in their Swedish data that the fathers who used parental leave were more likely to reduce their working days during their child's first years, compared to fathers who did not use the leave.

Research on father involvement and father well-being

Worldwide research on fathering practices suggests that father involvement may be related to fathers' own well-being. For example, some results from Canada show that devoted fathers have higher social capital (Ravanera, 2007), that fatherhood rebalances the importance of self and other, and that it can lead to a reorientation towards time and scheduling in fathers' everyday lives (Daly et al, 2013). However, unexpectedly little research has examined the impact of father involvement on fathers' own well-being on a large scale in general, and in Finland in particular. Hence, there is very little information available concerning this issue.

A recent study based on a sample of Finnish fathers in nuclear families emphasised that close social ties and networks increase father involvement and fathers' sense of well-being at the early stages of their fatherhood (Lähteenmäki and Neitola, 2014). This research shows that strong support from the fathers' relatives, especially from their own parents or parents-in-law, was very important in helping fathers manage their daily lives and in providing psychological support. Father involvement and father well-being appeared to be related in such a way that those men who were most concerned about their parental engagement were also those most willing to look for support as a strategy to preserve and improve their well-being. Hence, it might be stated that the men who take care of themselves are best able to care for their children as well.

Work-related behaviour

Balancing employment with family obligations is still one of the most problematic concerns for fathers of young children. According to the OSF (2014a), men with young children (under seven years) spend more time at work per week (38 hours) than fathers of older children or childless men.[1] In addition to family-related factors prompting fathers of young children to work long days and overtime, there are also workplace-related motives that may affect the behaviour of fathers. For example, many young fathers experience the workplace as so competitive that they do not risk asking for accommodations to reduce work–family conflict (Salmi and Lammi-Taskula, 2004).

A recent study (Salmi et al, 2009) found that fathers face less work–family conflicts than mothers (20% versus 40%). Work-related travelling was mentioned by fathers as a major problem. Fathers working in the public sector experienced the workplace as more father-friendly than fathers working for private employers. This may be due to the higher priority given to equality issues in the public sector. Father-friendliness implies, above all, support for taking family leaves, but also encouragement to share family-related problems. Another study (Lahelma et al, 2005) revealed that the gender differences in perceived work–family conflicts disappeared among well-educated working mothers and fathers in leading positions: both reported relatively high amounts of work–family conflicts.

Finnish fathers with young children tend to work full-time and they also do more overtime work than other groups (Lyly-Yrjänäinen, 2013). As men's time spent in childcare has grown, this has led to a higher total number of hours spent in employment and care work for men than women in families with young children (Miettinen and Rotkirch, 2012). This shows that Finnish fathers increasingly face challenges in coordinating their work and family time, and, consequently, this work–life conflict can pose serious risks for father involvement and well-being.

The term 'burned-out father' has not yet been part of the general public discourse on parents' coping abilities, but it may become a topic in the near future. These challenges are reflected in data showing that about one in every three working fathers with children from birth to six years old felt that they do not have enough time to spend with their child or their spouse. Also, the same proportion of fathers was concerned about their own coping ability, and over 40% felt that they had neglected their housework (Lammi-Taskula and Salmi, 2014).

Fatherhood programmes

Finland has a long tradition of promoting shared parenting and 'new fatherhood' by introducing a number of family leave options for fathers, but much less has been done to find new ways to support fathers in their choices and behaviours for shared parenting. Even if different kinds of fatherhood programmes may offer a solution to the challenge of how to get fathers to take parental leaves and increase their childcare activities, there have not been any systematic, countrywide programmes. Some local maternity and child welfare clinics offer classes for expectant fathers, but this is mostly on a small scale and is dependent on locally available resources. In practical terms, this kind of programme plays only a minor role in the general maternity classes for expectant women, and father-focused activities usually involve only two or three meetings in a small group of men under the leadership of a nurse from the local clinic. The resources vary at the local level and depend on the overall state of the economy; in times of a recession, funds for this type of programme are often cut.

An important agency in this area has been the *Mannerheimin Lastensuojeluliitto* (Mannerheim League for Child Welfare) (MLL).[2] This voluntary organisation, founded in 1920, is the largest child welfare organisation in Finland. MLL is a non-profit non-governmental organisation (NGO) and membership is open to everyone. The MLL offers families an opportunity to get acquainted with and take part in volunteer work, and to participate in a diverse range of activities. Local associations arrange clubs, groups for parents, excursions, training and special events. Most of the activities – like father–child groups – are based on volunteer work and are organised by local associations. Father–child groups are typically peer groups led by experienced fathers. Although quite new, this is a growing form of peer group activity at the local level. However, studies on men participating in father–child groups have not been conducted yet.[3]

As Grusec (2006) maintains, it is vitally important to provide parent education programmes that teach about the factors that increase effective parenting in general rather than to focus exclusively on 'problem parenting' stemming from a lack of knowledge or skills. Thus, the inclusive nature of MLL's fatherhood programme and its cultural sensitivity is important because fathers voluntarily enter the group with the intention of having an enjoyable time with other fathers and their children. In the MLL programmes, as in some other NGO programmes,[4] no assumptions are made about the history or background of the families attending group activities. For example, the father–child group activities are targeted at all fathers – not only at those in families with problems. The support programmes focus on the general challenges of everyday parenting rather than specific problems. However, there are also programmes in the NGO field specifically for fathers in fragile families, such as groups for alcoholic or violent fathers, and for divorced fathers.[5]

Unfortunately, there are currently no studies evaluating the outcomes of fatherhood programmes in Finland, so the overall effectiveness of these programmes is unclear. Due to the voluntary nature of these programmes, it appears likely that participating fathers may be more enthusiastic and positive about nurturing issues compared to non-participants.

The Finnish fatherhood regime

In this book, the concept of fatherhood regime is utilised to bring to light the institutional and cultural framework for fatherhood in a particular national context because policy regimes are thought to potentially affect everyday fathering practices. Policies can encourage measureable changes in fathers' behaviour in circumstances where financial support for active fatherhood is high and workplaces are supportive of fathers who want to use their entitlements to family leaves or nurture their father–child relationship after divorce (Brandth and Kvande, 2009).

Previous studies (Hobson and Morgan, 2002; Gregory and Milner, 2008) construct fatherhood regimes based on fathers' rights and obligations, breadwinner regimes, care regimes, family policies, and gender arrangements. With respect to fathers' rights and obligations, the long policy history of making gender equality a priority has had a significant influence in Finland. Thus, in governmental family policies, parental rights and obligations are generally the same for both parents. However, there is still an exception: at present, maternity leave is approximately twice as long as paternity leave. Compared to many other advanced countries, a paid paternity leave of nine weeks is regarded as very generous, but from the Finnish perspective of gender equality, this arrangement means that mothers are given more opportunities to establish an intimate parent–child relationship than fathers from the very onset of parenthood.

In terms of breadwinner regimes Finland is a 'solidaristic gender equity regime' (Mutari and Figart, 2001), which means that it features a relatively high proportion of married women in paid work and a small gender wage gap. Thus, breadwinning is no longer a crucial male-specific obstacle to father involvement because it is shared. In addition, shared parenting can be perceived as a key feature of the Finnish fatherhood regime in terms of fathers' time use with childcare (Miettinen and Rotkirch, 2012) and fathers' own accounts of their father involvement (Eerola and Mykkänen, 2013; Eerola, 2014). It is quite well-documented that in families with young children in which both parents are employed, the parents do share childcare and other parental duties relatively equally. In families with a stay-at-home mother, the majority of fathers also do their share of childcare outside of their working hours. Finnish fathers stress the importance of involvement in childcare and in hands-on nurturing as being part of their basic paternal duties from the very beginning of a child's life (Eerola and Mykkänen, 2013; Eerola, 2014).

As Gregory and Milner (2011) have put it, a shift towards a more egalitarian sharing of care responsibilities requires a new alternative male model among existing models of appropriate masculinity. The 'new fatherhood' model is intended to offer this alternative, and it appears that in the Finnish context, it is gaining general acceptance. The data presented here highlight how a father-friendly culture and policies have been successful in influencing fathers' practices and their understanding of active fatherhood as part of contemporary masculinity. Current studies imply that the cultural atmosphere accept and even emphasises active fathering as a desirable expression of modern masculinity. Recent studies (Eerola and Huttunen, 2011) capture a portrait of the nurturing father as one of the most common types of father as the current understanding of appropriate masculinity allows men to narrate fatherhood in a more familistic and emotionally rich way. Interestingly, all fathers in this study narrated themselves as 'family men' and emphasised the importance of 'being there' for the family (Eerola and Huttunen, 2011).

Nevertheless, a narrow focus on the image of the nurturing father would exclude some crucial features of the Finnish fatherhood regime. Foremost is fathers' relatively low uptake of leave during the first years after the birth of a child, especially when compared to mothers. Although the Finnish family leave system enables equal participation in stay-at-home periods during parental and home-care leaves, this has not been a popular choice for fathers. Only in few cases is the father's share of family leave equal to that of the mother. Hence, like in other countries, it appears that this imbalanced uptake of family leave reflects the continued importance of fathers' breadwinning obligations in families with young children. Despite the fact that in Finland, official policies, high women's LFP rates and fathers' own accounts support the dual-earner model, male-breadwinning patterns are resisting government efforts for change. Together, fathers' extensive LFP and mothers' higher uptake of family leave show the continued gap between real-life practices and family policy ideals.

Within the Finnish fatherhood regime, it appears that fatherhood is more diverse than ever. While a growing number of men want to be involved fathers, there are also more fathers who step into the background or out of their child's life. This happens most often through divorce because children usually reside with the mother after divorce (Hakovirta and Broberg, 2014). Simultaneously, as family forms have become more diverse over the last decades, men live out their role as fathers in increasingly varied situations. For example, single, remote and stepfathers have already become increasingly common types of fathers, and fathers living in same-sex couples or different kinds of lesbian, gay, bisexual and transgender (LGBT) families have become more visible and culturally accepted. This diversity in the forms of fatherhood has to be understood better by researchers because shifts in the current types of fathers may have a major impact on the Finnish fatherhood regime.

Conclusion and recommendations for policy

As a Nordic welfare state, Finland has been an early adopter of egalitarian policies within a dual-earner family model and a family leave system including high levels of income replacement, reduced work hours for parents, family income support and a system of publicly provided childcare. These policies are believed to positively affect men's share of childcare, maternal employment and women's relative earnings and household bargaining power (Hook, 2006).

This review points to several implications for research, policy and practice. Although Finnish men's share in childcare is at an internationally comparatively high level (Miettinen and Rotkirch, 2012), there is an urgent need to expand men's participation in early care further. Thus, the next phase would involve support for and the encouragement of fathers to realise that they can deal with childcare without any gendered restrictions. Fathers' increased engagement in early care benefits fathers, mothers, children and the entire society, especially in terms of well-being and gender equality in work and family life. To realise fathers' potential in nurturing, the most important factor would be to encourage fathers' own effort. However, support from mothers, other women and men, the workplace, and family policies would make it substantially easier.

Finnish fathers' work hours in families with small children appear to be high, whether due to families' financial restrictions, workplace constraints or fathers' own preferences. From both the US (Gerson, 2010) and the Nordic (Esping-Andersen, 2009) perspective, there remain numerous real and perceived barriers in the workplace that prevent cutting back fathers' work hours. Moreover, economically disadvantaged fathers may consider a reduction of their work hours unfeasible for their family's budget, even if workplace circumstances permit it.

In addition to norms of masculinity or workplace restrictions, 'intensive mothering', or mothers as gatekeepers, have been barriers to faster progress towards involved fathering (Hays, 1997). The high level of parental leave uptake by mothers shows that mothers are willing to sacrifice their careers and much of their personal time for their children, disregarding their employment history. Also, public discourse – among parents as well as family experts – continues to debate whether the care of very young children remains 'woman's work', and whether exclusive mothering should remain the dominant parental ideal and practice rather than shared parenting (Vuori, 2009). The discourse of exclusive mothering is still strong among young women.

Although the cultural shift towards involved fathering is noticeable, the terms 'unfinished revolution' (Gerson, 2010), 'incomplete revolution' (Esping-Andersen, 2009) or even 'stalled revolution' (England, 2010) aptly characterise the contemporary Finnish state of new fatherhood. The theory of 'lagged adaptation' (Gershuny et al, 1994) is useful in understanding the behaviour of fathers. The authors postulate that men will devote more time to domestic and childcare work if women are not there to do it, for example, because they are engaged in full-time employment. The LFP rate of Finnish women with children under age three is significantly lower (66%) than that of women with children aged three to six (81%). The Finnish family leave system offers the opportunity to stay at home until the child is three years old, which keeps many mothers out of the labour force for several years, and which, in turn, lets fathers devote themselves to employment. This situation cannot be blamed on the father – or the mother – but is mainly due to the financial situation of the family. Furthermore, even in Finland, a 'woman's Euro' is still less than a 'man's Euro' (Napari, 2007).

The lagged adaptation argument derives from three common sociological approaches to the understanding of individual behaviour: habits, skills and meanings (Gershuny et al, 2005). The skills of care work need to be built up gradually, and the change of conventional habits and meanings concerning participation in the various care activities may be slow. According to this theory, while observed changes are likely to be in the positive direction, the scale of such changes may be uneven and much smaller than anticipated. The imbalance between mothers' and fathers' use of parental leaves supports the lagged adaptation view in fathers' – as well as in mothers' – behaviour, so that the path towards completely realising new fatherhood may be long and uneven.

Gaps in research

Finnish research has focused mostly on the uptake of parental leave and the effect on women's LFP, as well as on men's leave uptake. This kind of research has mainly been completed by individual researchers, and systematic follow-up studies are often lacking. Recent research has compared leave schemes, their uptake and their consequences in the Nordic countries, and has also widened the focus to workplace attitudes and practices in connection with leave-taking. However, the connection to fathers' agency in daily practice is missing. Furthermore, more research examining the impact of father involvement on fathers' own well-being is needed.

In addition, there are studies that examine decision-making patterns between parents, men's and women's reasons for leave-taking, as well as the consequences of leave-taking on the economic position of families. However, longitudinal panel studies designed to understand the effects of fathers' leave-taking on their activities with children or on their own well-being are lacking. Moreover, there are currently no studies evaluating the outcomes of fatherhood programmes in Finland, so the overall effectiveness of these programmes is unclear. This is an important issue because more and more fatherhood programmes are on the agendas of various NGO actors, and they are competing with each other for the minimal resources that are available.

Promising initiatives and suggestions for change

At the level of family policies, action towards more equally shared infant care should be taken. As the statistics imply, men do use the leaves that are allocated for them. Thus, extending fathers' paid quotas would most probably increase men's share of the leaves, just as it has in Norway and Iceland. Brandth and Kvande (2009) found that in the Norwegian context, fathers' quotas represent the crucial break with the dominant gender order, and, thus, may present the most promising path towards more equality in family issues.

A new parental leave arrangement could be implemented along with the so-called '6 + 6 + 6-model' sketched by Salmi and Lammi-Taskula (2010; 2013) from the National Institute for Health and Welfare. Their proposal is based on three six-month periods: one for the mother, one for the father and one to be arranged as the parents wish. While this model would probably be highly effective in terms of increased father involvement and child and family well-being, it might also be too expensive to implement in the current economic climate. However, as a first step towards the equal sharing of family leaves, the proposed model could be applied with shorter time periods. For example, one option might be to maintain the three periods but to make them each for fewer months, which would not raise the total duration of parental leave radically, but could significantly improve men's opportunities to invest in early care.

According to the European Foundation for the Improvement of Living and Working Conditions (2007), an autonomous body of the EU, the basic building blocks for a shift in the existing gender division of labour via increasing fathers' uptake of parental leave are generous financial support and a period of leave dedicated to fathers. While only a minority of workplaces report problems with parental leave, it remains a policy concern (European Foundation for the Improvement of Living and Working Conditions, 2007), and companies have to pay attention to work–life conflicts, men's family leaves and other family-related absences. In recent years, workplaces have become more family-friendly, but many employer policies remain mostly directed at women, and, thus, men who take leave may fear being considered lazy and disengaged workers (Salmi et al, 2009). However, compared to other European fathers, Finnish men find it easier to take parental leave, mainly because only 16% of Finnish fathers consider their job situation insecure (Hobson and Fahlen, 2009).

An efficient way to reduce fathers' work–family conflict would be a joint initiative of employers and labour organisations to promote father-friendliness at work, spearheaded by family and child organisations, such as the MLL and the Finnish Parents' League. These kinds of initiatives can encourage fathers to take family leaves, to invest in family life and to reduce their work hours. In fact, the current atmosphere in Finnish workplaces, especially in the public sector, appears to be quite receptive to men's taking paternity and parental leaves. According to Salmi, Lammi-Taskula and Närvi (2009), around 80% of men who had used at least some weeks of parental leave said that they had not noticed any effects in terms of their working conditions or work prospects.

With such projects, it would be possible to enhance men's awareness of their possibilities to reconcile work and family. This would also promote a father- and family-friendly work culture, with the message that fathers can be replaced at work, but not at home. In addition, those employers who are successful in promoting family-friendly work cultures could be rewarded with a 'father-friendly workplace' certification that acknowledges their efforts and enhances their reputation.

Another way to increase father involvement with young children is the clear acknowledgement of fathers in maternity and child welfare clinics, which have a long history in Finland of producing excellent outcomes in terms of mothers' and newborns' well-being. First, men's participation in the activities of the clinics should become the norm, and, second, the name 'maternity clinic' should be changed to 'parental clinic', in which fathers participate on an equal footing. The visits before childbirth can encourage men to embrace shared parenting, to prioritise family responsibilities over other activities and to gain independent nurturing experiences. At the same time, mothers could be advised to more readily share parenting with the father. For example, parents should learn to discuss childcare and stay-at-home arrangements before the birth so that the early care can be shared by both parents. As child welfare clinics provide the most respected source of information on childcare, fathers' active participation in the clinics would be one of the most efficient ways to engage both them and mothers with shared parenting.

Notes

[1] See also: http://www.stat.fi/til/akay/2009/07/akay_2009_07_2014-04-16_kat_003_fi.html

[2] See: http://www.mll.fi/en/

[3] See: http://varsinaissuomenpiiri.mll.fi/vapaaehtoisille/isalapsitoiminta/

[4] See: https://ensijaturvakotienliitto-fi.directo.fi/tyomuodot/miehena-ja-isana/intoa-isatyohon/

[5] See: http://www.miessakit.fi/en

References

Anttonen, A. (1998) 'Vocabularies of citizenship and gender: Finland', *Critical Social Policy*, 18(3): 355–73.

Brandth, B. and Kvande, E. (2009) 'Gendered or gender-neutral care politics for fathers?', *The ANNALS of the American Academy of Political and Social Science*, 624: 177–89.

Broberg, M. (2010) *Uusperheen voimavarat ja lasten hyvinvointi* [*The resources of the stepfamily and the children's well-being*], Helsinki: Population Research Institute.

Daly, K.J., Ashbourne, L. and Brown, J.L. (2013) 'A reorientation of worldview: children's influence on fathers', *Journal of Family Issues*, 34(10): 1401–24.

Datta Gupta, N., Smith, N. and Verner, M. (2008) 'Perspective article: the impact of Nordic countries' family friendly policies on employment, wages, and children', *Review of Economic Households*, 6: 65–89.

Duvander, A.-Z. and Jans, A.-C. (2009) 'Consequences of fathers' parental leave use: evidence from Sweden', *Finnish Yearbook of Population Research*, pp 49–62.

Duvander, A.-Z. and Lammi-Taskula, J. (2011) 'Parental leave', in I.V. Gíslason and G.B. Eydal (eds) *Parental leave, childcare and gender equality in the Nordic countries*, TemaNord 562, Copenhagen: Nordic Council of Ministers, pp 31–64.

Eerola, P. (2014) 'Nurturing, breadwinning and upbringing: paternal responsibilities by Finnish men in early fatherhood', *Community, Work & Family*, 17(3): 308–24.

Eerola, P. (2015) *Responsible fatherhood: A narrative approach*, Jyväskylä: Jyväskylä studies in education, psychology and social research. Available at: https://jyx.jyu.fi/dspace/bitstream/handle/123456789/45600/978-951-39-6111-4_vaitos24042015.pdf?sequence=1

Eerola, P. and Huttunen, J. (2011) 'Metanarrative of the "new father" and narratives of young Finnish first-time fathers', *Fathering*, 9(3): 211–31.

Eerola, P. and Mykkänen, J. (2013) 'Paternal masculinities in early fatherhood: dominant and counter narratives by Finnish first-time fathers', *Journal of Family Issues*, DOI: 10.1177/0192513X13505566.

England, P. (2010) 'The gender revolution: uneven and stalled', *Gender & Society*, 24(2): 149–66.

Esping-Andersen, G. (2009) *Incomplete revolution: adapting welfare states to women's new roles*, Cambridge: Polity Press.

European Foundation for the Improvement of Living and Working Conditions (2007) *Parental leave in European companies, establishment survey on working time 2004–2005*, Luxembourg: Office for Official Publications of the European Communities. Available at: http://www.eurofound.europa.eu/pubdocs/2006/87/en/1/ef0687en.pdf

Forsberg, H. (2005) 'Finland's families', in B.N. Adams and J. Trost (eds) *Handbook of world families*, Thousand Oaks, CA, London and New Delhi: Sage, pp 262–82.

Forsberg, L. (2007) 'Negotiating involved fatherhood: household work, childcare and spending time with children', *NORMA: Nordic Journal for Masculinity Studies*, 2(2): 109–26.

Gershuny, J.I., Godwin, M. and Jones, S. (1994) 'The domestic labour revolution: a process of lagged adaptation?', in M. Anderson, F. Bechoffer and J.I. Gershuny (eds) *The social and political economy of the household*, Oxford: Oxford University Press, pp 151–97.

Gershuny, J.I., Bittman, M. and Brice, J. (2005) 'Exit, voice, and suffering: do couples adapt to changing employment patterns?', *Journal of Marriage and Family*, 67(3): 656–65.

Gerson, K. (2010) *The unfinished revolution: how a new generation is reshaping family, work, and gender in America*, New York, NY: Oxford University Press.

Gregory, A. and Milner, S. (2008) 'Fatherhood regimes and father involvement in France and the UK', *Community, Work & Family*, 11(1): 61–84.

Gregory, A. and Milner, S. (2011) 'What is "new" about fatherhood? The social construction of fatherhood in France and the UK', *Men and Masculinities*, 14(5): 588–606.

Grusec, J.E. (2006) 'Parents' attitudes and beliefs: their impact on children's development', in R.E. Tremblay, R.G. Barr and R.De.V. Peters (eds) *Encyclopedia on early childhood development*, Montreal: Centre of Excellence for Early Childhood Development. Available at: http://research4children.com/theme/common/document_launch.cfm?ItemId=5523#page=84

Haagensen, K.M. (2012) *Nordic statistical yearbook 2012, Vol.50*, Copenhagen: Nordic Council of Ministers.

Haataja, A. (2007) 'Parental leaves, child care policies and mothers' employment in Finland and Sweden: a comparison', in R. Myhrman and R. Säntti (eds) *Opportunities to reconcile family and work*, Report 16, Helsinki: Ministry of Social Affairs and Health, pp 99–111.

Haataja, A. (2009) *Fathers' use of paternity and parental leave in the Nordic countries*, Helsinki: The Social Insurance Institution of Finland (Kela), Research Department. Available at: www.kela.fi/research

Hakovirta, M. and Broberg, M. (2014) 'Isyys eron jälkeen' ['Fatherhood after divorce'], in P. Eerola and J. Mykkänen (eds) *Isän kokemus* [*Father's experience*], Helsinki: Gaudeamus, pp 114–26.

Halme, N. (2009) *Isän ja leikki-ikäisen lapsen yhdessäolo* [*Time spent together by fathers and small children*], Research 15, Helsinki: National Institute for Health and Welfare. Available at: http://tampub.uta. fi/handle/10024/66396/browse?order=DESC&rpp=20&sort_ by=3&etal=-1&offset=40&type=dateaccessioned

Halme, N., Åstedt-Kurki, P. and Tarkka, M.-T. (2009) 'Fathers' involvement with their preschool-age children: how fathers spend time with their children in different family structures', *Child Youth Care Forum*, 38: 103–19.

Hawkins, A.J. and Dollahite, D.C. (1997) *Generative fathering: beyond deficit perspectives*, Thousand Oaks, CA: Sage.

Hays, S. (1997) 'The ideology of intensive mothering: a cultural analysis of the best-selling gurus of appropriate childrearing', in E. Long (ed) *From sociology to cultural studies: new perspectives*, Malden, MA: Blackwell, pp 286–321.

Hearn, J. and Lattu, E. (2002) 'The recent development of Finnish studies on men: a selective review and a critique of a neglected area', *NORA: Nordic Journal of Women's Studies*, 10(1): 49–60.

Hobson, B. and Falen, S. (2009) 'Competing scenarios for European fathers: applying Sen's capabilities and agency framework to work–family balance', *The ANNALS of the American Academy of Political and Social Science*, 624: 214–33.

Hobson, B. and Morgan, D. (2002) 'Introduction', in B. Hobson (ed) *Making men into fathers. Men, masculinities and the social politics of fatherhood*, Cambridge: Cambridge University Press, pp 1–21.

Holli, A.M. (2003) *Discourse and politics for gender equality in late twentieth century Finland*, Acta Politica 23, Helsinki: Department of Political Science, University of Helsinki.

Hook, J. (2006) 'Care in context: men's unpaid work in 20 countries, 1965–2003', *American Sociological Review*, 71(4): 639–60.

Johansson, T. (2011) 'Fatherhood in transition: paternity leave and changing masculinities', *Journal of Family Communication*, 11: 165–80.

Kela (The Social Insurance Institution of Finland) (2013) 'Home and family. Families with children: benefits and housing allowances'. Available at: http://www.kela.fi/web/en/families

Kela (2014) 'Maternity, paternity and parental allowances: number of recipients and allowances paid out', Kelasto Reports. Available at: http://raportit.kela.fi/ibi_apps/WFServlet?IBIF_ ex=NIT124AL&YKIELI=E

Knoester, C., Petts, R.J. and Eggebeen, D.J. (2007) 'Commitments to fathering and the well-being and social participation of new fathers', *Journal of Marriage and Family*, 69: 991–1004.

Lahelma, E., Winter, T., Martikainen, P. and Rahkonen, O. (2005) 'Työn ja perheen väliset ristiriidat ja niiden taustatekijät naisilla ja miehillä' ['Work–family conflicts and the background factors of men and women'], in K. Kauppinen (ed) *Työ, perhe ja elämän moninaisuus I* [*Work, family and diversity of life I*], Tampere: University of Tampere, pp 34–48.

Lähteenmäki, M. and Neitola, M. (2014) 'Isien tukiverkostot vauvaperheissä' ['Fathers' support network in families with small infants'], in P. Eerola and J. Mykkänen (eds) *Isän kokemus* [*Father's experience*], Helsinki: Gaudeamus, pp 65–74.

Lammi-Taskula, J. (2003) 'Isät vapaalla: Ketkä pitävät isyys- ja vanhempainvapaata ja miksi?' ['Fathers on leave: who take paternal and parental leaves and why?'], *Yhteiskuntapolitiikka*, 68(3): 293–8.

Lammi-Taskula, J. (2006) 'Nordic men on parental leave: can the welfare state change gender relations?', in A.L. Ellingsæter and A. Leira (eds) *Politicising parenthood in Scandinavia: gender relations in welfare states*, Bristol: The Policy Press, pp 79–99.

Lammi-Taskula, J. (2007) *Parental leave for fathers? Gendered conceptions and practices in families with young children in Finland*, Research Report 166, Helsinki: National Research and Development Centre for Welfare and Health. Available at: http://tampub.uta.fi/handle/10024/66396/browse?order=DESC&rpp=20&sort_by=3&etal=-1&offset=40&type=dateaccessioned

Lammi-Taskula, J. (2012) 'Introduction', in S. Parrukoski and J. Lammi-Taskula (eds) *Parental leave policies and the economic crisis in the Nordic countries*, Helsinki: National Institute of Health and Welfare, pp 1–11. Available at: http://www.julkari.fi/handle/10024/80133

Lammi-Taskula, J. and Salmi, M. (2014) 'Isät, työ ja perhe' ['Fathers, work and the family'], in P. Eerola and J. Mykkänen (eds) *Isän kokemus* [*Father's experience*], Helsinki: Gaudeamus, pp 75–90.

Leira, A. (2002) *Working parents and the welfare state: family change and policy reform in Scandinavia*, Cambridge: Cambridge University Press.

Lyly-Yrjänäinen, M. (2013) *Työolobarometri* [*Working life barometer*], Helsinki: Ministry of Employment and the Economy.

McGill, B.S. (2014) 'Navigating new norms of involved fatherhood: employment, fathering attitudes, and father involvement', *Journal of Family Issues*, 35(8): 1089–106.

Miettinen, A. and Rotkirch, A. (2012) *Yhteistä aikaa etsimässä: Lapsiperheiden ajankäyttö 2000-luvulla* [*Time use of Finnish families with children*], Helsinki: Population Research Institute.

Ministry of Education and Culture (2014) 'Child day care'. Available at: http://www.minedu.fi/OPM/Koulutus/varhaiskasvatus/paivahoitomaksut/?lang=fi

Ministry of Social Affairs and Health (2013) *Child and Family Policy in Finland*, Helsinki: Brochures of the Ministry of Social Affairs and Health. Available at: http://www.stm.fi/en/publications/publication/-/_julkaisu/1849724#en

Mutari, E. and Figart, D.M. (2001) 'Europe at a crossroads: harmonization, liberalization, and the gender of work time', *Social Politics*, 8(1): 36–64.

Napari, S. (2007) 'Is there a motherhood wage penalty in the Finnish private sector?', *Labor: Review of Labour Economics and Industrial Relations*, 24(1): 55–73.

O'Brien, M. (2009) 'Fathers, parental leave policies, and infant quality of life: international perspectives and policy impact', *The ANNALS of the American Academy of Political and Social Science*, 624(1): 190–213.

OECD (Organisation for Economic Co-operation and Development) (2010) 'Gender brief. Version: March 2010'. Available at: http://www.oecd.org/els/social

OECD (2011) 'Doing better for families', OECD Publishing. Available at: http://dx.doi.org/10.1787/9789264098732-en

OECD (2012) 'OECD family database'. Available at: http://www.oecd.org/els/family/PF1.6%20Public%20spending%20by%20age%20of%20children.xls

OSF (Official Statistics of Finland) (2013) 'Kelan lapsiperhe-etuustilasto 2012' ['The Social Insurance Institution of Finland: benefit statistics of families with children in 2012']. Available at: http://www.kela.fi/it/kelasto/kelasto.nsf/NET/040613100800AS/$File/Lapsiperhe-etuustilasto_2012.pdf?OpenElement

OSF (2014a) 'Time use survey 2009'. Available at: http://www.stat.fi/til/akay/2009/07/index_en.html

OSF (2014b) 'Families 2012, annual review'. Available at: http://www.stat.fi/til/perh/2012/02/perh_2012_02_2013-11-22_en.pdf

Paajanen, P. (2005) *Perhebarometri 2005: Eri teitä vanhemmuuteen* [*Family barometer 2005: various paths to parenthood*], Helsinki: Population Research Institute.

Paajanen, P. (2006) *Perhebarometri 2006. Päivisin leiväntuoja, iltaisin hoiva-isä. Alle 3-vuotiaiden esikoislasten isien näkemyksiä ja kokemuksia isyydestä* [*Family barometer 2006. Breadwinner in the daytime, nurturing father in the evening. Under 3 years old first born children's fathers' views and experiences about fatherhood*], Helsinki: Population Research Institute.

Palkovitz, R. (2002) *Involved fathering and men's adult development*, Mahwah, NJ: Lawrence Erlbaum.

Pascall, G. and Lewis, J. (2004) 'Emerging gender regimes and policies for gender equality in a wider Europe', *Journal of Social Policy*, 33(3): 373–94.

Programme of the Finnish Government (2011) *An open, fair and confident Finland*, Helsinki: Prime Minister's Office. Available at: http://valtioneuvosto.fi/documents/10184/367809/Programme+of+Prime+Minister+Katainen%E2%80%99s+Government/64238eca-58cd-43bb-81dc-963a364a422e

Rantalaiho, M. (2003) 'Pohjoismaisen isyyspolitiikan isäkuva' ['The father image in Nordic fathering policies'], in H. Forsberg and R. Nätkin (eds) *Perhe murroksessa: Kriittisen perhetutkimuksen jäljillä* [*The family in transition: on the trail of critical family studies*], Helsinki: Gaudeamus, pp 202–29.

Ravanera, Z. (2007) 'Informal networks social capital of fathers: what does the social engagement survey tell us?', *Social Indicators Research*, 83(2): 351–73.

Reich, N. (2012) 'Fathers' childcare: the difference between participation and amount of time', HWWI Research Paper, No 116. Available at: http://hdl.handle.net/10419/55510

Rønsen, M. (2004) 'Fertility and public policies – evidence from Norway and Finland', Demographic Research, 10:6, Max-Planck-Gesellschaft, Rostock. Available at: www.demographic-research.org

Säkkinen, S. and Kuoppala, T. (2011) *Lasten päivähoito 2011* [*Children' day care 2011*], Tilastoraportti 30, Helsinki: National Institute of Health and Welfare. Available at: http://urn.fi/URN:NBN:fi-fe2012122010330

Salmi, M. and Lammi-Taskula, J. (1999) 'Parental leave in Finland', in P. Moss and F. Deven (eds) *Parental leave: progress or pitfall?*, Brussels: NIDI CBGS Publications, pp 85–12.

Salmi, M. and Lammi-Taskula, J. (2004) *Puhelin, mummo vai joustava työaika? Työn ja perheen yhdistämisen arkea* [*Phone, grandmother or flexible work time? The everyday reconciliation of work and family*], Helsinki: National Institute of Health and Welfare.

Salmi, M. and Lammi-Taskula, J. (2007) 'Family policy, labour market and polarization of parenthood in Finland', in R. Myhrman and R. Säntti (eds) *Opportunities to reconcile family and work*, Reports of the Ministry of Social Affairs and Health, 16, Helsinki: Ministry of Social Affairs and Health, pp 87–101.

Salmi, M. and Lammi-Taskula, J. (2010) *6+6+6 -malli vanhempainvapaan uudistamiseksi [6+6+6-model for renewal of parental leave]*, Helsinki: National Institute of Health and Welfare. Available at: http://urn.fi/URN:NBN:fi-fe201205084953

Salmi, M. and Lammi-Taskula, J. (2013) 'Finland country note', in P. Moss (ed) *International review of leave policies and research 2013*. Available at: http://www.leavenetwork.org/lp_and_r_reports/

Salmi, M., Lammi-Taskula, J. and Närvi, J. (2009) *Perhevapaat ja työelämän tasa-arvo [Family leaves and the equality in work life]*, Työ ja yrittäjyys 24, Helsinki: Ministry of Employment and the Economy. Available at: http://www.google.fi/url?sa=t&rct=j&q=&esrc=s&source=web&cd=3&ved=0CDoQFjAC&url=http%3A%2F%2Fwww.tem.fi%2Ffiles%2F22983%2FTEM_24_2009_tyo_ja_yrittajyys.pdf&ei=hjF3U5SkJuz54QTknICgDQ&usg=AFQjCNEp-BfbOfyZ3_kizldFKirGpi_Ibw

Schwab, K. (ed) (2013) *The global competitiveness report 2013–2014: full data edition*, Geneva: World Economic Forum. Available at: http://www.weforum.org/issues/global-competitiveness

Takala, P. (2005) 'Use of family leaves by fathers – the case of Finland', paper presented at the Childhoods 2005 Conference: Children and Youth in Emerging and Transforming Societies, 29 June–3 July, Oslo.

Välijärvi, J., Kupari, P., Linnakylä, P., Reinikainen, P., Sulkunen, S., Törnroos, J. and Arffman, I. (2007) *The Finnish success in PISA – and some reasons behind it*, Jyväskylä: Institute for Educational Research, University of Jyväskylä.

Vikat, A., Thomson, E. and Prskawetz, A. (2004) 'Childrearing responsibility and stepfamily fertility in Finland and Austria', *European Journal of Population/Revue européenne de Démographie*, 20(1): 1–21.

Vuori, J. (2009) 'Men's choices and masculine duties. Fathers in expert discussions', *Men and Masculinities*, 12(1): 45–72.

WEF (World Economic Forum) (2013) *The global gender gap report 2013*, Berkeley, CA: Harvard University and the University of California. Available at: http://www.weforum.org/reports

Ylikännö, M. (2009) 'Fathers' time use: the rise of new fatherhood', *Yhteiskuntapolitiikka*, 74(2): 121–31.

TWO

Germany

Marina A. Adler, Karl Lenz and Yve Stöbel-Richter

The cultural and policy context of fatherhood

Contemporary perceptions of German fatherhood and fathering are rooted in the unique history of the division and reunification of two independent states, the Federal Republic of Germany (FRG, now the Western states) and the German Democratic Republic (GDR, now the Eastern states). German unification in 1990 combined the West German 'ideal-typical' conservative welfare state and strong male-breadwinner system with the East German socialist full-time dual-earner system. The West German male-breadwinner model, with an exclusive 'family phase' for mothers, but not for fathers, was based on a strong maternalist ideology, which was also reflected in family policies. By contrast, in the former GDR, the 'mother as worker' ideal dominated, and both parents were expected to focus on employment, while the state cared for their children. The German merger resulted in a combined one-and-a-half-breadwinner system, with continued major regional variation, and recent efforts to include fathers more actively in leave policies (Erler, 2011). As a result, in the East German states, more parents continue to be dual-earner couples with two full-time earners, while in the West, most parents still have either one full-time and one part-time earner or only one earner; two full-time earning parents are uncommon.

Family policies in both German states were targeted at mothers rather than fathers: in the GDR, mothers received support to combine motherhood and employment to become full-time working mothers, while in the West, mothers were encouraged to leave the labour market for three years to become full-time mothers and then re-enter on a part-time basis (Adler, 2002, 2004; Adler and Brayfield, 2006). The different policy and cultural contexts that developed in the two separate states have lingering effects on the gendered 'culture of care' in the contemporary Eastern and Western states (Ostner, 2002; Adler and Brayfield, 2006; Lenz and Adler, 2010) and also reflects regional variations in the inclusion of fathers in care work (Erler, 2011; Meuser, 2014).

While recent legislation has improved institutional support for work–life reconciliation via public childcare and paternal leave, including 'daddy months', the cultures of time, care and workplace remain in favour of 'mother care' for young children, particularly in the West. Hence, despite recent family policy reforms towards more gender-egalitarian goals, most would still classify contemporary Germany as a conservative welfare state, albeit perhaps not as the classic case anymore. German general social spending in 2009 was 31% of gross domestic product (GDP), which was above the Organisation for Economic Co-operation and Development (OECD) average of 24.8%.[1] For family benefits, spending was 3.7%, also above the OECD average of 2.6%, and the proportion spent on early childhood was 0.5%, compared to the OECD average of 0.7%.[2]

Due to the unique historical circumstances, this chapter begins by describing the differing 'gender arrangements' (Pfau-Effinger, 1998), 'cultures of care' (Adler and Brayfield, 2006) and 'statutory father-care-sensitive leave models' (O'Brien, 2009) both east and west of the former border. Between the Second World War and 1990, the FRG was characterised by relatively generous social spending on family and employment-related social benefits, and a tax system based on a male-breadwinner gender regime. Until German unification in 1990, the FRG provided extensive family leave to mothers at low compensation and a public childcare system that targeted children older than age three. It promoted a family model where mothers stayed at home for three years to care for children and fathers devoted most of their time to employment (Kreyenfeld and Geisler, 2006; Cooke, 2011). Even though fathers became entitled to take part of a 10-month shared parental leave in 1986, very few fathers participated (Bünning, 2014).

The GDR featured a state-supported dual-earner regime with generous benefits for employed mothers and extensive free public childcare. Women were integrated into the labour market to almost the same degree as men, even when they were mothers. At the same time, women also did the lion's share of the housework and childcare, which has led to the 'double burden' for women in the East. There were no special state policies for fathers; father involvement was considered a family matter (Pabst, 2008). While the West German government supported families and protected families as independent private units, the GDR state considered child-rearing a shared responsibility between the state and family (Hettlage and Lenz, 2013).

Thus, at the time of reunification in 1990, a number of discrepant structures, norms and expectations regarding the relationship between employment and parenthood clashed. The Eastern tradition of facilitating women's reconciliation of employment and family responsibilities via state support collided with the Western legacy of a state-supported strong male-breadwinner system (Adler and Brayfield, 2006). Even today, contradictory family policies prevail. The German tax system, with its exemptions for home childcare provision and 'income splitting' rules, favours male-breadwinner families (Cooke, 2006; Kreyenfeld and Geisler, 2006). Married couples can file a combined tax return, which privileges couples in which one partner earns nothing or very little. In addition, the controversial 'Betreuungsgeld' (childcare allowance) was initially designed to allow parents to care for their children at home and, thus, only allowed limited hours of employment (Spieß, 2012). This meant that mothers mainly provided home care. In 2014, this was reformed by removing the employment restrictions and also allowing childcare provision by others as long as it is not publicly funded care (Spieß, 2012). In 2014, this monthly allowance was a flat rate of €150 per child for 22 months per child (BMFSFJ, 2013b, 2013c; Bujard, 2014).[3]

Ostner (2002) describes the treatment of fathers in both German post-war family policy regimes as guided by 'two logics' and as 'unfavourable'. The government of the former GDR disempowered the care and provider capabilities of fathers by becoming the default 'surrogate father', taking over parental and breadwinning responsibilities. In West Germany, employed 'husband-fathers' were privileged as traditional family breadwinners rather than carers. Hence, in the West, being a father did not reduce men's working hours. Despite the different policies, it appears that fathers on both sides of the German border were remarkably similar in terms of relatively low involvement with their children. German unification has brought more opportunities for father involvement through flexibility in parental leave policies and more fathers' rights in custody battles (Ostner, 2002). These legislative changes have increased fathers' access to children and have moved the fatherhood model from relatively exclusive 'father-breadwinner' towards the direction of 'father-carer'. Nevertheless, East German men may be more open to 'new masculinities' because of a longer tradition of dual-earner gender arrangements (Ostner, 2002). In the West, maternalist values and maternal gatekeeping appear to be persisting barriers to increased father care (Meuser, 2014).

Leave provisions

In 1992, shared parental leave was extended to three years, of which the parent received a flat rate of €300 a month for the first two years, allowing parents to alternate taking leave (Statistisches Bundesamt, 2013a). Since 2001, both parents are able to take parental leave simultaneously and to work up to 30 hours per week while on leave (Gerlach, 2010). Furthermore, since 2002, there are tax breaks for private childcare. However, it was not until 2007 when the *Bundeselterngeld with partner months* was introduced that significantly more fathers became motivated to take leave. This parental allowance, or *Elterngeld*, was part of a policy package called 'sustaining family policy', which was designed to reverse falling birth rates, to increase women's labour force participation (LFP) and to promote gender equality by incentivising fathers' participation in care work (Reimer, 2014). Parents receive 67% of their average previous net earnings (65% since 2011, up to a maximum of €1,800 a month) for 14 months, starting with the day of the child's birth (Bujard and Fabricius, 2013). This period can be divided between both parents, though one parent can only ask for a maximum of 12 months. Two of the 14 months are mandatory maternity leave with full pay and two are the so-called '*Vätermonate*', or '*daddy months*', which are a bonus not transferable to mothers (Bujard and Fabricius, 2013). However, if fathers do not take these two 'daddy months' of paid dedicated leave, they forfeit the benefit. Those who were not working before they became parents, for example, students or homemakers, receive the minimum amount of €300 monthly added to the family income. A single parent is eligible to take the full 14 months (BMFSFJ, 2011).

In addition, *Elternzeit* (parental time) allows parents to take (unpaid) childcare leave until the child is three (BMFSFJ, 2011). During this period of time, parents are eligible to take a leave of absence from work with a guaranteed right to return to the same job or a comparable position within the company. In order to align the end of parental leave with the availability of day care for children under age three, a 2007 law spurred the expansion of public childcare for children in that age group. This has increased the proportion of children aged two and younger in public childcare from 16% in 2007 to 28% in 2012 (Statistisches Bundesamt, 2012b), and 15% of children younger than age three now spend 30 or more hours per week in formal childcare arrangements (Eurostat, 2012). This proportion is higher in the Eastern states than in the West. Beginning in January 2015, *Elterngeld Plus* will expand parental choice regarding early childcare, will incentivise an earlier return to employment and will reward the equal sharing of parental leave and employment for four months between partners.[4]

Contextual demographic and family trends related to fatherhood

The regional differences in gender culture and policy are also reflected in different demographic trends, family structure and LFP. While internationally comparative statistics do not distinguish between the Eastern and Western states, Table 2.1 presents regionally specific data for indicators where regional information is available.

Table 2.1 shows that not only did German marriage rates decline from 5.1 to 4.6 since 2000, but so did divorce rates (2.4 to 2.3). While marriage rates are similar in the East German and West German states, divorce is more prevalent in the West (2.2) than the East (1.9). The total fertility rate has not changed much over the last decade, but the crude birth rate has decreased from 9.3 to 8.1 and fertility is slightly higher in the Eastern than the Western states. One reason that fewer children are being born is the increase in mothers' average age at first birth, which is currently older than 29. Overall, the proportion of German women who have their first child when they are older than 35 has risen to 24% in 2010 (Euro-Peristat, 2013). While the average age at first birth has increased dramatically in the Eastern states since unification, it is still lower in the East (27.4) than in the West (29.2). In addition, non-marital births have increased in all of Germany quite drastically from 15% to 34% over the last decade; however, whereas 62% of women in the Eastern states have babies outside of marriage, only 28% of Western women do (BMFSFJ, 2012a; Statistisches Bundesamt, 2013a).

Hence, several Eastern family-related life-course patterns have survived unification: women still become mothers earlier, have more children and are more likely have children outside of marriage in the East than in the West. In addition, family forms, gender arrangements and gendered LFP continue to vary by region. Today, many German couples remain unmarried at the birth of their first child – in 2010, 43% of first children (36% in the West and 74% in the East) were born to unmarried parents. This is because traditional married families have decreased as alternative forms of living together, such as cohabitation and solo parenting, have gained popularity. Table 2.1 reflects that the share of households with children composed of married couples and children decreased from 77% to 71%, while that of cohabiting couples with children rose from 7% to 9%. Whereas the number of solo

Table 2.1: Selected indicators related to parenting for Germany, circa 2000 and circa 2012

Indicator	2000			2012		
	Total	East	West	Total	East	West
Crude marriage rate (per 1,000 population)	5.1	3.9	5.4	4.6 (2011)	4.6	4.7
Crude divorce rate	2.4	2.3	2.4	2.3 (2011)	1.9	2.2
Total fertility rate	1.4	1.2	1.4	1.4 (2011)	1.43	1.36
Crude birth rate	9.3			8.1		
Mothers' mean age at first birth	29[a]			29.2	27.4	29.2
% non-marital births	15			34	62	28
% of family households with kids <18 that are:						
Husband/wife with children	76.8 (2002)			70.7		
Unmarried couple with children	6.9 (2002)			9.4		
Mother only with children	14.2 (2002)			17.9		
Father only with children	2.1 (2002)			2.0		
% of children < 18 living with:						
Two married parents	80.5	65.2	83.9	74.5	56.9	78
Father only		2.5	2.6		1.9	1.7
Mother only		20.7	13.5		22.8	14.2
% of married-couple families that are:						
Dual-earner families	NA			52.2	55.8	51.6
Male-provider families	NA			36.6	31.0	37.6

Table 2.1: continued

Indicator	2000			2012		
	Total	East	West	Total	East	West
LFP						
LFP rate, men (age 15–64)	78.9			82.4		
Fathers (15+) of kids under 18	98.8 (1996)	87.9	90.4	84.1	81.8	84.6
Fathers of < 3 year olds	88.8 (1996)	82.6	89.7	82.2	78.1	83.1
Fathers of 3–5 year olds	90.8 (1996)	88.6	91.2	85.1	83.5	85.4
Men, % full-time	95.2			91.3		
Men, % part-time	4.8			8.7		
Men, mean number of hours/week	41.1			39.8		
Fathers, mean number of hours/week	NA			39 (2010)		
LFP rate, women (15–64)	63.6			71.7		
Mothers (15+) of kids under 18	55.0 (1996)	69.5	50.5	60.3	62.9	59.7
Mothers of < 3 year olds	26.6 (1996)	32.5	25.6	31.7	38.7	30.0
Mothers of 3–5 year olds	50.0 (1996)	63.8	46.9	61.8	66.4	60.7
Women, % full-time	66.1			62.2		
Women, % part-time	33.2			37.8		
Women, mean number of hours/week	31.9			30.5		
Mothers, mean number of hours/week	NA			25 (2010)		

Note: [a] 2000 mean age at birth UNECE Statistical Database, compiled from national and international (Eurostat and UNICEF TransMONEE) official sources.

Sources: Datenreport 2013; Statistisches Jahrbuch 2013; Eurofound (2014); BMFSFJ (2012a, 2013a); Pötzsch (2012); OECD Data Base, available at http://stats.oecd.org/'; Eurostat; Statistisches Bundesamt (2012c); Huerta et al (2013); http://www.sozialpolitik-aktuell.de/familie-datensammlung.html#i-familien-und-kinder; OECD.StatExtracts; Keller and Haustein (2013).

mother households has increased from 14% to 18%, solo father families remain rare at around 2%. Between 2000 and 2012, the proportion of children who live with two married parents also shrank from 81% to 75%. In addition, the share of children who live with two married parents continues to be much lower in the East (57%) than in the West (78%). Conversely, in the East, more children live with a solo parent than in the West.

Table 2.1 also illustrates the persistent regional differences in the preferred gender arrangement in families. While more than half of all German married couples are dual-earner families (52%), the rate is higher in the Eastern (56%) than in the Western states (52%). Mikrozensus data of 2012 (presented in Keller and Haustein, 2013) show that in 29% of German couples with children, the father is the only breadwinner: 31% in the West compared to 23% in the East. In addition, mothers in the East are much more likely to work full-time (55%), including those with children under age three (53%), than Western mothers (25% and 22%, respectively) (Keller and Haustein, 2013). In only 19% of West German working couples with children did both parents work full-time, compared to 54% of East German couples, and while in 76% of Western couples, fathers worked full-time and mothers part-time, this was the arrangement in only 41% of Eastern couples (Keller and Haustein, 2013). Thus, as was the norm in the former GDR, in the Eastern states, the dual-earner arrangement includes two full-time employed parents even when the children are younger than age three. In contrast, mothers in the Western states still tend to be employed part-time, and, thus, the dual-earner arrangement is mostly a one-and-a-half-earner model.

In 2012, the LFP for German men aged 15–64 was 82%, and 91% worked full-time. There is little difference regardless of the age of the fathers' children: the LFP of fathers in general was at 84%, for fathers of children younger than age three, it was 82%, and the rate was 85% for fathers with children aged three to five. These statistics are somewhat higher in the East than in the West. Men's part-time employment rate has increased to 8.7% in recent years. It also becomes clear that German men do not significantly reduce their full-time work status when they become fathers. Based on Mikrozensus data of 2012, about 95% of all fathers worked full-time (95% in the West and 93% in the East); this was almost as high for fathers of children younger than age six (94%). While only 5.6% (under three years old) to 5.8% (three to five year olds) of Western fathers of young children work part-time, in the East, 8.3% to 9.1% do so. Among fathers, the percentage working reduced hours increases with the number of children: only 6.2% of fathers with one child younger than age six work reduced hours, while 7.8% of those with three children do (Statistisches Bundesamt, 2014a). Overall, men's weekly average number of hours worked has decreased over the last decade from 41.1% to 39.8%.

While the LFP rate of German women has increased from 63% to 72% over the last decade, there is quite a gap between mothers (60%) and women in general. When examining the LFP of women with children under age three (32%), it becomes clear that mothers of infants and toddlers prefer to care for their children at home, particularly in the West. Once the children are older than age three, women re-enter the labour market (62%) and use public childcare. What is most striking is that German women have very high part-time employment rates (38%), which are now even higher than they were in 2000. About 69% of all German mothers work part-time, but the rate is much higher in the West (75%) than the East (44%) (Keller and Haustein, 2013). This pattern is mirrored by statistics on day-care use for children younger than age three in Germany, which is only 26% – this is below the European Union (EU) target of 33%. One obstacle for women's full-time LFP when children reach school age is that in the German school system, classes end at lunchtime and mothers are expected to provide lunch for their children. Efforts to increase school time to full-day coverage are in progress, including providing afterschool care and lunch; however, by 2012, only about 56% of schools offered afternoon programmes and only about one third of students participated in them (Bundesministerium für Bildung und Forschung, 2014).

Fathers and parental leave

While Germany does not provide statutory paternity leave, the current parental leave provision, which includes unofficial 'daddy months', can be considered a 'father-care-sensitive leave model' (O'Brien, 2009) because it is a measure intended to facilitate father involvement. The 2007 policy package appears to have at least partially worked as intended: it has increased the proportion of fathers who take parental leave dramatically from 3.5% in 2006 to 28% in 2012; those who took parental leave used, on average, about 3.3 months (Bujard und Fabricius, 2013). The majority of leave-taking fathers took up to two months (78%), 14% took three to nine months and 8.2% took 10–12 months (Statistisches Bundesamt, 2012a; 2014b). In 2012, fewer than 8% of all parental leave months were taken by fathers (Reimer, 2014). The compensation during the leave remains, on average, about one third higher for men than women (Statistisches Bundesamt, 2013b).

Pfahl und Reuyß (2009) distinguish among five types of fathers who take parental leave, using six criteria related to fathers' and their partners' length of leave and level of financial support, level of employment, combination with unpaid leave, and previous experience with taking leave. Their survey sample included 624 leave-taking fathers and 52 in-depth interviews and resulted in the following father types (Pfahl und Reuyß, 2009: 227–8): (1) 46% were 'cautious fathers', who were career-oriented first-time leave-takers and took short leave mainly to help their partners; (2) 14% were 'semi-egalitarian' fathers, who were also career-oriented but took three to eight months of leave while their partner worked in order to support their partner's work; (3) 9% were 'family-oriented' fathers, who considered the child the focus of their leave and took one to eight months leave while their partners worked, plus took unpaid leave to care for a child younger than age two; (4) 6% were 'reversed' fathers – they had higher-earning partners, were less interested in a career, had previous leave experience and stayed home for nine to 12 months, while their partners did not use much leave; and (5) 5% were 'family-centred' fathers, who prioritised family long-term, took nine to 12 months leave (as well as additional unpaid leave), had previous leave experience and often reduced their working hours when returning to work. In general, two thirds of leave-taking fathers stated that their main motive for taking leave was to establish a close relationship with their children; fewer than one quarter of leave-taking fathers primarily wanted to support their partner's working career (Pfahl and Reuyß, 2009). This indicates that child involvement is more important to fathers' uptake of parental leave than attitudes about gender egalitarianism (Bekkengen, 2006).

The decision regarding which type of leave combination will be taken by parents depends on financial conditions, career aspirations, gender attitudes and the availability of childcare (Pfahl and Reuyß, 2009; Richter, 2012). In addition, fathers' decisions can depend on workplace culture, the size of the workplace, sector and occupation, and the attitudes of employers and colleagues (Pfahl and Reuyß, 2009; Richter, 2012). Even when firms provide a supportive environment, highly qualified fathers often hesitate to announce their parental leave plans because they fear negative repercussions for their careers (Richter, 2012).

A number of quantitative analyses investigate the determinants of fathers' parental leave use. In general, fathers who take parental leave tend to be more educated, have only one child and live in Eastern Germany (Geisler and Kreyenfeld, 2011, 2012). Geisler and Kreyenfeld (2011) examined German Mikrozensus data from 1999 to 2005 to show that while men's level of education does not affect their likelihood of taking leave, their lower 'relative education' vis-a-vis that of their partners does increase fathers' leave-taking. Similarly, Trappe (2013) concluded that relative earnings within couples affect fathers' leave-taking behaviour.

Fathers and childcare

Availability of affordable public childcare for young children, especially those under age three, is a precondition for the integration of both parents into the labour market. While the provision of childcare for very young children has been the norm in the East, in West and unified Germany, this has only recently emerged as a major demand on the policy agenda. In 2007, it was decided that, by 2013, public childcare should be available nationwide for 35% of all children younger than age three (Statistisches Bundesamt, 2013b). Since 2013, all children who have completed their first year also have a legal right to public childcare. In Germany, most parents (mainly mothers) care for their children themselves during the first year while on leave, and in about 25% of cases, integrate grandparents into caring for the infants (see data from Nationale Untersuchung zur Bildung, Betreuung und Erziehung in der frühen Kindheit [NUBBEK] and Aufwachsen in Deutschland: Alltagswelten [AID:A] studies). Non-family childcare is generally provided through formal institutions or 'day mothers/ fathers' (women or men who are paid to care for the young children of working parents during the day, usually in their own home and with their own children).

In 2012, 28% of German children under three were in formal childcare; in the Eastern states, this childcare coverage included 49%, compared to 22% of children younger than age three in the Western states (Statistisches Bundesamt, 2013b). More than half of those under three years old are generally in childcare for the entire day (more than 30 hours per week); in the East, this applies to 68% of children younger than age three, while in the West, it only applies to 30% (Statistisches Bundesamt, 2013b). While this appears to be relatively high, the rate of under two year olds in childcare is very low because the typical age of entry is older than 24 months – this is younger in the East (about 21 months) than the West (about 29 months) (Tietze et al, 2012). For three to five year olds, day-care coverage increases dramatically: nationwide, about 93% of children were in childcare in 2012 (Statistisches Bundesamt, 2013b).

Due to the mother-centred care culture, long mother-focused leave provisions, high female part-time employment and relatively high non-family childcare availability, 'father care' as a childcare arrangement is not even a subject of surveys and statistical estimates in Germany. While grandparent care is estimated, neither the Mikrozensus nor family-focused surveys, such as NUBBEK (Tietze et al, 2012) or AID:A (Rauschenbach und Bien, 2011), deal with fathers as the *primary family childcare provider* when mothers work. In fact, the word 'fathers' is not mentioned in the most recent NUBBEK survey and report on childcare in early childhood (Tietze et al, 2012). Hence, no data are available for fathers as a possible childcare arrangement during mothers' work hours and for how many children fathers are the primary carer during the week.

Research on father involvement

German research on father involvement began making inroads in the 1980s with the work of Fthenakis (1985), who initially examined the psychological aspects of the father–child relationship and later characterised involved fatherhood as a 'gentle revolution in the family' (Fthenakis, 1999). While a lot of early German scholarship tended to focus on the lack of father involvement (ie the effect of absent fathers on children), more recently, father typologies and the concepts of 'new fathers', 'responsible fathers' and 'positive fathering' have gained popularity (Cyprian, 2007; Mühling, 2007; Abel and Abel, 2009; Possinger, 2013). These changes in focus were related to societal shifts from more disciplinarian models towards more emotion-based child-rearing ideals, more 'child-centred' families and more egalitarian gender attitudes and policies. Yet, there is ample evidence that contemporary German fathers, even when they are on parental leave, assume the role of an assistant or 'co-parent' in the performance of direct childcare activities (Possinger, 2013; Meuser, 2014). It appears that there are generally three kinds of German father engagement: the traditional-caring father, the partnership-caring father and the egalitarian-caring father (Possinger, 2013). The first group, also called 'after-work dads', is the largest segment and includes men who mostly 'help' mothers perform childcare activities that they find pleasurable. The second group of fathers is more engaged in more aspects of childcare, which are still considered mothers' territory, but they will reduce some of their workplace involvement under special circumstances. The last group is the smallest group, being most engaged in all aspects of childcare and inclined to shift time-use patterns from work to family. Overall, about 20% of German fathers spend 'substantial' paternal time with their children, defined as more than 28 hours per week (Koslowski Smith, 2007).

Time engaged with children

Based on national time-use survey data, in 2001/02, employed fathers of children under age seven who spend any time performing childcare spent, on average, 62 minutes per day with childcare as a primary activity and another 25 minutes with childcare as a secondary activity (Gauthier and De Gusti, 2012). For children younger than age three, primary childcare activities took 1 hour and 17 minutes (Mühling, 2007). In addition, in 2001/02, fathers of children younger than age seven in dual-earner couples spent, on average, 1 hour and15 minutes per day with primary childcare and 25 minutes with childcare as a secondary activity (Gauthier and De Gusti, 2012). Fathers with non-employed or part-time employed partners spent only 62 minutes primarily caring for their young children. Overall, during that time, fathers spent about 10 hours per week in primary and secondary childcare with preschoolers while they were employed full-time (Gauthier and De Gusti, 2012).

Unfortunately, there are no German time-use survey data like those from 2001/02 available for the time after the 2007 enactment of parental leave, only non-representative survey data or qualitative studies. In general, German fathers appear to spend substantially more time with children when they are on leave (Wrohlich et al, 2012). Furthermore, using AID:A survey data from 2009, Zerle and Keddi (2011) found that German fathers in full-time dual-earner couples share in childcare to a high degree, especially when it comes to playing, going on outings with children and spending family time on Sundays. This is also confirmed by qualitative research that shows Germany to have a 'Sunday is family day' culture (Grunow, 2007). About 74% of fathers state that they spend three or more hours with their children on Sundays and two thirds spend one to two hours on childcare during the average weekday. Grunow (2007) concludes that there has been relatively little change in fathers' time involvement with young children, and that both parents have declared Sunday as 'family day' and thus both devote more hours to their children. Recent surveys from 2011–2013 (IfD Allensbach, 2011, 2012, 2013) also show that working fathers generally appear to do about one hour of primary childcare per day and that 59% of fathers spend less than two hours a day on primary childcare.

Grunow (2007) used longitudinal German Socio-Economic Panel (SOEP) data to compare the total time (in whole hours) fathers spend with their under three year olds in the Eastern and Western states. The analysis only included fathers who spend any time with childcare. In 2004, West German fathers spent, on average, 2.7 hours on weekdays and 5.7 hours on Sundays (in 2003) on total childcare activities (primary and secondary activity) of small children. For East German fathers, it was 2.5 and 6.6 hours, respectively. These statistics reflect only minor changes in time use since 1991. The data also show that men do about 20% of routine care activities for children under age six. The analysis of the proportion of time fathers spent with childcare of the total childcare among the parents reflects greater differences by region. In 2004, West German men spent 22% on weekday childcare and 32% (2003) on weekend care, compared to 28% and 36%, respectively, in the East.

Older data from the 'Bamberger study' of 1988–2002 also show that East German men do a larger share of care work during the week and on weekends (27–36%) than West German men (22–32%) (see Grunow, 2007; Grunow et al, 2007, 2012). Various qualitative analyses confirm that father involvement is higher in the Eastern states than in West Germany (Behnke, 2012; Behnke et al, 2013; Meuser, 2014). In particular, it is argued that in the West, fathering is framed much more in gendered terms – any care work done by fathers is considered a 'special effort' and is praised, but it remains in the realm of 'assisting' mothers (Behnke and Meuser, 2013). In the East, fathers' agency in care work is considered a normal, expected and unquestioned activity rather than something special, and fathers are not considered 'assistants' of mothers to the same extent as in the West. Behnke and Meuser (2013) interpret this as a by-product of the double full-time employment of most East German parents and their coordinated efforts to reconcile work and family. In addition, Zerle and Krok (2008) show that 38% of Western fathers compared to only 30% of Eastern fathers held 'traditional' gender role attitudes.

Level of father engagement

According to Nickel (2002), a longitudinal study of pregnancy, birth and parent–child interaction during the first year after birth showed that, in 2000, about 91% of fathers attended the birth and 78% were with the mothers in the delivery room. Those fathers who took preparatory courses on birth and the care of newborns were found to be more involved in the first six weeks with changing nappies, carrying infants and pushing prams. According to a 2013 survey (FORSA,

2013), 83% of fathers were present in the delivery room for the birth of at least one of their children. It appears that, unlike in the past, father participation before, during and right after birth is now considered an expected part of becoming a father rather than a sign of especially engaged fatherhood.

Fthenakis und Minsel (2002) examined childcare activities and subjective constructions of fatherhood along four dimensions: social function, breadwinner function, instrumental function and willingness to reduce career ambitions. The first and third functions relate to fathers as nurturers, and the second and fourth to fathers as providers. Results show that two thirds of men defined themselves as nurturers, and considered the social function as the most important father function, especially among new fathers and those of children under age six. The study also shows that only half of fathers of children younger than six participated in care work, which means that they were not fulfilling their own aspirations (Fthenakis et al, 2002). The fathers mostly did tasks that were not time-sensitive and those that involved play. Only about 20% of fathers did physical care work. Most of the time spent with infants involved physical care (35 minutes) and playing (34 minutes), while for children between the ages of three and six, the overall time spent was 52 minutes, with physical care requiring 16 minutes and playing 19 minutes (see Mühling, 2007).

In surveys from 2011–2013 (IfD Allensbach, 2011, 2012, 2013), men self-reported doing the following tasks by themselves 'regularly' for children younger than age 16: about 10% transport children, help with homework, read, play music, go to a playground or play with their children; about 14% transport children to and from day care/school; 25% organise family outings; and 50% play sports with their children. A 2013 survey (Forsa Institute, 2013) shows that for younger children, men self-report doing the following 'regularly': 71% participate in baby care; 58% get up at night; 54% play with their children; and 50% cuddle with children. Similarly, Krok and Zerle's (2008) analysis of 2007 data indicates that 92% of fathers play with their children and 62% check their children's homework 'often or very often'. Overall, it is noticeable that the German research literature is quite vague when it comes to how engaged fathers are in specific activities, how often they are performed and how much time they involve. Non-specific descriptions of fathers stating that they 'often or very often' spend time with their children or that they 'regularly' supervise or care for their children prevail.

Determinants of father engagement with young children

While research in Germany has examined the determinants of fathers' uptake of parental leave (Geisler and Kreyenfeld, 2011, 2012; Trappe, 2013), less attention has been given to the consequences of parental leave on fathers' childcare time. Even a relatively short time outside the workplace should allow fathers to bond with their children and to develop parenting skills and confidence (Rehel, 2014). While Schobers's (2014) analysis suggests that fathers increased their participation in childcare only temporarily during the first year after taking parental leave, Bünning's (2014) research indicates a longer-term effect. An online survey suggests that about 19% of fathers worked reduced hours after taking parental leave, and fathers who took leave stated in interviews that they would prefer more opportunities to integrate work and family (Pfahl and Reuyß, 2009).

Unfortunately, because there are no representative German time-use data after 2007 indicating father participation in specific childcare tasks, this review focuses on studies of previous data and those multivariate analyses focusing on time spent with childcare in general. Multivariate examinations of changes in time use between 1991/92 and 2001/02 show that while fathers do not spend different amounts of time at work than non-fathers, fathers of children younger than age five do more housework and childcare than non-fathers, especially on weekends (Neilson and Stanfors, 2014). The authors suggest that there is evidence for the emergence of more active 'weekend fathers' in Germany. Based on their analysis, the authors argue that for the time period studied, German extended parental leave targeting mothers, the cultural preference for mother care at home in the early years and joint taxation reinforced a traditional division of labour regarding childcare.

Hook and Wolf (2011) also used the German Time Use Survey (TUS) 2001 data in a multivariate analysis predicting father involvement, but focused on active time used for childcare as a primary activity rather than general time use that includes children. Their three dependent variables were the number of minutes fathers actively spent with children in physical care, interactive care and time alone with children. The analyses were run separately for weekdays and weekends and included fathers of children younger than age 15. Variables in the equations included fathers' age, education, work hours, partners' employment status, number and ages of children, and whether a male child is present. Results indicate that during the week, more educated men and those with a youngest child under age six (compared to those with a youngest child who is aged six to nine) spent significantly more time with physical childcare. Interestingly, on the weekend, older men, those with small children and those with a male child increased their time alone with children. The authors conclude that German fathers are not very responsive to their own and their partners' specific employment characteristics. German fathers may be less likely to change their own childcare time based on their partners' work time, mainly because German culture favours maternal caring for young children.

In a decomposition analysis comparing Austria and Germany, Berghammer (2013) used the German TUS data for families with children under age six and examined the time fathers spent with childcare as a primary activity. This study controlled for variations in gender arrangements (six types of full-time/part-time/not employed constellations), the number of children and the education of both partners. Disregarding whether their partners worked 40 hours a week or not at all, German fathers cared for their children for five to seven hours per week, and this was about half the time of mothers' care work time. Full-time working fathers (and mothers) and those with higher education increased their childcare time. The finding that German parents have not significantly changed their time involvement with children between 1991/92 and 2001/02 is particularly interesting, especially considering the controls included.

Bünning (2014) analysed data of the SOEP between 2006 and 2012 and the Families in Germany (FID) between 2010 and 2012 to assess the effect of parental leave on fathers' time allocation. Results show that leave-taking fathers increased their participation in childcare by more than 1.5 hours and reduced their work hours by more than three hours per week, and that this change in time use persisted for at least two or three years after taking leave. The longer the period of paternal leave taken, the more fathers shifted their time allocation so that those who took more than the two 'daddy months' reduced their total working time by about six hours per week. Conversely, the non-leave-taking fathers increased their work time by about one hour per week. In addition, leave-takers 'also do a higher share of child care and housework if their partners work more hours and they themselves work shorter hours' and 'after taking long and solo parental leaves' (Bünning, 2014: 10). When partners alternated their leave-taking, the reductions in working hours were larger then when couples took the leave simultaneously. Overall, Bünning concludes that parental leave, especially if it is extended and taken solo, encourages fathers to shift some of their time from the workplace to their family.

Research on father involvement and father well-being

The examination of the relationship between parenthood and health often centres on the positive effects of children on the quality of life of parents related to the experience of intense emotional bonding and the everyday routine structure of life (Stöbel-Richter, 2010; Von der Lippe and Rattay, 2014). Research indicates that parenthood is generally related to reduced mental health issues, especially depression and substance use (Helbig et al, 2006). Only a few German studies focus on the relationships between fatherhood and health directly. A study by the Robert Koch Institut (2003) found that both solo fathers and married fathers consider their health as equally good, but solo fathers worry less about their health. This is interesting because other studies document that single parents are usually at higher risk of mental health issues (Hagen and Philipps, 2012; Helbig et al, 2006). Furthermore, analyses of Gesundheit in Deutschland aktuell (GEDA) data from 2009 and 2010 (Von der Lippe and Rattay, 2014) show that only about 8% of fathers feel psychologically burdened and 8% have severe physical problems. Risk factors related to health impairment for fathers (as for mothers) were lower social status, lower social support, unemployment and the lack of a partner in the household. In general, there are few gender differences and fathers are not different from non-fathers in health status.

Most research assessing fathers' subjective well-being finds more positive than negative effects of fatherhood. For example, a 2013 survey of fathers (Forsa Institute, 2013) indicates that 58% of respondents and 65% of fathers of children younger than age six consider their life more happy and complete since the birth of their child(ren). In addition, the fathers of young children also report becoming more self-confident (28%). Nevertheless, the respondents also mentioned a perceived lack of time for themselves (39%) and feeling overwhelmed or stressed (41%) since becoming fathers. Furthermore, while 29% thought the relationship with their partner was strengthened, 20–30% were also dissatisfied with various aspects of their relationship after becoming fathers.

Pollmann-Schult (2010; Pollmann-Schult and Diewald, 2007; Pollmann-Schult and Wagner, 2014) recently assessed the effects of fatherhood on men's well-being via multivariate analysis of SOEP data. Measures of well-being included life satisfaction, civic engagement, relationships to the family of origin and friends, and religious participation. Most dimensions of well-being were affected positively by the transition to fatherhood. The multivariate analyses found that fathers of under six year olds are more satisfied with life since becoming fathers, visit relatives more frequently, have a closer relationship to their own father and participate in religious events more often, disregarding work status, education and partner characteristics. The involvement in clubs and attendance at sporting events is enhanced by having children older than age 14, but on the negative side, children of all ages reduce restaurant visits and visits with friends. The author concludes that, overall, the subjective well-being of men is increased by fatherhood.

Work-related behaviour

The effect of fatherhood on men's working lives depends on their individual characteristics, the labour market behaviour of their partners and family policies. Pollmann-Schult (2009) examined the effect of fatherhood on German men's income using SOEP data from 1984 to 2006. When controlling for various employment-related characteristics, fathers of one child increase their income by about 1.2% and this effect is raised by additional children. However, once the employment status of the partner is included, the pay-off of children for fathers disappears – it is replaced by a payoff of having a partner who is not employed over one who is. Specifically, married fathers in a dual-earner family with a full-time employed partner earn significantly less than those in a male-breadwinner family.

While the German work culture is quite time-demanding, there are a number of worker protections in place that are relevant to parents. By law, firms with more than 15 employees have to provide opportunities for part-time work and family-related leave for their employees. Most German companies also have special initiatives on workplace flexibility, such as flexitime, education programmes and work opportunities from home for employees returning from parental leave (BMFSFJ, 2006). While these programmes apply to both genders, men are still less likely than women to request reduced work hours. One respondent in Possinger's (2013: 31–2) research discussed the high pressure to do 'care work' for firm and clients, and refers to the company as a 'greedy child'. Hence, it appears that both firm and family compete over the time and attention of fathers.

Reimer's (2014) research on work organisations shows that they can mediate fathers' leave-taking by making requests for leave uncomfortable. Fathers fear negative consequences for their careers from their employer or colleagues. Men may feel that they have to justify leaving early and that it is not 'manly' to be a carer (Possinger, 2014). It appears that norms of masculinity and care work still have compatibility issues when it comes to workplace culture. According to Oechsle (2014), for fathers, taking leave is often regarded as taking a holiday, which makes fatherhood and related care work less visible and less important. Parental leave for fathers is not viewed as an entitlement or right, but as a favour that is negotiable. Thus, fathers are uncertain about the reactions from employers and co-workers to their leave. Interestingly, research has shown that this fear is mostly unfounded. In fact, about 37% of men were working in some flexible working time arrangement in 2010 (compared to 36% of women) (Körner et al, 2012). In addition, Germans work fewer hours and enjoy more job security than workers of the majority of Western countries: Germany has the third-lowest total work hours of all OECD countries (OECD, 2011).

The 2013 Forsa Institute survey shows that 64% of fathers prefer to work full-time and another 22% would like to work 30–35 hours a week. The majority of respondents (58%) also state that their workplace offers opportunities for such reduced hours and 43% would like more time with their family. Yet, 89% of the sample works full-time, and only 18% had taken parental leave. One reason for these conflicting results is the perceived effect of reducing work hours on their career: 41% thought that taking parental leave would have a negative effect. According to another recent survey on the time use of employed parents (IfD Allensbach, 2012), 65% of fathers state that their employment involvement prevents them from spending time on other things, and 52% feel that they do not have enough time to do everything that needs to be done. Half of fathers would feel less stressed if they could work less, 53% if they had more flexible working times and 32% if they could work from home.

According to Possinger (2013), German fathers attempt to solve these work–family conflicts through 'boundary management', which involves the active creation of quality time for family, especially at meal times and weekends. In addition, fathers may avoid working overtime, reserve early evenings for 'family time' and defend their free time against demands to engage in work activities.

Overall, German men appear to be hesitant to reduce their working time when they become fathers, and if they do, they do not reduce their hours by very much. A multivariate analysis of fathers' preferred work hours in the Western states (Pollmann-Schult, 2008) in different gender arrangements shows that the employment status and income of the mother is a more important consideration than positive caring attitudes. In general, Western fathers with young children whose partners are not employed or employed part-time increased the number of preferred work hours by one and two-and-a-half hours, respectively. When their partners work full-time, fathers decrease their preferred work hours by three quarters of an hour. Similarly, in couples where mothers have no or low income, fathers increase their preferred work time, while higher-earning mothers lead fathers to reduce their preferred work time.

Fatherhood programmes

In addition to men's and fathers' groups and associations of subgroups of fathers (solo fathers, fathers with custody), magazines directly targeting fathers have emerged in Germany. Some of these associations are subsidised by the government and support reforms in family law (*Verein Väteraufbruch für Kinder*) and improvements in the reconciliation of work and family for fathers (*Väter e. V.*). The organisation *Väter e. V.* has an online information system and training programmes for fathers to learn about rights and strategies for work–family reconciliation. Another association (*Verein Väter und Karriere*) focuses on research and the implementation of work and family integration programmes in the workplace (Huber and Schäfer, 2012). Huber (2014: 203) argues that men often have an information deficit when it comes to their own rights as fathers. Thus, for example, many fathers do not even think of taking time off to take care of their sick child because they do not realise that they have this right.

While there has also been an increase in self-help groups, father-focused parenting books and father–child meets, fathers appear to be mainly interested in easily accessible information. Internet chat rooms in which specific subjects are discussed are becoming particularly popular among fathers. Internet sites like *Vatersein* or *Väteraufbruch* offer forums where fathers can exchange experiences and receive advice from trained moderators on topics such as separation, divorce and custody (Nakhla et al, 2010). Nevertheless, it appears that these spaces are mainly reserved for middle-class men's concerns and rarely involve vulnerable populations with specific needs, such as unemployed, low-income, migrant or substance-abusing fathers. For these special groups of fathers, several outreach programmes have been developed that attempt to provide services under the rubric of father education or counselling.

In terms of preparation for parenthood, high schools are beginning to offer programmes – such as 'Project Daddy Cool' – that aim to present a multitude of role models of being a father (Zerle and Krok, 2008). Using events, activities and forums for discussion, these programmes hope to demystify relationships and family for young men. In addition, father modules are offered as part of birth preparation and family formation programmes, which offer seminars specifically for fathers (eg *Väterbildung in Deutschland*).[5] Unfortunately, it has been shown that only about 17% of participants in family education programmes are men (Lösel et al, 2006). In order to specifically increase the participation of fathers, some programmes have changed their philosophy from 'let them come to us' to 'let us go to them'. Hence, the format shifted from the so-called 'come-structure', where potential participants are invited to come to meetings, to one where family educators perform home visits ('go-structure') for new parents (Nakhla et al, 2010). However, even with this innovation, fathers often avoid being present at the visits.

Barriers to father participation in programming include time scheduling, feelings of incompetence and insecurity, and the rejection of activities considered outside the male gender role. It appears that many fathers feel uncomfortable in a space that they perceive as mothers' or women's space. In addition, some fathers resent the assumption that they need help being a good father or that they are incapable of proper fathering or fathering their own way (Nakhla et al, 2010). The idea that they are deficient as parents or that they are help-seekers often puts men on the defensive. Thus, it is important to have fathers themselves be involved in creating programming and designing spaces based on their preferences, needs and competencies (Schäfer and Schulte, 2009). The *Väterzentrum* in Berlin is considered a model of a centre for fathers because its infrastructure is designed specifically by and for fathers (Nakhla et al, 2010).

With respect to workplace programmes, almost 90% of German firms now offer flexible working times and family-friendly policies that include fathers. Initiatives like flexitime, education programmes and telework for returning leave-takers have become widely accepted (BMFSFJ, 2006). The 30 largest German companies have all adopted initiatives that are designed to integrate work and family needs, and a number of companies, such as Bayer, Volkswagen and Siemens, even offer on-site day-care centres, job sharing, sabbaticals and extended leave. These efforts have been evaluated through a non-profit work and family audit certification process by the *Hertie Foundation* since the late 1990s, which certifies workplaces that offer support to working families (Hertie-Stiftung, 2010). The leading German trade associations and governmental institutions promote this management tool as a strategy to identify promising initiatives and best practices, and to target areas of improvement (Hertie-Stiftung, 2014).

In 2012, 18% of companies offered special father-support policies, which encourage parental leave-taking and working reduced hours (BMFSFJ, 2013d). A number of workplaces have also introduced father representatives, father networks or father advisory boards. For example, these advocacy groups hold lunch meetings or seminars that help fathers understand their rights and competencies, learn about strategies to reconcile work and family, connect with each other, and make fatherhood visible at work. One of the issues is that when fathers are more involved with their children, the probability of work–family conflict increases, but this conflict is often not part of public or workplace discourse. Huber (2014: 202) refers to this phenomenon as the 'hidden reconciliation problem' facing involved fathers.

The German fatherhood regime

It appears that Germany is a 'mixed' or moderate fatherhood regime because while parental leave policies now include fathers, and the take-up rate of fathers leave of two months or more has increased, it remains below 30% due to several counterproductive policies. While taking two months of leave would seem like a good amount of time to become proficient in infant care and to help German fathers break out of their 'apprentice' or 'co-parenting' role, these fathers are often not solely responsible for their children's care because the leave is taken concurrently with mothers. German fathers tend to spend relatively little time alone with their young children, especially in the Western states and when it comes to performing 'typical' mothers' activities. While there is a common public discourse on the desirability of the 'active father', data on the engagement, accessibility and responsibility of fathers with young children reflect a low incidence of such fathers in general, and in the West in particular. It appears that available well-compensated parental leave is used mainly by women and for longer periods of time, after which public childcare is available, so that most fathers are buffered from more actively caring for their children. Most German women stay at home for more than a year after the birth of a child. The fact that West German women stay at home with their children for around two years and then often only return to work part-time reinforces the gendered division of childcare. This pattern is less pronounced in the Eastern states, where women tend to exit the labour market for a shorter time and then are more likely to work full-time. This is a continuation of the 'baby year' pattern prevalent in GDR policy, after which mothers were expected to be full-time workers. The evidence presented also shows that East German men are somewhat more involved fathers than West German men.

It appears that contemporary fathers understand their own fatherhood as being both nurturer and provider (Schiefer and Bujard, 2012), and the 2007 policy reform allows fathers more freedom to pursue these competing goals. Survey data show that more than half of full-time working fathers would like to spend more time with their children (IfD Allensbach, 2010a, 2010b). Yet, there is a split between egalitarian attitudes and the daily reality after a child is born. In other words, fathers' behaviour lags behind their intentions and available policy provisions. While there has been a sharp increase in men's leave participation since 2007 and fathers' proportion of time spent with their children has increased vis-a-vis mothers', the numbers are still relatively low by international comparison.

This chapter has presented considerable evidence of the continuing prevalence of the 'after-work dad', the 'weekend father' and the father as 'assistant' in Germany. What is astonishing is that in a context of comparatively low work hours, increasing workplace flexibility to accommodate family responsibilities, increasing policy support for fathers and more egalitarian attitudes in general, there has been relatively little change in the amount of hands-on childcare tasks performed by fathers over the last few decades. While the proportion of childcare performed by fathers in dual-earner couples has increased and men in the East are somewhat more involved than those in the West, overall, German fathers do significantly less routine care work every day than mothers. The reasons for this pattern are related to economic realities, family policies and gender culture. First, economic pressures based on work performance result in fathers' high work orientation in terms of preferred work hours and a reluctance to reduce hours. When the workplace is considered the 'greedier child' (Possinger, 2013), less time is available to engage with real children. Second, the continued popularity of a gender arrangement with a non-working or part-time working mother in the early years is reinforced by long parental leave that is primarily taken by mothers. By encouraging women to stay at home with children for one to three years, childcare becomes defined as their main activity, reinforcing men's provider role. Third, a persisting maternalist culture relegates fathers to 'assistants' rather than parents in their own right because childcare is still not considered a 'male domain'. Specifically, according to Meuser (2014), as long as childcare work is associated with women and mothering, it will be viewed through a 'maternal lens', and, thus, other forms of nurturing children, such as fathering, are less visible or are devalued.

The German policy framework and labour market feature a number of safeguards that reduce the financial risks for men wanting to decrease their work hours. However, couples make decisions about their family budget together and the gender wage gap and the complication of coordinating two full-time earners with childcare arrangements often lead to a traditional division of labour (Zerle and Krok, 2008). In addition, while mothers' employment is considered acceptable, it remains in the position of 'secondary earner' rather than main earner, especially in West Germany and when the children are young (Mühling, 2007). However, while men are the main providers who receive major incentives to meet the cultural expectation to be involved fathers, the means for integrating work and family often remain hidden and undiscussed in public. About 68% of men who were unable to take parental leave stated that reducing their work hours was not an option (BMFSFJ, 2011). Other fathers who take leave may end up in a 'father trap', where they want success at work but also want to be engaged fathers (Jurczyk and Thiessen, 2008). In order to escape this trap, fathers engage more with their children without losing or reducing their work identity as providers (Jurczyk and Thiessen, 2008). This contrasts with mothers, who reduce their hours at work to retain their identity as mothers and time with their children (Zerle and Krok, 2009).

Conclusion and recommendations for policy

As fatherhood is currently being redefined, German fathers find themselves negotiating an insecure territory between the breadwinner and carer aspects of fathering. They have moved from the 'absent father' of the past to a more present 'co-parent' (Meuser, 2014), who knows how to change nappies and feed a child when necessary, but who considers childcare work essentially still mothers' work. Yet, truly involved fatherhood implies a father who actively participates in direct routine childcare every day and considers those tasks to be part of his own repertoire, his area of competence and commitment. Currently, most fathers do not reduce their work hours significantly, and they mostly return to the same work hours after parental leave, indicating that childcare is a temporary or side-job for them.

When fathers not only take leave concurrently to their partners, but also alternate and become solo carers, fundamental changes in the gender division of labour are possible (Richter, 2012). It appears that the more mothers are involved in the labour market and the more they earn, the higher the involvement of fathers at home, and vice versa (BMFSFJ, 2012b). This means that when women leave the labour market for one to three years and then re-enter only part-time, they not only reduce their financial contribution to family income, but also reinforce the idea that care work is their area of competency and that they are 'secondary earners'. At the same time, fathers remain the main earners as they are relegated to the position of 'secondary parent'. However, a consistent finding presented here is that there is a relatively small group of fathers – about 20% – who consciously take parental leave and reduce their work hours because they want to care for their children (Pfahl and Reuyß, 2009; Bünning, 2014).

Even though Germany has recently seen dramatic shifts in gender attitudes and policies that aim to facilitate providing and nurturing behaviours for both parents, the basic gender arrangement has not kept pace with these changes. German family policies have moved from an exclusive focus on supporting women and mothers to gender mainstreaming with the goal of the equality of both genders in family and employment. While this implies a demand for an increased involvement of full-time working fathers in care work at home, it has not included a corresponding demand for an equal full-time LFP of mothers. The wish to be an active father clashes with the provider image. Softening ideas about masculinity coexist with the traditional maternalist division of care work – men spend most of their time at work and women spend most of their time at home (Zerle and Krok, 2009). 'In the past, Germany had been labeled a prototypical conservative welfare state regime.... The new regulations raise the question of whether this reform represents a turning point in German family policies. Is Germany losing its identity as a conservative welfare state?' (Geisler and Kreyenfeld, 2012: 5). The evidence reflects an incomplete move from the ideal-typical conservative welfare state towards a more social-democratic one.

Gaps in research

Unfortunately, lack of current data on specific tasks prevents the testing of hypotheses related to the effect of policy changes on the daily activities performed with children by fathers on leave and by those not on leave. Data-collection efforts need to target the essential hands-on tasks required for the well-being of children at various young ages, how often they have to be performed and how much time they require. This review has found a lack of specificity in German research on father involvement, and clear comparable data are necessary.

This review also points to a lack of research on paternal well-being. Another important research area worth expanding relates to testing the co-parenting thesis of Meuser (2014). The relationship between parents in terms of main and secondary carer and main and secondary earner needs exploration, particularly with respect to the degree of maternal gatekeeping. In addition, why are fathers reluctant to work fewer than 30 hours and why do women prefer to work part-time? What are the dynamics of decision-making within couples given that the context for egalitarian leave-taking has improved significantly in recent years?

Promising initiatives and suggestions for change

One of the important findings is that when fathers are involved early in their child's care, they tend to remain involved. Hence, birth preparation courses and new father programmes should be expanded, with special emphasis on making them 'father-friendly' environments. The *Väterzentrum* in Berlin provides a good model for how to create comfortable spaces for men in which they feel supported. Similarly, the idea of having 'father representatives' in the workplace appears promising. Once established, these positions should be widely advertised to attract fathers' participation. In particular, it would be helpful if fathers could be encouraged to take solo and prolonged parental leave so that fatherhood would be visible and important.

Other important innovations are on-site day-care centres and efforts to accredit workplaces that have father-friendly environments. Nevertheless, mothers also need to be targeted − after-school programmes should be expanded so that women can work full-time. While German society has done a lot to facilitate father involvement in childcare, it lags behind in facilitating mother involvement in the labour market. If the goal is to have families where both parents share provider and carer responsibilities in an egalitarian manner, both mothers and fathers have to be involved. Currently, German policy is contradictory − while moving away from exclusive mother care, it also reinforces the traditional division of labour through the tax system and caring allowance. Hence, policy should move in one direction − away from supporting exclusive mother care and male breadwinners towards egalitarian care sharing.

Notes

[1] See: www.oecd.org

[2] See: www.oecd.org

[3.] See also: http://www.bmfsfj.de/BMFSFJ/Service/themen-lotse,did=199286. html#fragment

[4.] See: http://www.elterngeld.net/elterngeldplus.html

[5.] See: http://elternbildung-tirol.at/bild/veranstaltung/vaeterbildung_1.pdf

References

Abel, F. and Abel, J. (2009) 'Zwischen neuem Vaterbild und Wirklichkeit. Die Ausgestaltung der Vaterschaft bei jungen Vätern. Ergebnisse einer qualitativen Studie', in K. Jurczyk and A. Lange (eds) *Vaterwerden und Vatersein heute. Neue Wege – neue Chancen!*, Gütersloh: Bertelsmann Stiftung, pp 231–49.

Adler, M. (2002) 'German unification as a turning point in East German women's life course: biographical changes in work and family roles', *Sex Roles: A Journal of Research*, 47: 83–98.

Adler, M. (2004) '"Child-free" and unmarried: changes in the life planning of young East German women', *Journal of Marriage & Family*, 66: 1167–76.

Adler, M. and Brayfield, A. (2006) 'Gender regimes and cultures of care: public support for maternal employment in Germany and the United States', *Marriage & Family Review*, 39: 229–53.

Behnke, C. (2012) *Partnerschaftliche Arrangements und väterliche Praxis in Ost-und Westdeutschland. Paare erzählen*, Opladen: Berlin–Toronto.

Behnke, C. and Meuser, M. (2013) 'Aktive Vaterschaft. Geschlechterkonflikte und Männlichkeitsbilder in biographischen Paarinterviews', in P. Loos, A.M. Nohl, A. Przyborski and B. Schäffer (eds) *Dokumentarische Methode. Grundlagen, Entwicklungen, Anwendungen*, Opladen: Berlin–Toronto, pp 75–91.

Behnke, C., Lengersdorf, D. and Meuser, M. (2013) 'Egalitätsansprüche vs. Selbstverständlichkeiten. Unterschiedliche Rahmungen väterlichen Engagements bei Paaren aus den westlichen und den östlichen Bundesländern', in A. Rusconi, C. Wimbauer, M. Motakef, B. Kortendiek and P. Berger (eds) *Paare und Ungleichheit(en). Eine Verhältnisbestimmung*, Opladen: Berlin–Toronto, pp 192–209.

Bekkengen, L. (2006) 'Men's parental leave: a manifestation of gender equality or child orientation?', in L. Gonäs and J. Karlsson (eds) *Gender segregation. Divisions of work in post-industrial welfare states*, Burlington, VT: Ashgate, pp 149–62.

Berghammer, C. (2013) 'Keine Zeit für Kinder? Veränderungen in der Kinderbetreuungszeit von Eltern in Deutschland und Ősterreich', *Zeitschrift für Soziologie*, 42: 52–73.

BMFSFJ (Bundesministerium für Familien, Senioren, Frauen, und Jugend) (ed) (2006) 'Facetten der Vaterschaft'. Available at: http://www.bmfsfj.de/BMFSFJ/Service/Publikationen/publikationsliste,did=70116.html

BMFSFJ (ed) (2011) 'Familienreport 2010. Leistungen, Wirkungen, Trends'. Available at: http://www.bmfsfj.de/BMFSFJ/Service/publikationen,did=140786.html

BMFSFJ (ed) (2012a) 'Geburten und Geburtenverhalten in Deutschland'. Available at: http://www.bmfsfj.de/BMFSFJ/Familie/demografischer-wandel,did=190036.html

BMFSFJ (ed) (2012b) 'Zeit für Familie. Familienzeitpolitik als Chance einer nachhaltigen Familienpolitik', 8, Familienbericht, Bonn. Available at: http://www.bmfsfj.de/RedaktionBMFSFJ/Abteilung2/Pdf-Anlagen/Achter-familienbericht,property=pdf,bereich=bmfsfj,sprache=de,rwb=true.pdf

BMFSFJ (ed) (2013a) 'Familienreport 2012. Leistungen, Wirkungen, Trends'. Available at: http://www.bmfsfj.de/BMFSFJ/Service/publikationen,did=195578.html

BMFSFJ (ed) (2013b) 'Elterngeld-Monitor 2012'. Available at: http://www.bmfsfj.de/BMFSFJ/Service/Publikationen/publikationsliste,did=184556.html

BMFSFJ (ed) (2013c) 'Politischer Bericht zur Gesamtevaluation der ehe- und familienbezogenen Leistungen'. Available at: http://www.bmfsfj.de/BMFSFJ/familie,did=195944.html

BMFSFJ (ed) (2013d) 'Unternehmensmonitor Familienfreundlichkeit 2013'. Available at: http://www.bmfsfj.de/BMFSFJ/Service/publikationen,did=199418.html

Bujard, M. (2014) 'Elterngeld – Wie Agenda Setting und neue Interessenkoalitionen den familienpolitischen Paradigmenwechsel ermöglichten', Duisburg. Available at: http://regierungsforschung.de/elterngeld-how-agenda-setting-and-new-stakeholder-coalitions-facilitated-a-paradigm-shift-in-german-family-policies/

Bujard, M. and Fabricius, K. (2013) 'Mehr Väter mit Elternzeit: Beteiligungsquoten und Bezugsdauer von Elterngeld im Bundesländervergleich', *Bevölkerungsforschung Aktuell* 34(6): 2–10.

Bundesministerium für Bildung und Forschung (ed) (2014) 'Bildung in Deutschland 2014', 5, Bildungsbericht, Bonn.

Bünning, M. (2014) 'What remains after the "daddy months"? The impact of taking parental leave on fathers' subsequent participation in paid work, child care and domestic work in Germany', paper presented at the Workshop 'Practices and Policies around Parenthood: Towards New Models of Fatherhood?', Torino (Italy), 8 May.

Cooke, L.P. (2006) 'Policy, preferences and patriarchy: the division of domestic labor in East, West Germany and the United States', *Social Politics: International Studies in Gender, State and Society*, 13(1): 1–27.

Cooke, L.P. (2011) *Gender-class equality in political economies*, New York, NY: Routledge.

Cyprian, G. (2007) 'Väterforschung im deutschsprachigen Raum – ein Überblick über Methoden, Ergebnisse und offene Fragen', in T. Mühling and H. Rost (eds) *Väter im Blickpunkt. Perspektiven der Familienforschung*, Opladen: Leske & Budrich, pp 23–48.

Erler, D. (2011) 'Germany: taking a Nordic turn?', in S.B. Kamerman and P. Moss (eds) *The politics of parental leave policies. Children, parenting, gender and the labour market*, Bristol: The Policy Press, pp 119–34.

Eurofound (ed) (2014) '3rd European quality of life survey'. Available at: http://www.eurofound.europa.eu/surveys/european-quality-of-life-surveys-eqls/european-quality-of-life-survey-2012

Euro-Peristat (ed) (2013) 'European perinatal health report. Health and care of pregnant women and babies in Europe in 2010'. Available at: http://www.europeristat.com/images/doc/Peristat%202013%20V2.pdf

Eurostat (2012) 'Database'. Available at: http://ec.europa.eu/eurostat/data/database

Forsa Institute (ed) (2013) 'Meinungen und Einstellungen der Väter in Deutschland', Gesellschaft für Sozialforschung und statistische Analyses mbH, Berlin.

Fthenakis, W.E. (1985) *Väter. Zur Psychologie der Vater-Kind Beziehung*, Band 1 and 2, München: Deutscher Taschenbuch Verlag.

Fthenakis, W.E. (1999) *Engagierte Vaterschaft. Die sanfte Revolution in der Familie*, Opladen: Leske & Budrich.

Fthenakis, W.E. and Minsel, B. (2002) *Die Rolle des Vaters in der Familie*, Stuttgart: Kohlhammer.

Fthenakis, W.E., Kalicki, B. and Peitz, G. (2002) *Paare werden Eltern. Die Ergebnisse der LBS-Familien-Studie*, Opladen: Leske & Budrich.

Gauthier, A.H. and De Gusti, B. (2012) 'Time allocation to children by parents in Europe', *International Sociology*, 27(6): 827–45.

Geisler, E. and Kreyenfeld, M. (2011) 'Against all odds: fathers' use of parental leave in Germany', *Journal of European Social Policy*, 21: 88–99.

Geisler, E. and Kreyenfeld, M. (2012) 'How policy matters. Germany's parental leave benefit reform and fathers' behavior 1999–2009', MPIDR Working Paper, WP 2012-021.

Gerlach, I. (2010) *Familienpolitik*, Wiesbaden: VS Verlag für Sozialwissenschaften.

Grunow, D. (2007) 'Wandel der Geschlechterrollen und Väterhandeln im Alltag', in T. Mühling and H. Rost (eds) *Väter im Blickpunkt. Perspektiven der Familienforschung*, Opladen: Leske & Budrich, pp 49–76.

Grunow, D., Schulz, F. and Blossfeld, H.-P. (2007) 'Was erklärt die Traditionalisierungsprozesse häuslicher Arbeitsteilung im Eheverlauf: Soziale Normen oder soziale Ressourcen?', *Zeitschrift für Soziologie*, 36: 162–81.

Grunow, D., Schulz, F. and Blossfeld, H.-P. (2012) 'What determines change in the division of housework over the course of marriage?', *International Sociology*, 27: 289–307.

Hagen, C. and Philipps, V. (2012) 'Lebensformen und gesundheitliche Ungleichheit', in T. Lampert and C. Hagen (eds) *Armut und Gesundheit. Theoretische Konzepte, empirische Befunde, politische Herausforderungen*, Wiesbaden: VS-Verlag.

Helbig, S., Lampert, T., Klose, M. and Jacobi, F. (2006) 'Is parenthood associated with mental health?', *Social Psychiatry and Psychiatric Epidemiology*, 41: 889–96.

Hertie-Stiftung (2010) 'Beruf unf Familie. Eine Initiative der gemeinnuetzigen Hertie-Stiftung'. Available at: http://www.beruf-und-familie.de/

Hertie-Stiftung (2014) 'Unternehmens- und Beschäftigtenumfrage: "Beruf und Pflege"'. Available at: http://www.beruf-und-familie.de/system/cms/data/dl_data/6e4d8cc73f3669024ec927da5ee94d2e/2014_Befragung_Beruf_und_Pflege.pdf

Hettlage, R. and Lenz, K. (2013) *Projekt Deutschland*, München: Wilhelm Fink.

Hook, J.L. and Wolf, C.M. (2011) 'New fathers? Residential fathers' time with children in four countries', *Journal of Family Issues*, 33(4): 415–50.

Huber, J. (2014) 'Vater, wo bist du? Eine sozialwissenschaftliche Annäherung an das dialektische Phänomen väterlicher An- und Abwesenheit', PhD dissertation, Fakultät für Erziehungswissenschaften der Technischen Universität Dresden, Dresden, Germany.

Huber, J. and Schäfer, E. (2012) 'Väterpolitik in Deutschland', in H. Walter and A. Eickhorst (eds) *Das Väter-Handbuch*, Gießen: Psychosozial, pp 127–46.

Huerta, M.C., Adema, W., Baxter, J., Han, W.-J., Lausten, M., Lee, R. and Waldfogel, J. (2013) 'Fathers' leave, fathers' involvement and child development: are they related? Evidence from four OECD countries', OECD Social, Employment and Migration Working Papers No 140. Available at: http://www.oecd.org/officialdocuments/publicdisplaydocumentpdf/?cote=DELSA/ELSA/WD/SEM%282012%2911&docLanguage=En

IfD Allensbach (Institut für Demoskopie Allensbach) (2010a) 'Monitor Familienforschung. Das Wohlbefinden von Eltern im Auftrag des BMFSFJ'. Available at: http://www.bmfsfj.de/BMFSFJ/Service/publikationen,did=158762.html

IfD Allensbach (2010b) 'Monitor Familienleben 2010. Einstellung und Lebensverhältnisse von Familien'. Available at: http://www.bmfsfj.de/BMFSFJ/familie,did=155818.html

IfD Allensbach (2011) 'Monitor Familienleben 2011'. Available at: http://www.ifd-allensbach.de/uploads/tx_studies/Monitor_Familienleben_2011.pdf

IfD Allensbach (2012) 'Monitor Familienleben 2012'. Available at: http://www.bmfsfj.de/RedaktionBMFSFJ/Abteilung2/Pdf-Anlagen/monitor-familienleben-2012,property=pdf,bereich=bmfsfj,sprache=de,rwb=true.pdf

IfD Allensbach (2013) 'Monitor Familienleben 2013'. Available at: http://www.ifd-allensbach.de/uploads/tx_studies/7893_Monitor_Familienleben_2013.pdf

Jurczyk, K. and Thiessen, B. (2008) 'Väterbilder-Mütterbilder. Die Kluft zwischen Leitbildern und Alltag', *DJI-Bulletin*, 83/84: 27–9.

Keller, M. and Haustein, T. (2013) 'Vereinbarkeit von Familie und Beruf. Ergebnisse des Mikrozensus 2010', in Statistisches Bundesamt (ed) *Wirtschaft und Statistik*, Wiesbaden: Statistisches Bundesamt, p 34.

Körner, T., Puch, K. and Wingerter, C. (2012) *Qualität der Arbeit. Geld verdienen und was sonst noch zählt*, Wiesbaden: Statistisches Bundesamt. Available at: https://www.destatis.de/DE/Publikationen/Thematisch/Arbeitsmarkt/Erwerbstaetige/BroschuereQualitaetArbeit0010015129001.pdf?__blob=publicationFile

Koslowski Smith, A. (2007) 'Working fathers in Europe. Earning and caring?', CRFR Research Briefing 30, Centre for Research on Families and Relationships, University of Edinburgh. Available at: http://www.socialpolicy.ed.ac.uk/__data/assets/pdf_file/0004/6538/rb30.pdf

Kreyenfeld, M. and Geisler, E. (2006) 'Müttererwerbstätigkeit in Ost- und Westdeutschland', *Zeitschrift für Familienforschung*, 18: 333–60.

Krok, I. and Zerle, C. (2008) 'Was wünschen sich junge Männer und junge Väter von Politik und Arbeitgebern?', *DJI Bulletin*, 83/84: 16–19.

Lenz, K. and Adler, M.A. (2010) *Geschlechterverhältnisse. Einführung in die sozialwissenschaftliche Geschlechterforschung. Band 1 (Reihe Geschlechterforschung)* [*Gendered structures. Introduction to social science gender research. Volume I (Gender Research Series)*], Weinheim: Juventa Verlag.

Lösel, F., Schmucker, M., Plankensteiner, B. and Weiss, M. (2006) *Bestandaufnahme und Evaluation der Elternbildung*, Berlin: Bundesministerium für Familie, Senioren, Frauen und Jugend.

Meuser, M. (2014) 'Care und Männlichkeit in modernen Gesellschaften – Grundlegende Überlegungen illustriert am Beispiel involvierter Vaterschaft', in B. Aulenbacher, B. Riegraf and H. Theobald (eds) *Sorge: Arbeit, Verhältnisse, Regime. Soziale Welt – Sonderband 20*, Baden-Baden: Nomos: pp 159–74.

Mühling, T. (2007) 'Wie verbringen Väter ihre Zeit? Männer zwischen "Zeitnot" und "Qualitätszeit"', in T. Mühling and H. Rost (eds) *Väter im Blickpunkt. Perspektiven der Familienforschung*, Opladen: Leske & Budrich, pp 115–42.

Nakhla, D., Eickhorst, A. and Schwinn, L. (2010) 'Catch them if you can?! Angebote zur psychosozialen Unterstützung von Vätern mit Säuglingen und Kleinkindern unter besonderer Berücksichtigung der Teilnahmemotivation', *Praxis der Kinderpsychologie und Kinderpsychiatrie*, 59: 629–39.

Neilson, J. and Stanfors, M. (2014) 'It's about time! Gender, parenthood, and household divisions of labor under different welfare regimes', *Journal of Family Issues*, 35(8): 1066–88.

Nickel, H. (2002) 'Väter und ihre Kinder vor und nach der Geburt', in H. Walter (ed) *Männer als Väter*, Giessen: Psychosozial Verlag, pp 555–84.

O'Brien, M. (2009) 'Fathers, parental leave policies, and infant quality of life: international perspectives and policy impact', *The Annals of the American Academy of Political & Social Science*, 624: 190–213.

OECD (Organisation for Economic Co-operation and Development) (2011) 'Family database'. Available at: www.oecd.org/els/family/database.htm

Oechsle, M. (2014) 'Hidden rules and sense of entitlement – working fathers within organizations', paper presented at the WFRN Conference, New York, June.

Ostner, I. (2002) 'A new role for fathers? The German case', in B. Hobson (ed) *Making men into fathers – men, masculinities and the social politics of fatherhood*, Cambridge: Cambridge University Press, pp 150–67.

Pabst, I. (2008) Übergang zur Vaterschaft – *ein Vergleich zwischen der DDR und der BRD*, Saarbrücken: VDM-Verlag.

Pfahl, S. and Reuyß, S. (2009) *Das neue Elterngeld. Erfahrungen und betriebliche Nutzungsbedingungen von Vätern*, Düsseldorf: Hans-Böckler-Stiftung.

Pfau-Effinger, B. (1998) 'Gender cultures and the gender arrangement – a theoretical framework for cross-national gender research', *Innovation: The European Journal of Social Science Research*, 11(2): 147–66.

Pollmann-Schult, M. (2008) 'Familiengründung und gewünschter Erwerbsumfang von Männern – Eine Längsschnittanalyse für die alten Bundesländer', *Zeitschrift für Soziologie*, 37(6): 498–515.

Pollmann-Schult, M. (2009) 'Vatersein "zahlt" sich aus. Einflüsse der Familiengründung auf das Einkommen von Männern', in K. Jurczyk and A. Lange (eds) *Vaterwerden und Vatersein heute*, Gütersloh: Verlag Bertelsmann Stiftung, pp 173–91.

Pollmann-Schult, M. (2010) 'Wenn Männer Väter warden – über die Auswirkungen der Vaterschaft auf Freizeit, Lebenszufriedenheit und familiäre Beziehungen', *Zeitschrift für Familienforschung*, 22(3): 350–69.

Pollmann-Schult, M. and Diewald, M. (2007) 'Auswirkungen der Familiengründung auf den Berufsverlauf von Männern', *Kölner Zeitschrift für Soziologie und Sozialpsychologie*, 59: 440–58.

Pollmann-Schult, M. and Wagner, M. (2014)'Vaterschaft im Kontext. Wie die familiengründung die Erwerbstätigkeit von Männern beeinflusst', *WZB Mitteilungen*, 143: 19–22.

Possinger, J. (2013) *Vaterschaft im Spannungsfeld von Erwerbs- und Familienleben. 'Neuen Vätern' auf der Spur*, Wiesbaden: Springer VS.

Possinger, J. (2014) 'Total availability – involved fathers between breadwinning and care', paper presented at the WFRN Conference, New York, June.

Pötzsch, O. (2012) *Geburten in Deutschland. Ausgabe 2012*, Wiesbaden: Statistisches Bundesamt, Destatis.

Rauschenbach, T. and Bien, W. (eds) (2011) *Aufwachsen in Deutschland. AID:A – Der neue DJI-Survey*, Muenchen: Beltz Juventa.

Rehel, E.M. (2014) 'When dad stays home too: paternity leave, gender, and parenting', *Gender & Society*, 28: 110–32.

Reimer, T. (2014) 'Work organizations as mediators for fathers' entitlements and fathers' wishes to take paid parental leave', paper presented at the WFRN Conference, New York, June.

Richter, R. (2012) 'Väter in Elternzeit. Innenansichten aus Familien und Unternehmen. Gleichstellungserfahrungen in der "Gewinnzone"'. Available at: http://www.gwi-boell.de/sites/default/files/assets/gwi-boell.de/images/downloads/Robert_Richter_Vaeter_in_Elternzeit.pdf

Robert Koch Institut (ed) (2003) *Gesundheit alleinerziehender Mütter und Väter*, Gesundheitsberichterstattung des Bundes, 14, Berlin: Robert Koch-Institut.

Schäfer, E. and Schulte, M. (2009) 'Kicker, Carrera und "care": Wie die Generation Papa tickt und wo sie sich trifft', *Frühe Kindheit*, 12: 35–8.

Schiefer, K. and Bujard, M. (2012) '"Papa arbeitet viel": Lange Arbeitszeit von deutschen Vätern und mögliche Ursachen', *Mitteilungen aus dem Bundesinstitut für Bevölkerungsforschung*, 33(November): 10–16.

Schober, P.S. (2014) 'Parental leave and domestic work of mothers and fathers: a longitudinal study of two reforms in West Germany', *Journal of Social Policy*, 43: 351–72.

Spieß, C.K. (2012) 'Betreuungsgeld widerspricht den Zielen nachhaltiger Familienpolitik', *DIW-Wochenbericht*, 79(24): 24–6.

Statistisches Bundesamt (2012a) *Elterngeld – Wer, wie lange, wie viel?*, Wiesbaden: Statistisches Bundesamt. Available at: https://www.destatis.de/DE/PresseService/Presse/Pressekonferenzen/2012/Elterngeld/begleitmaterial_PDF.pdf?__blob=publicationFile

Statistisches Bundesamt (2012b) *Kindertagesbetreuung in Deutschland 2012*, Wiesbaden: Statistisches Bundesamt. Available at: https://www.destatis.de/DE/PresseService/Presse/Pressekonferenzen/2012/kindertagesbetreuung/begleitmaterial_PDF.pdf?__blob=publicationFile

Statistisches Bundesamt (2012c) 'Mikrozensus 2011: Familien und Haushalte'. Available at: https://www.destatis.de/DE/ZahlenFakten/GesellschaftStaat/Bevoelkerung/Mikrozensus.html

Statistisches Bundesamt (2013a) 'Statistisches Jahrbuch 2013'. Available at: https://www.destatis.de/DE/Publikationen/StatistischesJahrbuch/StatistischesJahrbuch2013.pdf

Statistisches Bundesamt (2013b) 'Datenreport 2013. Ein Sozialbericht für die Bundesrepublik Deutschland', Bundeszentrale für politische Bildung. Available at: www.wzb.eu/publikationen/datenreport

Statistisches Bundesamt (2014a) Öffentliche Sozialleistungen. *Statistik zum Elterngeld. Beendete Leistungsbezüge für im Jahr 2012 geborene Kinder*, Wiesbaden: Statistisches Bundesamt. Available at: https://www.destatis.de/DE/Publikationen/Thematisch/Soziales/Elterngeld/ElterngeldGeburtenJ_5229201129004.pdf?__blob=publicationFile

Statistisches Bundesamt (2014b) 'Destatis 2014'. Available at: https://www.destatis.de/DE/ZahlenFakten/Indikatoren/QualitaetArbeit/Dimension3/3_7_ElternTeilzeitarbeit.html

Stöbel-Richter, Y. (2010) *Fertilität und Partnerschaft. Eine Längsschnittstudie zu Familienbildungsprozessen über 20 Jahre*, Gießen: Psychosozial-Verlag.

Tietze, W., Becker-Stoll, F., Bensel, J., Eckhardt, A.G., Haug-Schnabel, G., Kalicki, B., Keller, H. and Leyendecker, B. (eds) (2012) 'Nationale Untersuchung zur Bildung, Betreuung und Erziehung in der frühen Kindheit', NUBBEK. Available at: http://www.nubbek.de/media/pdf/NUBBEK%20Broschuere.pdf

Trappe, H. (2013) 'Väterzeit – das Elterngeld als Beschleuniger von Gleichstellung?', *Zeitschrift für Familienforschung*, 25: 238–64.

Von der Lippe, E. and Rattay, P. (2014) 'Seelische und körperliche Belastung von Müttern und Vätern in Deutschland – Ergebnisse der GEDA-Studie 2009 und 2010', *Praxis Klinische Verhaltensmedizin und Rehabilitation*, 93: 5–20.

Wrohlich, K., Berger, E., Geyer, J., Haan, P., Sengul, D., Spieß, C.K. and Thiemann, A. (2012) *Elterngeld Monitor*, Politikberatung Kompakt, Berlin: DIW.

Zerle, C. and Keddi, B. (2011) '"Doing Care" im Alltag Vollzeit erwerbstätiger Mütter und Väter. Aktuelle Befunde aus AID:A', *GENDER–Zeitschrift für Geschlecht, Kultur und Gesellschaft*, 3(3): 55–72.

Zerle, C. and Krok, I. (2008) *Null Bock auf Familie? Der schwierige Weg junger Männer in die Vaterschaft*,Gütersloh: Verlag Bertelsmann Stiftung.

Zerle, C. and Krok, I. (2009) 'Väter in der Zerreißprobe', *DJI Bulletin*, 88: 14–15.

THREE

Italy

Elisabetta Ruspini and Maria Letizia Tanturri

The cultural and policy context of fatherhood

Italy occupies a rather peculiar position among Western countries when it comes to family policy in general, as well as to policies directed at fathers in particular. The historical development of the Italian welfare state does not derive from a consistent policy line or recognisable cultural matrix. The original liberal and later corporatist welfare state was politically discredited in the post-war years, and it was never replaced with a coherent model (Trifiletti, 1999). There has been a generalised gradual increase of provisions of labour market protections for specific categories of workers.

While the state does not take on the responsibility of guaranteeing a family wage, it allows nuclear or extended families to pursue strategies to ensure that at least one member has a well- protected job (Petmesidou, 1996). Saraceno (1995: 279–80) argues that:

> the Italian familist welfare regime is not exclusively nor even primarily based on a strong breadwinner model, but on the family as perceived as a unit of income and resources, to which everyone contributes according to his/her opportunities, although they may differ by gender. What is assumed is not the figure of breadwinner but family solidarity – including kin – and the primary responsibility of women – married and mothers – in the provision of care.

This is also reflected in low levels of state support for families: in 2009, Italy spent only 1.58% of gross domestic product (GDP) on family benefits, as compared to the Organisation for Economic Co-operation and Development (OECD) average of 2.61% (OECD, 2014). Furthermore, Italy spent 27.8% of GDP on public social expenditures (compared to the OECD average of 22.1%), and only 24.1% of that was spent on early education and childcare.

Italian culture may be defined as *familistic. Familism* refers to a set of normative beliefs that describes a strong attachment and loyalty to one's family, emphasises the centrality of the family unit, and stresses the obligations and support that family members owe to both nuclear and extended kin (Saraceno, 2003; Rossi, 2009). This includes a strong reliance on family members for material and emotional help. For example, in Italy, young adults of both sexes live with their parents until they get married, and they are supported by their parents as long as they stay within the family – even in families with a single breadwinner – regardless of whether the young person has a separate income or not (Facchini, 2002). Children, after leaving home to establish new families, still maintain strong relationships with their parents and in-laws, usually live in close proximity, and visit them regularly. This phenomenon is referred to as the *famiglia lunga* (the 'long' family) (Scabini and Donati, 1988) and the slow transition process to adulthood has been defined as 'problematic' (Sironi and Rosina, 2012).

The survival of the familistic cultural system depends on 'traditional' gender relations. This is reflected in increased investment of personal resources in family life, a sense of hostility towards formal childcare arrangements and a reluctance to adopt an egalitarian division of household labour. Even among young couples, the traditional division of labour predominates and wives/mothers/daughters, in general, remain the main carers for children. Rather than relying on Italian men, care services for the elderly, sick and children are increasingly provided by foreign women (and men) in Italian families (see, eg, Perra and Ruspini, 2013). In order to balance the shortage of formal care services and the cultural resistance to external care, migrant women often replace family carers and thus play a very crucial role in the maintenance of Southern European care systems (Lyberaki, 2008; Ambrosini and Beccalli, 2009; Wall and Nunes, 2010). Some authors talk about a distinctive Southern European immigration pattern (King, 2001; Bettio et al, 2006) in which a new 'migrant-in-the-family' care model emerges.

As Dalla Zuanna (2001) explains, familism persists even where the traditional family model with male breadwinners declines. This is the case in contemporary Italy, where fertility is low and alternative marital and reproductive behaviours (divorce, cohabitation, extramarital fertility) are increasing (Ruspini, 2011a). The familistic culture has contributed to creating the model of 'few but high-quality children' (Dalla Zuanna, 2001; Livi Bacci, 2001), and couples invest very high energies and expectations in their only child. In Italy, the family has acted as an informal support network (a social security cushion), offering care services for children, the elderly and sick people – services provided by the welfare state in other countries. This family economy model prioritises the needs of the family over those of women (Saraceno, 1994), reduces men's contribution to housework and childcare, and hides changes in men's lives.

Leave provisions

In response to the 1996 European Union (EU) directive on parental leave, new legislation (Law 53/8 March 2000: Provisions for the Support of Maternity and Paternity, for the Right to Care and Training and for the Coordination of Urban Temporalities) was enacted in 2000 that provided parents with the option of parental leave and introduced the individual, rather than non-transferable, right of male employees to take time off work in order to care for their children during the first eight years. Both parents are now guaranteed the right to take leave from work for up to a maximum of six months each and 10 months together. Fathers deciding to make use of leave for a period of at least three months (even if not consecutive) allow the couple an additional 'bonus' month. In total, parents could take up to 11 months of leave: for example, six months for the mother and four months for the father, which become five months thanks to the 'bonus' month. This measure is not well-compensated because it gives parents an allowance of only 30% of their salary up to the child's third year of life. However, it introduced an option for fathers to be more involved with their children.

In addition to the 2000 legislation on parental leave, Law 54/8 February 2006 introduced shared custody as the preferred model in custody cases of divorced parents. This law was demanded by various associations of separated fathers in order to combat what was described as 'inequality of treatment in lawsuits for separation and custody of minors'. With the new law, the judge normally entrusts the children to both parents without having to choose between them. For questions of ordinary administration, parental power would then appear as a shared right, with a number of duties attributed to both parents according to the areas of competence linked to their past experience, their aptitudes and the indications of preference made by the children.

In contrast to parental leave, maternity leave is mandatory in Italy: Italian employed women can stay at home with 80% of their wage (in the public sector, with full pay) during the last two months of pregnancy and the first three months after giving birth (or, alternatively, during the last month of pregnancy and the first four months after the birth of the child), and can go home to nurse their babies during work hours for a maximum of two hours a day (full-time work; one hour if the work day is less than six hours) in the baby's first year of life.

Italian fathers have only been entitled to specific paternity leave (one day) since 2012. Before 2012, maternity leave could be transferred to fathers under certain conditions. The father has the right to paternity leave in all those cases when the mother did not make use (or made only partial use) of maternity leave because of the mother's death or serious illness, her abandoning of the family, or sole custody of the father in case of separation or divorce. In such circumstances, the father is entitled to three months' leave, paid at 80% of salary (see, eg, Addabbo and Giovannini, 2013). In case of adoption, the working mother can transfer (totally or partially) her maternity leave to the father.

Following the request of the EU Parliament, a parliamentary debate began in June 2010 regarding the introduction of a compulsory and fully paid paternity leave. The very recent employment law reform (Law 92/2012: The Reform of Italian Employment Law) introduced, on a trial basis for the years 2013–15, an important innovation. Starting in January 2013, employees who become fathers are entitled to a one-day compulsory paternity leave and two days of voluntary leave from work, which can be used as an alternative to the mother's compulsory maternity leave and with her consent. That is, fathers can take two additional days if the mother agrees to transfer these days from her maternity leave allocation. The above days of leave should be used within the fifth month after the child's birth and the employee must notify the employer of his intention to take the leave at least 15 days in advance. This leave is paid for by the *Instituto Nazionale della Previdenza Sociale* (INPS; the Italian Social Security Body) and compensated at 100% of pay (Addabbo, Giovannini and Mazzucchelli, 2014).

Within this context, the social construction of paternity in Italy is the story of the absence of fathers from family policy (Ruspini, 2006). Italian legislation has dealt very little with paternity and support to the fathers' care functions. While a 1971 law (Law 1204/30 December 1971) on the protection of working mothers defined the policy of mandatory maternity leave, until very recently, no reference was made to paternity leave or to any kind of exemption from work for the father.

Contextual demographic and family trends related to fatherhood

This section describes the most relevant demographic trends, the main characteristics of family composition and fathers' labour force participation (LFP) patterns. Where useful, data is differentiated by geographical, cultural and economic differences between Northern and Southern Italy. Official data on reproductive behaviour are provided only for women because data on fathers are traditionally considered less important or even uncertain. Thus, micro-level survey data are substituted where macro-data are not available; however, those data may be biased even when weighted and usually differ from the macro-data.

Italian marriage rates have been decreasing sharply over the last decade (see Table 3.1). This is, in part, a side effect of population aging, but also of the growing preference for less institutionalised forms of union. Over the last decade, marriages have been partially replaced by cohabitation *more uxorio* and an increasing proportion of out-of-wedlock births (especially in the North), which totalled less than 10% in 2000 but are now close to 30%. Italy differs from other Western countries in that divorce rates – despite their increase over the last decade – are among the lowest in Europe.

The Italian case has been amply studied as a paradox in the demographic literature because of the combination of very low and late fertility in the context of strong family values. Period fertility has been below replacement since the mid-1970s, and was one of the first in the world to reach 'lowest-low' levels (Total Fertility Rate, TFR = 1.19) in the mid-1990s (Kohler et al, 2002). Since 2000, a small recovery has brought the Italian TFR close to 1.46. However, the economic recession after 2009 stopped this positive trend and fertility has stalled at around 1.4 in more recent years, with a marked decrease in the number of births (ISTAT, 2014). It is interesting to note that the Southern regions of Italy – those most anchored in traditional family and gender values – have been showing lower total fertility rates than those observed in Northern Italy. Mothers' age at first birth is now 31 and the rate of births to mothers over the age of 30 is close to 70%. Linked to the delay of childbearing, there is also an increase in the prevalence of childlessness, both temporary and permanent (Miettinen et al, 2014).

In Italy, low fertility interplays with strong family ties and values (Reher, 1998; Livi Bacci, 2001), familism, and high parental investments in child quality (Dalla Zuanna, 2001; Dalla Zuanna and Micheli, 2004), and with the increase in both the direct and indirect costs of children (De Santis and Livi Bacci, 2001). The lack of gender equity in the division of domestic tasks and childcare (McDonald, 2000a, 2000b; Mencarini and Tanturri, 2004; Mills et al, 2008; Anxo et al, 2011) is also found to be a reason for preventing couples from having additional children.

Table 3.1: Selected indicators related to parenting for Italy in 2000 and 2012

Indicator	2000	2012
Crude marriage rate (per 1,000 population)	5	3.5
Crude divorce rate	0.66	0.91
Total fertility rate	1.26	1.42
Crude birth rate	9.5	9
Mothers' mean age at first birth	28.6	31
% non-marital births	12	24.8
Births per 1,000 men	19.7	18.6
% of family households that are:		
Husband/wife	27.7	28.7
Unmarried couple	3.1	7.6
Husband/wife with children	56	50
Mother only with children	10.8	11.2
Father only with children	2.2	2.3
% of children < 5 living with:		
Two parents	NA	94.5
Father only	NA	0.5
Mother only	NA	5.3
% of married-couple families that are:		
Dual-earner families	29.2	29.4
Male-provider families	29	40.9
Labour force participation (LFP)		
LFP rate, men (age 15–64)	61.8	62.2
Fathers (> 15) of kids under 18	74.5	86
Fathers of under 6 year olds	NA	92
Men, % full-time	92.6	92.2
Men, mean number of hours/week	41.3	40.5
Fathers, mean number of hours/week	41.6	NA
LFP rate, women (15–64)	49.2	51.5
Mothers (> 15) of kids < 18	47.2	55.3
Mothers of under 6 year olds	NA	53.2
Women, % full-time	76	67.6
Women, mean number of hours/week	35.4	33.1
Mothers, mean number of hours/week	34.6	NA

Sources: ISTAT, demographic indicators (various years); population censuses (2001, 2011); Multipurpose Survey – 'Family and social survey' (2009); OECD family database; calculations from the Italian Labour Force Survey (2000, 2012) and the Multipurpose Survey – 'Aspects of daily life' (2012); Eurostat Labour Force Survey (1995, 2005, 2009, 2011).

Family structures have not changed significantly over the last decade, but the proportion of unmarried couples has more than doubled (see Table 3.1). Husband–wife constellations remain the predominant family forms and most children under age five today are living with both parents (more than 94%). While 5.3% of children live with their mother either in a solo mother family or with other family members, solo father families are still very rare (less than 0.5%). The male-breadwinner model still prevails among married couples in contemporary Italy, accounting for 41% of that population. Conversely, dual-earner families represent less than 30% of the couples in Italy.

The LFP of fathers of children under 18 is high (86% in 2012) and it is even higher for fathers of preschool children (92%). In Italy, men typically work full-time and long hours, and fathers work more hours than men in general (62%). Women's LFP is currently one of the lowest in the EU, only 52%. The proportion is slightly higher among mothers of minor children, but this is a cohort effect because the mothers are part of cohorts of women having increased participation rates. The employment rate among Italian mothers decreases further as the number of children increases: for mothers with three children, employment rates are less than 40% (OECD, 2011). The target set by the EU (2020 Strategy for Development and Employment) calls for 75% of the population aged 20–64 to be employed by 2020. In 2010, the value of the indicator in Italy (61%) was 14 percentage points below this target and summed up an extremely large gender imbalance (73% for men; 50% for women) (ISTAT, 2010). Most working women have a full-time contract (67%), but, on average, women work fewer hours than men (33 per week).

Fathers and parental leave

A report by the National Institute of Statistics (ISTAT, 2011) shows that 'only' 749,000 working parents applied for parental leave (86% of whom were women) and 541,000 applied for sick leave (77% were women). The use of parental leave among fathers remains very low: only 6.9% of the entitled fathers with at least one child under age eight took leave in 2010 (the rate in 2005 was 7.5%) and fewer than one out of five fathers took at least one month of leave (ISTAT, 2011). Conversely, the take-up rate increased for women (45% of mothers in 2010) and most of them (70%) stayed at home for at least a month (ISTAT, 2008, 2011). The reasons most often reported by fathers for not using parental leave were: (1) that they did not need it because their partner or another person cared for their children (27%); (2)

that they preferred working as a personal choice (21%); (3) that their partner used the entire leave (13%); or (4) that they were not entitled (20%) (ISTAT, 2011). Only 4% of the fathers report financial reasons for not taking leave. As in other countries, public sector workers in Italy are more inclined to take parental leave: the take-up rate is high (around 50%) among fathers who are civil servants.

As Baker et al (2011) explain, in Italy, there is no real fiscal incentive supporting parental leave and the concept of fathers taking time off work to look after children remains stigmatised (see also Rossi, 2006; Mazzucchelli, 2011). While 65% of Italian fathers are aware of their right to take parental leave, the vast majority (87%) show no intention of exercising that right (Mazzucchelli, 2011). The difficulties of fathers in reconciling family and work are increased by the characteristics of the Italian labour market: high rates of self-employment, a high proportion of people employed in small firms, a high degree of employment protection for male breadwinners and a proliferation of atypical contracts that do not entitle young people to any protection (Tanturri, 2010).

Fathers and childcare

On the whole, Italian parents spend a lot of time caring for their children, in part, because of social pressure and expectations and, in part, because of the high value attributed to children (Dalla Zuanna, 2001), but also due to the scarcity of childcare services, especially for children under age three. Among under two-year-old children, only 24% go to crèche, while most of those aged three to five (96%) attend kindergarten (OECD, 2014). Crèches are not part of the state educational system and they can be either private or public. Public crèches are managed by the local municipality and are only partially subsidised. Geographical differences in their supply, cost and unmet needs are huge. Most kindergartens are managed by the state and are almost free.

When both parents are in the labour market, non-co-resident grandparents play a pivotal role in childcare: in 81% of cases, they take care of their grandchildren aged under 13 as a primary or secondary carer; the proportion is even higher for younger children (OECD, 2014). This family care is in line with Italian familist culture and reduces the pressure on fathers to get involved in childcare. The care of grandparents is generally preferred to formal childcare because private crèches and kindergartens are quite expensive; state kindergartens are often not available due to long waiting lists, and those that do not have waiting lists do not have a quality of care that is considered adequate (ISTAT, 2011).

Not surprisingly, in an international comparison, Italian men are among the least involved in family life. According to comparative research using the European Community Household Panel survey (Smith, 2004; Smith Koslowski, 2007), only 11% of Italian fathers of children under six dedicated a substantial amount of time to their children, defined as over 28 hours a week, while this proportion was 31% in Finland, 24% in Great Britain and 20% in Germany.

Research on father involvement

According to the Harmonized European Time Use Survey (HETUS),[1] in 2008/09, Italian men carried out, on average, a smaller proportion of unpaid household work than men in most other OECD countries. On average, Italian fathers devoted only 1 hour 48 minutes per weekday to total household labour, which is an increase of 26 minutes over the decade. The asymmetry index measuring the proportion of family work performed by mothers has decreased over the last 10 years, but this change was due mainly to mothers' reduction of domestic work.

The commitment of Italian fathers to family work seems to be responsive to their spouse's LFP (Mills et al, 2008; Craig and Mullan, 2010; Anxo et al, 2011; Sabbadini and Cappadozzi, 2011). In 2008/09, Italian fathers' involvement in family work, including childcare, was higher when fathers were highly educated (1 hour 45 minutes versus 1 hour 35 minutes for those having less than a high school degree) or if they live in Northern Italy (1 hour 59 minutes versus 1 hour 29 minutes for those living in the South). The most remarkable differences emerge when the father's partner is employed (2 hours 4 minutes versus 1 hour 29 minutes for those with a housewife partner) or in the presence of preschool children (2 hours 7 minutes versus 1 hour 34 minutes for those having older children) (Sabbadini and Cappadozzi, 2011).

Time engaged with children

The 2008/09 Italian Time Use Survey is a useful resource to measure father involvement in childcare and paid work according to family characteristics. This survey was administered by ISTAT to a sample of 44,606 respondents (belonging to 18,250 households). Of those, 40,944 respondents filled in the daily diary. The diary data are based on a grid of 10-minute intervals of time, with a description of the main activity carried out by the respondent, the secondary (or concurrent) activity, their location and the presence of other persons. One major strength of time-use data is that they include both men's and women's responses. This is particularly important for couples with children because fathers' reports were often unavailable in previous parenting research; therefore, many studies of father involvement relied exclusively on the mothers' reports.

Table 3.2 presents three values related to the daily time (in hours and minutes) that fathers dedicate to childcare according to the number of children and the age of the youngest child in 2008/09: the average time spent on childcare and paid work for the entire sample, the average time spent only by those who performed the activity on the interview day, and the proportion of those who perform a given activity on the date of the interview. The variables of interest are the daily time spent on childcare (including interactive childcare, physical care, transportation for the children and minding of children in the household) and the daily time spent on domestic work (including childcare, routine domestic tasks, maintenance, gardening, shopping, bureaucracy, management and transportation related to the family) by the father in different family typologies.

On an average weekday, 47% of fathers devote 1 hour 28 minutes to childcare and 75% devote 9 hours 16 minutes to paid employment. Fathers with one child under the age of six spend between 1 hour 28 minutes and 1 hour 42 minutes on childcare and more than 9 hours at work. The commitment of the fathers increases with the number of children. Fathers with two children under the age of six spend 1 hour 26 minutes to 1 hour 56 minutes on childcare, with the same number of employment hours. However, the most time spent was by fathers with three children under the age of six: they spend 1 hour 37 minutes to 1 hour 45 minutes on childcare and also increase their time at work to almost 10 hours.

Once the children are older, fathers invest less childcare time. Even when they have several children, fathers usually spend less time on each child. One possible reason behind this pattern is that there are some economies of scale in looking after several children together that allow fathers to save time: they can perform parental tasks simultaneously for all children (Paihlé et al, 2015). A second reason could be related to the role of older siblings, who might take care of their little brothers and sisters actively, so that their parents spend less time performing active childcare. Finally, a selection effect might also operate for parents with multiple children: they may choose to have more children because they feel that they can manage it, because their first experience of child-rearing was successful, because they are more efficient in performing childcare activities or, finally, because they are less able to invest in quality time with children due to the trade-off between the quality and quantity of time spent (Pahilé et al, 2014).

Table 3.2: Daily time (hours and minutes) fathers dedicate to childcare and paid work according to the number of children and the age of the youngest child in 2008/09 (sample average, average among doers, proportion doers, on an average weekday)

Number of children and the age of the youngest	Childcare			Paid work		
	Average time spent (entire sample)	Average time of doers	% doers	Average time spent (entire sample)	Average time of doers	% doers
Entire sample	00:41	01:28	46.5	06:57	09:16	75.1
Childless	00:00	0	0	06:54	09:28	72.9
1 child, 0–2	01:16	01:42	74	06:59	09:19	75
1 child, 3–5	01:01	01:28	69.4	07:14	09:14	78.3
2 children, 0–2	01:34	01:56	81.4	06:57	09:13	75.3
2 children, 3–5	00:55	01:26	63.8	06:32	09:10	71.3
3 children, 0–2	01:10	01:45	66.9	07:28	09:47	76.3
3 children, 3–5	01:03	01:37	65.5	07:20	09:55	74

Source: Italian Time Use survey (ISTAT), authors' calculations.

Level of father engagement

Tanturri and Mencarini (2009) carried out a study of fathers' involvement in daily routine childcare activities in Italy. Their empirical analysis is based on data from the 2002/03 Multipurpose Survey on Italian Families, carried out by ISTAT on a national representative sample of households. The indicators were: (1) helping the child dress; (2) feeding the child; (3) changing nappies; (4) bathing; and (5) putting the child to bed – all tasks that have been traditionally performed by mothers. The survey provides information on how frequently fathers carry out these daily childcare tasks (every day, a few times a week, once a week, a few times a month, a few times a year, never), with children younger than age six. In 2003, only a small minority of fathers was involved in everyday childcare activities: 7% with a child younger than age three and 6% with a child older than age three. The proportion of fathers who never performed any of the childcare tasks was around 4%. The proportion of 'inactive' fathers is higher in Southern Italy, in the islands and among fathers with lower levels of education.

Table 3.3 shows the frequency with which each activity was performed by fathers in 1998, 2003 and 2009. First, there is a remarkable increase in the proportion of fathers performing the tasks every day, regardless of the type of activity. Second, there is a general reduction of the share of fathers who never perform a certain activity, with the exception of changing nappies. This care activity is the least performed by Italian fathers: one third of Italian fathers have never changed a nappy and only one father in four reports changing his child's nappy every day. Another activity performed quite infrequently by fathers is bathing. However, in 2008, 37% of fathers of children younger than age three and 31% of fathers of older children put their child to bed daily. This task is one of the most relational activities among the routine tasks and, not surprisingly, it is preferred by men. Similarly, 35% of fathers of babies and toddlers and 26% of fathers of older children feed or eat with their child every day (see Table 3.3). Overall, using daily involvement in direct childcare, only between 16% and 37% of Italian fathers can be considered 'involved fathers'.

A comparison with the Multipurpose Survey carried out in 1988/89 indicates a slight increase in father involvement. An Index of Father Involvement (IFI) has been calculated to give an overall indication of fathers' participation in direct childcare tasks. If the value of the IFI is closer to 1, it indicates more commitment by fathers; an IFI value closer to 0 reflects less commitment (Tanturri and Mencarini, 2009). The focus of the analysis is on fathers' participation in the same routine care activities. The average IFI was higher in 2003 (0.62 for fathers of younger children and 0.56 for those of older children) than in 1998, and the proportion of never-active fathers (IFI = 0) has fallen from 8% to 4%) (Tanturri, 2006). In 2009, the proportion of inactive fathers remained stable, and the IFI increased only slightly to 0.64. Despite this positive trend, Tanturri and Mencarini (2009) conclude that in Italy, childcare is still performed almost completely by mothers. Even when fathers participate, they mainly support mothers by performing a few selective tasks among those essential for child-rearing. Consistent with other studies, it appears that even active fathers tend to prefer relational activities with children rather than the less rewarding, but extremely necessary, routine tasks (Di Giulio and Carrozza, 2003; Rosina and Sabbadini, 2006; ISTAT, 2007; Zajczyk and Ruspini, 2008). The literature shows that fathers, in general, prefer more interactive activities (eg playing), and Boscolo and Tanturri (forthcoming) show that the only type of childcare activity to which fathers devote more time than mothers is playing. The time devoted by fathers to all the other activities, including physical care and transportation, is much lower than the mother's time.

Table 3.3: Percentage of co-residential fathers of children younger than age six who perform a selection of routine activities in 1998, 2003 and 2008.

	Age of children (0–2 years old)			Age of children (3–5 years old)	
ACTIVITIES	1998 (%)	2003 (%)	2008 (%)	1998 (%)	2003 (%)
Bathing children					
Everyday	8.0	10.0	16.1	8.1	9.5
Few times a week	30.0	30.1	31.4	25.1	25.0
Never	37.8	29.3	26.4	39.0	30.6
Putting children to bed					
Everyday	25.6	34.9	37.4	23.3	30.7
Few times a week	41.1	42.8	38.6	39.5	43.8
Never	15.1	9.0	11.0	14.6	9.7
Feeding children					
Everyday	21.0	27.9	34.9	21.1	25.6
Few times a week	38.1	45.8	36.4	38.7	38.2
Never	20.8	12.5	15.7	18.9	15.5
Changing nappies					
Everyday	20.7	24.9	26.0	13.2	13.9
Few times a week	30.9	33.3	28.4	22.1	15.0
Never	31.0	26.2	32.6	49.3	58.8
Helping children dress					
Everyday	16.2	21.9	27.6	14.5	17.4
Few times a week	39.2	43.4	38.4	38.6	41.4
Never	24.8	14.2	13.7	20.4	14.0

Note: As not all the answer modalities have been included, the sum is less than 100%.

Source: Tanturri (2006), Tanturri and Mencarini (2009); 'Multipurpose Survey – family and social subjects' (2009).

The IFI was also calculated separately, according to the specific father's or couple's characteristics, such as both partners' education and type of household (dual-income or male-breadwinner) (Tanturri and Mencarini, 2009). Fathers' behaviour changes only slightly across categories: the maximum level above the mean IFI (0.62) is 0.68 and the minimum below the mean is 0.56. The variability in 2003 is about equal to that in 1998 (Tanturri, 2006). This suggests that Italian fathers' behaviour is shaped predominantly by gender norms, as opposed to men's characteristics. The level of father involvement is higher in Central and Northern Italy, where there are more egalitarian gender values and where more women are in the labour market. The hypothesis that younger fathers play a more important role in care activities does not seem to be confirmed by descriptive findings. However, more educated fathers have a higher IFI mean value than the less educated. As expected, teachers or white-collar professional fathers seem to be the most active; these professions may also be characterised by more compatible working time schedules for men. The lowest degree of father involvement is observed among managers, industrial professional men and entrepreneurs, whose jobs are usually very demanding in terms of time and commitment. The blue-collar and self-employed workers show lower-than-average levels of involvement. It is possible that very intense or irregular time schedules prevent them from spending much time with their young children.

Determinants of father engagement with young children

Ordinary Least Square analysis predicting time devoted to childcare by Italian men in 2008/09 shows that those fathers who do not have an employed wife/partner are remarkably less involved in childcare than men in dual-income families. As a consequence, it seems that they can relax their time constraints and enjoy more free time. The reverse is not true; women with a partner who is either working part-time or not working at all have less free time in Italy. More educated men devote more time to childcare – even if the time of highly educated parents is more expensive – showing that, among fathers, time with children might be perceived as an important parental investment in child well-being and success. More education and higher economic resources allow parents to avoid time squeeze by outsourcing some domestic tasks. While childcare time does not seem to be influenced by fathers' age, cohabiting fathers spend more time with their children than their married peers.

Multivariate results also confirm previous findings showing that there is an interesting substitution effect during weekends for childcare, with fathers taking care of children more frequently on weekends. The long hours worked by Italian men do not allow them to spend much time with their children during the week, while on weekends, they are more flexible. However, even on weekends, men tend to spend more time entertaining their children rather than engaging in routine care and the management of different schedules.

Our analyses also confirm other findings of geographical differences across Italy (Tanturri and Mencarini, 2009; Menniti et al, 2014). Southern men spend less time performing childcare because of a more traditional division of housework in the South. Additional models use data from the 2002/03 Italian Time Use Survey, combined with earnings information taken from the 2002 Bank of Italy Survey on Household Income and Wealth. The aim of this survey, which has been conducted annually or biannually since 1965, is to gather information about the economic behaviour of Italian families at the microeconomic level. The basic survey unit is the household, which is defined in terms of family relationships, that is, as a group of individuals linked by ties of blood, marriage or affection, sharing the same dwelling, and pooling all or part of their incomes. The analysis of the time allocation of Italian couples (Bloemen et al, 2010) shows that Italian fathers' childcare time allocation corresponds to their wages, the age of the children and their partners' education. Fathers' involvement in childcare increases with their own income and with the presence of young children, and this holds both for weekdays and weekends. Moreover, the higher the education level of their wives, the more time husbands allocate to childcare.

Despite major time constraints, more educated working fathers and mothers apparently do not reduce the time for care, as observed in some other countries, because of the high investment in child well-being and the familistic norms of what good parents have to do. Given this line of reasoning, it seems odd that Italian fathers dedicate so little time to caring for their children. Moreover, as children are so important in Italian familistic culture, it is possible that more involvement of fathers will become necessary in the future.

Research on father involvement and father well-being

The literature on Italian fathers shows that their behaviour is still predominantly shaped along traditional gender expectations, despite an increase in women's participation in the labour market (Rosina and

Sabbadini, 2006; Pinnelli et al, 2007; Romano and Bruzzese, 2007; Zajczyk and Ruspini, 2008). In Italy, the experience of parenthood reinforces a strong gender-specific division of labour, with an increase of women's time spent in housework and childcare (as well as a reduction of their time for paid work and free time), and an increase of men's time dedicated to paid work. The increase of men's working hours as a consequence of fatherhood is considered a rational response to the reduction of their partner's labour supply (and income) (ISTAT, 2007).

Research on fathers' well-being in connection with their involvement with children is quite scarce in Italy. The discourse is more focused on the programmes that attempt to increase father involvement in general and to demonstrate how important fathers' childcare contribution is to child development and to working mothers' stress reduction. According to fertility decline theories, children in developed countries provide mainly psychological, rather than financial, benefits to parents (Caldwell, 1982). Therefore, we can speculate that if fathers care for their children, their involvement with children may have a positive impact on father well-being. Moreover, fathers tend to choose the more entertaining and interactive activities to perform with their children, leaving to the mothers the less pleasant routine tasks.

The reconciliation of work and family appears not to be particularly problematic for Italian fathers. Empirical studies show that childbirth significantly increases stress levels for working women and reduces their satisfaction with the couple relationship (Mencarini, 2010). Mencarini (2012) also shows that only 8% of fathers are dissatisfied with the gender division of the care of children. Most fathers seem not to complain much about the time allocation at home. The reduction of free time (leisure and personal time) among fathers compared to childless men is mainly an issue for fathers of infants and toddlers, and is less so for those with older children.

Work-related behaviour

Among men who actively care for their co-resident children, 66% do not want to modify their work–life balance (ISTAT, 2010). Among those who do wish to change something, 5.3% would like to work more outside the home and perform care work less often, while 29% would prefer to dedicate less time to work outside the home and to do more care work inside the home. These responses suggest that about one third of working fathers experience a work–family reconciliation issue, and more than a quarter perceive their role of carer as so important that they would like to reduce their LFP. In particular, managers and entrepreneurs want to dedicate more time to their children. Studies on the organisational climate for working fathers suggest that the issue of work–family reconciliation is relevant for fathers and for their well-being.

Bosoni (2014) carried out a qualitative study in three Italian workplaces in 2011, which describes the challenges of reconciliation for working fathers in a context where work remains 'a pivotal trait shaping men's identity'. Interviews conducted with 32 fathers of children younger than age three indicate that fathers consider fathering not as a natural ability, but rather as a learned skill, and that the meaning of fatherhood was linked to being a provider rather than to being a nurturer. The study also shows the low level of support that workplaces provide for working fathers and their needs in terms of father involvement. Results support the view that paternal reconciliation strategies and fathers' expression of needs for family support can be influenced enormously by the workplace climate and attitude. Company culture emerges as being of paramount importance in shaping male reconciliation strategies (Bosoni, 2014).

Fatherhood programmes

Several initiatives aimed at supporting the changes observed in new family forms and at shifting traditional forms of masculinity towards a gender-egalitarian culture have been developed in Italy. A number of them are national initiatives, while others have a local focus. The policies are both official and unofficial (see Ruspini, 2011b). The legislative, educational and research initiatives reflect the emergence of 'new' types of masculinity that are more egalitarian and oriented to sharing and caring and the need to understand and support them.

The educational project *Condividiamo con i papà* (Let's share with fathers) is aimed at helping fathers become more involved with their children. This project, started in 2009, is sponsored by the province of Turin, the association *Il Cerchio degli uomini* (Men's Circle) and the maternity hospital S. Anna. Through childbirth education classes, fathers are offered the opportunity to discuss gender stereotypes in parenting and various parental leave opportunities.

Padri coraggiosi (Brave Fathers) is a web and media campaign, sponsored by the Provincia of Bologna and funded by the European Social Fund, aimed at raising awareness about the need to share caring activities among parents. The campaign started in May 2007 and especially targets young fathers. It aims to create a better appreciation of men's care activities and to reduce the practice of maternal gatekeeping in performing care. The media campaign uses a variety of strategies: billboards in public places; press releases for newspapers, TV and radio; and a free brochure with information for fathers on the 2000 parental leave law.

Another phenomenon that has emerged on the cultural and symbolic level is the movement for fathers' rights, which is part of the more general men's rights movement. The purpose of these groups includes 're-conquering' fathers' rights to custody of children after marital separation and proposing a reformed image of fatherhood compared with the 'traditional' uninvolved father model. Example of these organisations are: the *Associazione Nazionale Papà Separati Onlus*[2]; the *Associazione Padri Separati* (APS)[3]; the *Associazione PapàSeparati Lombardia Onlus*,[4] based in Monza; the *Associazione Padri Presenti* and the *Associazione Padri e Madri*, both in Verona; *Gesef-Genitori separati dai figli*,[5] based in Rome; and *Papà separati e Figli Onlus*,[6] based in Turin (Deriu, 2007). These groups meet regularly, join in movements (such as the *Armata dei Papà* [Dad's Army]) or organise appeals, demonstrations, marches, campaigns and other actions related to the issues of fatherhood and claims for men's rights.

The Italian fatherhood regime

The information presented in this chapter shows how the cultural and policy context relating to masculinities and fatherhood-related demographic trends shape the weak Italian fatherhood regime. While the concept of 'new fatherhood' is finding its way into Italian popular representations of fatherhood and appears to reflect a real change in family behaviours associated with generational changes in gendered attitudes, the extent of social change in Italy may be slower than the public debates and policies suggest or assume (Gregory and Milner, 2011).

Demands for change and challenges have multiplied even in the Italian familistic context. The forms of cohabitation and family formation are now changing (Rossi, 2006; Crespi, 2008; Ruspini, 2011a). Since the mid-1960s, a growing disaffection with the 'traditional' family model has emerged and, increasingly, there are childless families and single-parent households in Italy (Tanturri and Mencarini, 2008). These social changes vary by region, but also include more divorces, stepfamilies, multi-ethnic families and unmarried families. Concurrently and consequently, Italians are starting families later than the European average and fertility is low and in decline. A major reason for these changes is the recent change in women's identities, which increasingly and inevitably involve their male partners and the fathers of their children. Women, who had been mainly concerned with the management of the home and care work, have become less willing to be confined to dealing exclusively with family work. This decline in motivation to be mothers and homemakers is due to the lack of institutional family support, to women's new competences (particularly related to extensive education) and to their increasing access to the labour market. It appears that in Italy, men's identities and behaviour have not kept pace with these developments to the same degree as in other EU countries.

As expected, there are major tensions among traditional cultural norms of masculinity, changing laws slowly expanding paternal rights and obligations, and narratives of 'new fathers' and 'good fathers' (Magaraggia, 2013). Evidence suggests that in Italy, the 'new father', 'working father' or 'nurturing dad' is hesitant to emerge. Instead, it appears that it is necessary to prepare the new generations of men for new models of masculinity that include nurturing fatherhood and for the 'new women' who are reluctant to become mothers. The goal is to open up a wide range of actions to enable children, young boys and men to broaden the scope of their emotional and communicative skills.

In Italy, conceptions of the traditional and modern father coexist in a context of familism, a cult of motherhood and the millennial generation's demands for change in gender (and other) relations. These contradictions make it difficult to define Italian fatherhood and classify the contemporary Italian father in a typology. While, traditionally, Italian fathers have mainly been providers in the family, they also have to be 'present' in their child's life. According to Magaraggia (2013: 82) Italian fathers often 'remain "apprentices" who follow the instructions their partners give them regarding the everyday care of the young child'. This feeling of being only the 'helper' and an 'incomplete father' undermines fathers' motivation to become more involved with small children. The mother–centred culture does not easily make room for engaged fathers and prevents them from acquiring the skills and confidence to provide proficient childcare. This can lead to a sense of frustration and feelings of inadequacy among young fathers, who may then use increased commitment to paid employment as a way to avoid caring activities (Magaraggia, 2013). This may explain why so many Italian fathers work such long hours.

The Italian welfare state and gender regime is based on family subsidiarity, meaning that the family, enlarged to include the network of relatives, is 'obliged' to protect its members. In addition, the system relies on the indefinite prolonging of financial bonds between generations and on the provision of care work by women's intergenerational networks. Families, and women within families, are the 'invisible' but necessary and irreplaceable partners of Italian social policies: they fill the gaps in welfare state policies. Women's contributions play a vital role in protecting other members of the family from the consequences of illness, deprivation and poverty. This is closely linked to women's propensity to perceive their own needs as being less important than those of their children or of their husband/partner. Society and the women themselves often believe that they are better able to take care of children than are men. These cultural patterns prevent even willing fathers from becoming more involved in direct childcare.

This 'unsupported familism' (Saraceno, 1994) implies the scarce development of childcare services and insufficient measures for the reconciliation of work and family life. Both features impact negatively on the reshaping of gender relations among parents. Hence, Italy scores poorly on gender-equality indicators, both in the public (LFP) and in the private (share of unpaid work) realms. Italy currently faces a limited capacity to articulate transitions towards the 'dual-earner model' where both adult members of a family are in paid employment (León and Migliavacca, 2013: 26). Familistic practices reinforce the male provider role by encouraging women to reduce their employment hours when they become mothers and, at the same time, by not supporting men when they become fathers. Data on fathers' time spent with young children and details on the activities that they engage in show low levels of father involvement even in dual-earner households (Tanturri and Mencarini, 2009).

Over the last decade, the millennial generation has emerged as a powerful political and social force. This cohort has been defined as competent, highly qualified, technologically savvy and in search of a new form of citizenship (Taylor and Keeter, 2010; Rainer and Rainer, 2011). Millennials are more tolerant than previous generations of a wider range of 'non-traditional' behaviours related to marriage and parenting: from employed mothers of young children to unmarried adults living together. These trends are closely linked to changing gender identities, especially among younger men. The number of young men who are willing to question the traditional model of masculinity is growing (Ruspini et al, 2011), which is reflected in the growing popularity of 'female-dominated occupations' among men in Italy (Perra and Ruspini, 2013).

Younger men are also beginning to claim a greater share of responsibility in raising their children, but in daily interaction, playing remains the most important activity for fathers (Zajczyk and Ruspini,

2008; Zanatta, 2011). The desire to discover (or rediscover) the terms and values of one's own specific masculinity and to challenge the conditionings imposed by a one-dimensional model of masculinity seems to be increasing. While the growing involvement of husbands, partners and fathers in family life is undeniable (Rosina and Sabbadini, 2006), commitment to caring activities depends on fathers' level of education and applies to a minority of men who are younger and who have accepted a model of masculinity that includes active fatherhood.

Conclusion and recommendations for policy

The Italian fatherhood regime is in transition. While the father as a provider is far from losing its importance, the traditional identity of a good father as a good provider without direct involvement in nurturing is slowly eroding. The 'new fathers' or 'nurturing fathers' who are more involved in care activities are now emerging, but within a legal and cultural framework that is still predominantly shaped by traditional gender norms. Will the new fathers create a new environment of social diffusion that will change Italian family and work life? This is difficult to tell and will depend not only upon how effective new policy interventions will be, but also on how mothers will respond to this. A new Italian fatherhood regime requires fathers to reduce their work hours and give up their apprentice role in childcare in order to develop an independent relationship with their child. This requires that mothers relinquish their culturally and institutionally supported monopoly on childcare. Mainstreaming care work in Italy entails the erosion of familism, traditional masculinity norms and maternal gatekeeping. Social policies enabling fathers to be more involved are only the first step.

Gaps in research

There has been a general lack of attention to (and a lack of comparative research on) the complex relationship between 'old' and 'new' forms of masculinity, as well as the intersections among fatherhood, work–family integration, gender relations and children's well-being. How are contemporary fathers handling work–family conflict? How does this conflict challenge or reinforce their masculinity and gender identity? Many fathers face barriers, such as short paternity leave, few opportunities to reduce work hours and father-unfriendly workplaces.

While research (Gregory and Milner, 2011; Bosoni, 2014) shows that fathering and fathers' strategies to combine family and work are strongly influenced by the workplace, only a few studies assess this issue in Italy. Fathers' take-up of leave is the outcome of a complex dynamic between national fatherhood regimes, organisational and sector characteristics, and the individual employee. There is a need to implement research on fathers' experiences and options. Both research and policy on reconciling work and family have tended to focus on mothers' lives. As a result, men's fathering and their struggle with work–life issues have been neglected. Clearly, there is a need for research on the effects of incentivising paternity and parental leave for Italian fathers. Would more fathers stay home with their children if the leave were fully compensated or if they had effective parenting classes available?

In addition, very little research has examined the effect of father involvement with children on fathers' well-being. Both mental and physical health outcomes need to be studied because parenthood is a major event in men's lives, not just in women's lives. More programmes need to be developed and assessed in Italy in order to understand how fathers' feelings of competency and self-esteem in terms of their fathering capabilities can be improved. Overall, an investment in research on fathers, including the collection of consistent data on their activities with children, would uncover different types of men's difficulties with, and/or resistance to, embracing active fatherhood in all its forms. It would allow the design and implementation of measures to support father involvement effectively. Policies could also increase the life satisfaction and well-being of fathers, reduce parental stress levels, and have a positive effect on children's well-being.

Promising initiatives and suggestions for change

Legal mechanisms to encourage fathers to take parental leave may be necessary because available statistics suggest that parental leave is mainly taken by mothers. The parental leave law of 2000 (Law 53/8, March 2000) was a step in the right direction. However, in order to provide the opportunity for fathers to take leave, analyses are needed to determine why this law is so ineffective in facilitating a more equal share of childcare between parents. Fathers appear to need stronger incentives to take their entitlements and increased reassurances about their capabilities to care for small children (Crespi and Ruspini, 2016 forthcoming).

The extension of compulsory and paid paternity leave could be useful in encouraging fathers to stay at home with their children. Through a process of learning–by–doing, they could become skilled at being proficient care providers who are able to perform and share all routine tasks with the mother. Consistent policies on gender equity and a father's quota, as in Scandinavian countries, may contribute to fathers' understanding of their own rights regarding caring for their children. For instance, since the 1980s, several European countries have established different types of paternity leave or have reserved a part of the parental leave for fathers. Emerging evidence from a plurality of countries suggests that fathers' uptake of parental leave increases with higher incentives and a 'take it or lose it' clause, and that involvement of fathers in caring for the first child increases the probability of having a second child.

In addition, more flexibility in the conditions of uptake of parental leave could be important for fathers' work–family reconciliation. Some parents might choose to take all their parental leave together as a block, while others might use it on a piecemeal basis, utilising a full-time or part-time arrangement during the first few years of their child's life.[7] In terms of higher compensation and flexibility in taking leave, workplaces also have to become more supportive and 'father-friendly'.

The implementation of planned educational programmes designed to enhance fathering skills and to promote father involvement – with particular attention to critical moments of the life course, such as childbirth or separation/divorce – could be helpful in empowering fathers. Promoting active fatherhood in media campaigns is necessary in a context where motherhood is considered more central for children's well-being than fatherhood. Due to the mother-centred culture, even employed mothers maintain their childcare time by cutting back on their own leisure, personal care and sleep (Craig, 2007). This suggests that mothers may actively limit fathers' care opportunities through gatekeeping, thereby hampering their involvement with young children. Mothers might do this because they wish to retain control of a domain that they feel expert in, or because they do not trust fathers to deliver as high a standard of care as they themselves provide (Bianchi and Milkie, 2010; Craig and Mullan, 2011). Hence, the educational programmes and campaigns need to include mothers so that more egalitarian views of parenting are developed by both genders.

Increased adult male presence in schools and childcare centres and the revision of children's and school books so that both mothers and fathers are shown performing care work and paid work would help reduce traditional gender expectations regarding childcare. In order to reduce gender stereotypes, the development of new educational structures and processes for new generations should include education on the non-gendered preparation for parental and care functions, on the diversity of family relations, and on the plurality of gender identities.

Acknowledgements

The research leading to these results received funding from the European Union's Seventh Framework Programme (FP7/2007–13) under grant agreement no 320116 for the research project 'Families and Societies', and, from 2013, the University of Padova's Research Programme under grant agreement no CPDA139158 for the research project 'The Italian Families between Tradition and Innovation. New Types, New Challenges and New Opportunities'.

Notes

[1] See: https://www.h2.scb.se/tus/tus/Publications.html

[2] See: http://www.papaseparati.org/psitalia/

[3] See: http://www.padri.it/

[4] See: http://www.papaseparatilombardia.org/on_line/

[5] See: http://www.gesef.org/

[6] See: http://win.papaseparatitorino.it/

[7] See: http://www.coe.int/t/dghl/standardsetting/equality/03themes/women-decisionmaking/CDEG(2004)14final_en.pdf

References

Addabbo, T., Giovannini, D. and Mazzucchelli, S. (2014) 'Italy country note', in P. Moss (ed) *International review of leave policies and research 2014*, London: Institute of Education University of London: 178–91. Available at: http://www.leavenetwork.org/fileadmin/Leavenetwork/Annual_reviews/2014_annual_review_korr.pdf

Ambrosini, M. and Beccalli, B. (2009) 'Uomini in lavori da donne: il lavoro domestico maschile' ['Men in a woman's job: male domestic work'], in R. Catanzaro and A. Colombo (eds) *Badanti & Co, Il lavoro domestico straniero in Italia*, Bologna: Il Mulino.

Anxo, D., Mencarini, L., Pailhé, A., Solaz, A., Tanturri, M.L. and Flood, L. (2011) 'Gender differences in time use over the life course in France, Italy, Sweden, and the United States', *Feminist Economics*, 17(3): 159–95.

Baker, S., Miller, T., Bosoni, M.L. and Rossi, G. (2011) 'Men, work and family life: a study of policy and practice in the UK and Italy', December. Available at: https://radar.brookes.ac.uk/radar/file/e1fe167b-69c6-5f77-8615-66e3d73407cd/1/British_Academy_Fatherhood_literature_review%20May_2012_SBfinal.pdf

Bettio, F., Simonazzi, A. and Villa, P. (2006) 'Change in care regimes and female migration: the "care drain" in the Mediterranean', *Journal of European Social Policy*, 16(3): 271–85.

Bianchi, S. and Milkie, M. (2010) 'Work and family research in the first decade of the 21st century', *Journal of Marriage & Family*, 72: 705–25.

Bloemen, H.G., Pasqua, S. and Stancanelli, E.G.F. (2010) 'An empirical analysis of the time allocation of Italian couples: are Italian men irresponsive?', *Review of the Economics of the Household*, 8(3): 345–69.

Boscolo, I. and Tanturri, M.L. (forthcoming) 'Time for child care among fathers and mothers in Italy. Who does what?', Department of Statistical Science Working Paper Series. Available at: http://www.stat.unipd.it/

Bosoni, M.L. (2014) 'Men, fathers and work: the challenge of reconciliation. Case studies in some Italian companies', in E. Carrà (ed) *Families, care and work–life balance services: case studies of best practices*, Quaderno no 28, Milano: Vita e Pensiero, pp 11–30.

Caldwell, J.C. (1982) *Theory of fertility decline*, London: Academic Press.

Craig, L. (2007) *Contemporary motherhood. The impact of children on adult time*, Aldershot: Ashgate.

Craig, L. and Mullan, K. (2010) 'Parenthood, gender and work–family time in the United States, Australia, Italy, France and Denmark', *Journal of Marriage & Family*, 72: 1344–61.

Craig, L. and Mullan, K. (2011) 'How mothers and fathers share child care: a cross-national time-use comparison', *American Sociological Review*, 76(6): 834–61.

Crespi, I. (ed) (2008) *Identità e trasformazioni sociali nella dopomodernità: tra personale e sociale, maschile e femminile* [*Identities and social transformations in post-modernity*], Macerata: EUM.

Crespi, I. and Ruspini, E. (eds) (2016 forthcoming) *Balancing work and family in a changing society. The fathers' perspective, global masculinities series*, Basingstoke: Palgrave Macmillan.

Dalla Zuanna, G. (2001) 'The banquet of Aeolus: a familistic interpretation of Italy's lowest low fertility', *Demographic Research*, 4: 133–61.

Dalla Zuanna, G. and Micheli, G. (2004) *Strong family, familism and lowest-low fertility*, Dordrecht, Netherlands: Kluwer Academic Press.

Deriu, M. (2007) 'Disposti alla cura? Il movimento dei padri tra rivendicazione e conservazione' ['The father's movement between revindication and tradition'], in E. dell'Agnese and E. Ruspini (eds) *Mascolinità all'italiana. Costruzioni, narrazioni, mutamenti*, Torino: Utet, pp 209–40.

De Santis, G. and Livi Bacci, M. (2001) 'Reflections on the economics of the fertility decline in Europe', presented at the Euresco Conference: 'The second demographic transition in Europe', Bad Herrenalb, Germany, 23–28 June.

Di Giulio, P. and Carrozza, S. (2003) 'Il nuovo ruolo del padre' ['The new role of father'], in A. Pinnelli, F. Racioppi and R. Rettaroli (eds) *Genere e demografia*, Bologna: Il Mulino.

Facchini, C. (2002) 'La permanenza dei giovani nella famiglia di origine' ('The permanence of Italian young adults in the family'), in C. Buzzi, A. Cavalli and A. de Lillo (eds) *Giovani del nuovo secolo, V Rapporto IARD sulla condizione giovanile in Italia*, Bologna: Il Mulino, pp 159–86.

Gregory, A. and Milner, S. (2011) 'What is "new" about fatherhood? The social construction of fatherhood in France and the UK', *Men and Masculinities*, 14(5): 588–606.

ISTAT (National Institute of Statistics) (2007) *Essere madri in Italia*, Roma: ISTAT. Available at: http://www3.ISTAT.it/salastampa/comunicati/non_calendario/20070117_00/testointegrale.pdf

ISTAT (2008) 'Conciliare lavoro e famiglia – Una sfida quotidiana' ['The balance between work and family'], Rilevazione Aprile-Giugno 2005. Available at: http://www3.ISTAT.it/dati/catalogo/20080904_00/arg_08_33_conciliare_lavoro_e_famiglia.pdf

ISTAT (2010) *Employment rate (20–64 years)*, Roma: ISTAT. Available at: http://noi-italia2012en.istat.it/index.php?id=7&user_100ind_pi1%5Bid_pagina%5D=98&cHash=7410b059e61cae3bff4f10f6b61eaa6a

ISTAT (2011) *La conciliazione tra lavoro e famiglia. Anno 2010 [The balance between work and family. Year 2010]*, Statistiche report, 28 December, Roma: ISTAT. Available at: http://www.ISTAT.it/it/archivio/48912

ISTAT (2014) *Rapporto annuale. La situazione del paese nel 2010*, Roma: Istituto Nazionale di Statistica.

King, R. (ed) (2001) *The Mediterranean passage: migration and new cultural encounters in Southern Europe*, Liverpool: Liverpool University Press.

Kohler, H.-P., Billari, F.C. and Ortega, J.A. (2002) 'The emergence of lowest-low fertility in Europe during the 1990s', *Population and Development Review*, 28(4): 641–80.

León, M. and Migliavacca, M. (2013) 'Italy and Spain: still the case of familistic welfare models?', *Population Review*, 52(1): 25–42. Available at: http://www.academia.edu/2522477/Spain_and_Italy_still_the_case_of_familistic_welfare_models

Livi Bacci, M. (2001) 'Too few children and too much family', *Daedalus*, 130(3): 139–56.

Lyberaki, A. (2008) '"*Deae ex machina*": *migrant women, care work and women's employment in Greece*', GreeSE Paper no 20, Hellenic Observatory Papers on Greece and Southeast Europe. Available at: http://www2.lse.ac.uk/europeanInstitute/research/hellenicObservatory/pdf/GreeSE/GreeSE20.pdf

Magaraggia, S. (2013) 'Tensions between fatherhood and the social construction of masculinity in Italy', *Current Sociology*, 61(1): 76–92.

Mazzucchelli, S. (2011) 'The impact of Law 53/00 (regulation of parental leaves) on fathers: a good law disregard in daily life', in M. Cortini, G. Tanucci and E. Morin (eds) *Boundaryless careers and occupational wellbeing*, Basingstoke: Palgrave Macmillan, pp 241–55.

McDonald, P. (2000a) 'Gender equity in theories of fertility transition', *Population and Development Review*, 26(3): 427–39.

McDonald, P. (2000b) 'Gender equity, social institutions and the future of fertility', *Journal of Population Research*, 17(1): 1–16.

Mencarini, L. (2010) 'Asimmetrie di genere e bilanci tempo delle famiglie', in M. Livi Bacci (ed) *Demografia del capitale umano*, Coll. Prismi, Il Mulino: Bologna, pp 71–94.

Mencarini L. (2012) 'Soddisfazione personale e vita di coppia degli italiani:un'analisi dell'uso del tempo e della divisione dei compiti domestici', in M.C. Romano, L. Mencarini and M.L. Tanturri (eds) *Uso del tempo e ruoli di genere*, Argomenti no 43, Roma: ISTAT.

Mencarini, L. and Tanturri, M.L. (2004) 'Time use, family role-set and childbearing among Italian working women', *Genus*, LX(1): 111–37.

Menniti, A., Demurtas, P., Arima, S. and De Rose, A. (2014) 'Gender inequality at home when mothers work. The case of Italy', The University of Rome La Sapienza Working Paper, no 130 (May). Available at: http://www.memotef.uniroma1.it/sites/dipartimento/files/wpapers/documenti/FullTextWP130.pdf

Miettinen, A., Rotkirch, A., Szalma, I., Tanturri, M.L and Donno, A. (2014) 'Increasing childlessness in Europe: time trends and macro determinants', Families and Societies WP Series. Available at: http://www.familiesandsocieties.eu/?page_id=131

Mills, M., Mencarini, L., Tanturri, M.L. and Begall, K. (2008) 'Gender equity and fertility intentions in Italy and the Netherlands', *Demographic Research*, 18(1): 1–26.

OECD (Organisation for Economic Co-operation and Development) (2011) *Doing better for families*, Paris: OECD.

OECD (2014) *OECD family database*, Paris: OECD. Available at: www.oecd.org/social/family/database

Paihlé, A., Solaz, A. and Tanturri, M.L. (2015) 'The time cost of raising children in different fertility contexts: evidence from France and Italy', Families and Societies WP Series). Available at: http://www.familiesandsocieties.eu/?page_id=131

Perra, M.S. and Ruspini, E. (eds) (2013) 'Men who work in non traditional occupations', *International Review of Sociology-Revue Internationale de Sociologie*, 23(2). Available at: http://www.tandfonline.com/doi/abs/10.1080/03906701.2013.804288

Petmesidou, M. (1996) 'Social protection in Southern Europe: trends and prospects', *Journal of Area Studies*, 9(4): 95–125.

Pinnelli, A., Racioppi, F. and Rettaroli, R. (eds) (2007) *Genere e Demografia*, Bologna: Il Mulino.

Rainer, T. and Rainer, J. (2011) *The Millennials: connecting to America's largest generation*, Nashville: B&H Publishing Group.

Reher, D.S. (1998) 'Family ties in Western Europe: persistent contrasts', *Population and Development Review*, 24(2): 203–34.

Romano, M.C. and Bruzzese, D. (2007) 'Fathers' participation in the domestic activities of everyday life', *Social Indicators Research*, 84: 97–116.

Rosina, A. and Sabbadini, L.L. (eds) (2006) *Diventare padri in Italia. Fecondità e figli secondo un approccio di genere* [Becoming a father in Italy: fertility and children in a gender perspective], Collana Argomenti no 31, Roma: ISTAT.

Rossi, G. (2006) 'Work and family between idealism and reality: trends and choices of men and women in Italy', in G. Rossi (ed) *Reconciling family and work: new challenges for social policies in Europe*, Milano: FrancoAngeli.

Rossi, G. (2009) 'Development and dynamics of the family in the Southern Europe', in O. Kapella, C. Rille-Pfeiffer, M. Rupp and N.F. Schneider (eds) *Die Vielfalt der Familie. Tagungsband zum 3. Europäischen Fachkongress Familienforschung*, Opladen: Barbara Budrich, pp 365–89.

Ruspini, E. (2006) 'All'ombra delle cure materne. La costruzione della paternità' ['The social construction of fatherhood'], in F. Bimbi and R. Trifiletti (eds) *Madri sole e nuove famiglie. Declinazioni inattese della genitorialità*, Roma: Edizioni Lavoro, pp 257–78.

Ruspini, E. (ed) (2011a) *Studiare la famiglia che cambia* [*Changing families*], Roma: Carocci.

Ruspini, E. (2011b) 'And yet something is on the move: education to new forms of masculinity in Italy', in E. Ruspini, J. Hearn, B. Pease and K. Pringle (eds) *Men and masculinities around the world. Transforming men's practices*, Basingstoke: Palgrave Macmillan, pp 60–9.

Ruspini, E., Hearn, J. Pease, B. and Pringle, K. (eds) (2011) *Men and masculinities around the world. Transforming men's practice*, Basingstoke: Palgrave Macmillan.

Sabbadini, L.L. and Cappadozzi, T. (2011) 'Essere padri: tempi di cura & organizzazione di vita', unpublished contribution in the workshop 'Men, Fathers and Work from Different Perspective', Milan, 2 February.

Saraceno, C. (1994) 'The ambivalent familism of Italian welfare state', *Social Politics*, 1: 60–82.

Saraceno, C. (1995) 'Familismo ambivalente y clientelismo categórico en el Estado del bienestar italiano', in S. Sarasa and L. Moreno (eds) *El Estado del bienestar en la Europa del sur*, Madrid: Consejo Superior de Investigaciones Científicas/Instituto de Estudios Sociales Avanzados, pp 261–88.

Saraceno, C. (2003) *Mutamenti della famiglia e politiche sociali in Italia* (2nd edn), Bologna: Il Mulino.

Scabini, E. and Donati, P. (eds) (1988) *La famiglia 'lunga' del giovane adulto. Verso nuovi compiti educative*, Milano: Vita & Pensiero.

Sironi, E. and Rosina, A. (2012) 'The problematic transition to adulthood in Italy: comparison before and after the beginning of the global crisis', paper presented at the conference 'The transition to adulthood after the great recession', Bocconi University, Milan, Italy, 25–26 October. Available at: http://transitions.s410.sureserver.com/wp-content/uploads/2011/08/Rosina-_The-Problematic-Transition-to-Adulthood-in-Italy.pdf

Smith, A.J. (2004) 'Who cares? European fathers and the time they spend looking after their children', doctoral dissertation, University of Edinburgh.

Smith Koslowski, A. (2007) 'Working fathers in Europe. Earning and caring?', CRFR Research Briefing 30, Centre for Research on Families and Relationships, The University of Edinburgh. Available at: http://www.socialpolicy.ed.ac.uk/__data/assets/pdf_file/0004/6538/rb30.pdf

Tanturri, M.L. (2006) 'Ruolo paterno e caratteristiche della coppia', in A. Rosina and L.L. Sabbadini (eds) *Diventare padri in Italia. Fecondità e figli secondo un approccio di genere*, Collana Argomenti no 31, Roma: ISTAT.

Tanturri, M.L. (2010) 'Demografia e lavoro femminile: le sfide della conciliazione' ('Demography and women labour market participation: the reconciliation challenges'), in M. Livi Bacci (ed) *La demografia del capitale umano*, Coll. 'Prismi', Bologna: Il Mulino, pp 100–22.

Tanturri, M.L. and Mencarini, L. (2008) 'Childless or childfree? An insight into voluntary childlessness in Italy', *Population Development Review*, 34(1): 51–77.

Tanturri, M.L. and Mencarini, L. (2009) 'Fathers' involvement in daily child care activities in Italy: does a work–family reconciliation issue exist?', *Child*, no 22/2009. Available at: http://www.child-centre.unito.it/papers/child22_2009.pdf

Taylor, P. and Keeter, S. (eds) (2010) *Millennials: a portrait of generation next. Confident, connected, open to change*, Washington, DC: Pew Research Center, February. Available at: http://www.pewsocialtrends.org/files/2010/10/millennials-confident-connected-open-to-change.pdf

Trifiletti, R. (1999) 'Southern European welfare regimes and the worsening position of women', *Journal of European Social Policy*, 9(1): 49–64.

Wall, K. and Nunes, C. (2010) 'Immigration, welfare and care in Portugal: mapping the new plurality of female migration trajectories', *Social Policy & Society*, 9(3): 397–408. Available at: http://www.ics.ul.pt/rdonweb-docs/Karin%20Wall_2010_n4.pdf

Zajczyk, F. and Ruspini, E. (with B. Borlini and F. Crosta) (2008) *Nuovi padri? Mutamenti della paternità in Italia e in Europa* [*New fathers?*], Milano: Baldini Castoldi Dalai.

Zanatta, A.L. (2011) *Nuove madri e nuovi padri* [*New mothers and new fathers*], Bologna: Il Mulino.

FOUR

Slovenia

Nada Stropnik and Živa Humer

The cultural and policy context of fatherhood

Slovenia was part of the former Socialist Federative Republic of Yugoslavia until 1991, when it became an independent state. Yugoslavia was not a typical socialist country in terms of political regime, economic development or social conditions. It developed its own policies and allowed the federal republics to modify them. Slovenia began using Sweden as a model for parental leave and early childhood education and care (ECEC) policies in the 1970s and 1980s (Korintus and Stropnik, 2009). As a consequence, in Slovenia, it was possible to transfer the mother's right to childcare leave (now called parental leave) to the father as early as 1975. A family leave act was adopted in the same year (1974) that Sweden, the first country in the world, introduced paid parental leave to fathers. Unlike other former socialist countries, such as Hungary, Poland and the Czech Republic, Slovenia not only managed to preserve most of its achievements in the area of family and ECEC policies during the post-socialist period, but also continued to improve them. Over the last two decades, public spending on family and children has been between 1.7% and 2.2% of gross domestic product (GDP) (Jacović, 2012), which is lower than the 2009 Organisation for Economic Co-operation and Development (OECD) average of 2.6% (OECD Family Database[1]). However, family benefits (cash transfers, spending on services and tax savings) are well-targeted and efficient in Slovenia. These effective policies have resulted in one of the lowest relative child poverty rates (UNICEF, 2012).

During the socialist era, the Slovenian state granted women and men legal equality, provided women with reproductive and social rights, and offered social services that enabled women to fully participate in the labour market (Jalušič, 1999). Women's full-time employment, a well-developed system of public ECEC and generous maternity and parental leave and benefits were the main factors fostering a dual-earner model in Slovenia. In the private sphere, however, the division of care work remained quite traditional and gendered. Women performed most of the childcare and routine household labour, while men were mainly engaged in repair and maintenance work. With respect to childcare, men were involved in the more pleasant tasks, such as walking and playing with children (Boh, 1966; Ule, 1977). Today, a gendered and asymmetrical division of care work in the family still prevails (Rener et al, 2007; Sedmak and Medarič, 2007; Humer, 2009). The data on unpaid work in households, collected through the second European Quality of Life Survey (2007–08), confirms the persistence of gender inequality in the private sphere: employed women spent, on average, 42 hours per week on household tasks and childcare, compared to men's 28 hours per week (Eurofound, 2009). This gap can be interpreted as a 'second shift' for women, which equals almost two additional full-time working days per week. The birth of a child usually means a career pause for the mother even though she formally remains employed while on maternity and parental leave. For the father, however, it usually only involves relatively short absences from work when the child is born, when he takes the paternity leave and occasionally when he cares for a sick child (Humer, 2009). In 1997, fathers accounted for only 14% of all parents absent from work due to childcare responsibilities, and by 2007, fathers' share had increased to 16% (Rener et al, 2008). However, although the pace of change has been relatively slow, some aspects of fatherhood have been changing in both quantitative and qualitative terms (Rener et al, 2005, 2007, 2008; Humer, 2009).

The labour force participation of women, especially of those in full-time employment and of mothers, has been traditionally high in Slovenia. This has been due not only to the professional aspirations of women, but also to the need arising from low wages relative to the costs of living. Two wages have been necessary to support an adequate standard of living for a three- or four-member family (Stropnik and Šircelj, 2008). This has not changed despite considerable political, social and economic changes following the transition from socialism, mainly because aspirations and perceptions have been rising in step with rising income and changing opportunities.

Working full-time after parental leave, which is the norm for the majority of Slovenian mothers, is possible because of various policy measures: (1) a long, fully compensated parental leave; (2) well-regulated, widely available and affordable quality ECEC; and (3) labour market policies that facilitate the reconciliation of work and family obligations for parents with young children. The state policies supporting parents' participation in the labour market also ensure that income from work is high enough for parents to raise their children.

However, there is a lack of support for parents at the organisational level. There has been a clear increase in employers' demands on their employees' time as the economic system changed from socialism to capitalism. Specifically, employers in the private sector show less interest than public employers in work–family reconciliation measures, unless these measures contribute to their profit margin. Family life is becoming ever-more subordinated to working life, and along with persisting traditional gender ideologies in the private sphere, this prevents major changes in the gender division of care work in families and reinforces ideologies of motherhood and fatherhood in Slovenia (Rener et al, 2008). General trends in work intensity – such as longer working hours, work at high speed and tight deadlines – are difficult for employed people with family care responsibilities and obligations (Kanjuo Mrčela and Černigoj Sadar, 2007). While women are more likely to be affected, men are also engaged in care activities. Therefore, when dealing with the issue of father involvement in childcare, the relevant question is not 'Do men want to care?', but rather 'Do organizations want them to care?' (Scambor et al, 2013: 71).

According to a substantial body of literature, the most prominent changes in family life over the last several decades relate to changes in parenting. Changes in fathering and fatherhood are occurring on both the structural (policy) and individual (behaviour) level (Rener, 1993; Silva, 1999; Stacey, 1996; Segal, 1997; Dienhart, 1998; Švab, 2001; Rener et al, 2005, 2008; Kaufman, 2013). In Slovenia, the changes in fatherhood on an individual level are evident in the increased participation of fathers in childcare compared to previous generations of fathers (Rener et al, 2008; Humer, 2009). On a structural level, changes promoting active fatherhood are visible in developments in family and gender-equality policy, such as paternity leave provisions. In 2012, 84% of fathers used their basic entitlement to paid paternity leave (15 days) and 21% of these fathers took additional unpaid paternity leave (up to an additional 75 days) (MoLFSAEO, 2013, own calculations).

Leave provisions

Everyone covered by parental leave insurance (which is part of social security insurance in Slovenia) who is working at least one day prior to the first day of leave is entitled to maternity, paternity and parental leave with wage compensation. All employed and self-employed persons are covered (including farmers), as are their household members, other persons who have farming as their only or main occupation (if covered by mandatory pension and disability insurance), and unemployed persons included in public works, which is an active employment policy measure. Since 2005, in order to cover formerly insured persons who happen to be unemployed just before the start of the leave, persons who were insured for at least 12 months in the last three years before the start of the leave are now also covered.

Since 1986, the policy covered 105 days of maternity leave and 260 days of parental leave, to which 90 days of paternity leave were gradually added between 2003 and 2005. Fathers may use 15 fully paid days of paternity leave in the child's first six months, while the remaining 75 days can be used at any time before the child turns three years old. The Parental Protection and Family Benefits Act, adopted in April 2014, declares that when the economy recovers from the current financial crisis (ie from the year that will follow the year in which economic growth exceeds 2.5% of GDP), the fully paid paternity leave will last 30 days, with the second 15 days to be used before the child has completed the first grade of primary school). Parental leave is now an individual entitlement: 130 days belong to the mother and 130 days to the father. Thirty out of the mother's 130 leave days are non-transferrable, but the father may transfer to the mother all of his 130 days. Up to 75 days of the parental leave can be taken at any time before the child has completed the first grade of primary school. These 75 days, as well as the entire paternity leave, may be taken as individual days, but in that case, the length of the leave is equal to 70% of the eligible calendar days (because weekends are not counted).

During maternity leave, parental leave and the first 15 days of paternity leave, income compensation amounts to 100% of the average monthly gross wage of the entitled person during the 12 months prior to the leave (it is currently 90% due to temporary austerity measures implemented in mid-2012). Also, parents who have been insured for at least 12 months in the last three years before the start of the leave are eligible to some wage compensation. Generally, the minimum wage compensation is set at 55% of the minimum wage and the maximum compensation is 2.5 times the average wage in Slovenia (the upper limit is not applied to the compensation during maternity leave). The remainder of the 75 days of paternity leave are compensated with social security contributions (based on the minimum wage) paid from the state budget. Once the economy recovers from the economic crisis, these 75 days will be replaced by an additional 15 days with 100% wage compensation (adopted in April 2014).

Contextual demographic and family trends related to fatherhood

In order to better understand Slovenian fathers' involvement with young children, some contextual indicators are provided in Table 4.1. These are basic demographic indicators, Census data on family households and data on the labour force participation rate of men, women, fathers and mothers.

Table 4.1 shows that between 2000 and 2012, the Slovenian marriage rate has been reduced slightly from 3.6 to 3.4, which is one of the lowest in the European Union (EU). The divorce rate is also extremely low and has been rather stable, at just above one per thousand. Roughly one in three Slovenian marriages fails (SI-Stat Data Portal, 2013).

In the first half of the 2000s, about nine children were born per thousand population, which has increased to about 11 since 2008. Between 1995 and 2005, Slovenia was the country with the lowest-low total fertility rate (TFR), with its lowest level of 1.2 registered in 2003. The TFR increased to almost 1.6 by 2012, which was primarily due to the births of (postponed) second children. The postponement of childbirth is evident from the ever-higher average age of mothers at the birth of the first and the second child. Between 2000 and 2012, the average age of mothers at childbirth increased from 28.3 to 30.5 years.

Since 1976, both marital and non-marital children have enjoyed the same rights in Slovenia, when the Marriage and Family Relations Act was adopted. There is no stigma associated with having a child outside of marriage, and the share of non-marital births has been increasing quite dramatically over the last decade: they accounted for 37% of all births in 2000 and for 58% of all births in 2012. The percentage of non-marital births is much higher for first births (48% in 2000 and 68% in 2012) than for second (25% and 52%) and third births (18% and 36%) (SI-Stat Data Portal, 2013). While many couples used to marry after the birth of the first child, recent data for second and third children indicate this has become less typical (Šircelj, 2006). In addition, the percentage of fathers (not married to mothers of their children) who acknowledge paternity before the child is one month old has increased significantly from about 50% in 2001 to almost 95% of fathers in 2012 (SI-Stat Data Portal, 2013). Since 2005, it has been possible to acknowledge paternity of the child even before their birth; more than 71% of fathers did so in 2012.

Table 4.1: Selected indicators related to parenting for Slovenia, circa 2000 and circa 2012

Indicator	2000	2012
Crude marriage rate (per 1,000 population)	3.6	3.4
Crude divorce rate	1.1	1.2
Total fertility rate	1.3	1.6
Crude birth rate	9.1	10.7
Mothers' mean age at first birth	28.3	30.5
% non-marital births	37.1	57.6
Births per 1,000 men	18.7	21.6
% of family households that are:		**(2011)**
Husband/wife	20.7	22.1
Unmarried couple	2.3	2.1
Husband/wife with children[a]	53.0	41.8
Unmarried couple with children	5.3	8.7
Mother only with children	16.1	21.1
Father only with children	2.6	4.1
% of children <5 living with:		
Two parents	80.7	69.8
Father only	1.9	5.0
Mother only	17.4	25.2
% of married-couple families that are:		
Dual-earner families	76.8	76.8
Male-provider families	13.6	13.4
Labour force participation (LFP)		
LFP rate, men (age 15–64)	71.7	73.7
Fathers (15+) of kids under 18	93.9	96.2
Fathers (15+) of under 6 year olds	94.8	97.9
Men (15+), % full-time	94.3	94.1
Men (15+), % part-time	5.7	5.9
Mean number of hours/week, men (15+)	42.5	40.8
Mean number of hours/week, fathers (15+) of kids under 18	43.5	41.8
Mean number of hours/week, fathers (15+) of kids under 6	43.8	41.7
LFP rate, women (15–64)	63.1	67.0
Mothers (15+) of kids under 18	90.0	90.8
Mothers (15+) of under 6 year olds	90.6	88.5
Women (15+), % full-time	91.2	89.7
Women (15+), % part-time	8.8	10.3
Mean number of hours/week, women (15+)	40.7	38.6
Mean number of hours/week, mothers (15+) of kids under 18	41.1	39.4
Mean number of hours/week, mothers (15+) of kids under 6	41.0	38.4

Note: [a] The statistical definition of children in Slovenia does not have an age threshold.

Sources: SI-Stat Data Portal (2013); SORS (2002); Census data (provided by SORS, own calculations); EC (2010); LFS data (provided by SORS, own estimations); LFS data (estimations provided by SORS); OECD. Stat Extracts (see: http://stats.oecd.org/).

While family households consisting of a married couple with children is still the majority family form, in the period from 2002 to 2011, their share decreased by more than 11 percentage points. The share of unmarried couples with children and single-parent families has increased, particularly the share of solo mothers with children. This trend is reflected in the living arrangements of children younger than five years of age: while the share of young children living with two parents has decreased from 81% in 2002 to 70% in 2011, relatively more live with only one parent – more than a quarter with their mother. In the same period, the share of children aged under four living with unmarried parents increased to more than 25%.

Kanjuo Mrčela and Černigoj Sadar (2007) note that, in 2003, as many as 88% of men and 92% of women agreed with the statement: 'Both men and women should contribute to the family income'. Thus, it is not surprising that 76% of Slovenian families consisting of a couple with a child younger than age 18 were dual-earner families in both 2002 and 2011. The percentage was higher in married-couple families (77%) than in unmarried-couple families (about 70%). Male-provider families were more frequent among the unmarried-couple families (about 17%) than among married-couple families (about 13%).

The gender gap in labour force participation rates has been relatively small in Slovenia. In 2012, 67% of women aged 15–64 years (in general) and more than 88% of mothers aged 15 or older with a child younger than age six were employed, compared to 74% of men aged 15–64 years (in general) and almost 98% of fathers (aged 15 years or older) of children younger than six years old (Si-Stat Data Portal [2013] and evaluations by the Statistical Office of the Republic of Slovenia [SORS] based on the Labour Force Survey [LFS] data). In fact, in 2009, the employment rate of mothers aged 20–49 with a child aged under six was 3.7% higher than the employment rate of comparable women without a child (EC, 2010: 62). This pattern makes Slovenia unique. The employment impact of parenthood was even more pronounced for fathers aged 20–49 years with a child aged under six: their employment rate was 12.4% higher than the employment rate of comparable men without a child. In 2010, 85% of women and 94% of men with children younger than age 12 were employed, compared to 83% of women and 82% of men without children (Eurostat, 2011). This indicates that parents of both genders are more likely to be in the labour force than non-parents, and that fathers are much more likely to be employed than non-fathers, especially when the children are young.

While men are generally less likely than women to work part-time, the gender difference is relatively narrow in Slovenia. Specifically, in

2012, 94% of employed men aged 15 years and older worked full-time, which was true for 90% of comparable women (OECD.Stat Extracts[2]). In fact, the average number of hours worked per week was around 40.8 for men and 38.6 for women (own estimations based on the LFS data). Overall, part-time employment has increased over the last decade: 10% of all women and 6% of all men were employed part-time in 2012 (OECD.Stat Extracts[3]), compared to 9% and 6% in 2000 (own estimations based on LFS data), respectively. In 2010, women accounted for 72% of all persons who worked part-time due to parenting (Lah and Svetin, 2011). Nevertheless, in both 2000 and 2012, the mean number of hours worked per week was somewhat higher for fathers than for men in general, as it was for mothers of children younger than age 18 compared to all women, while it was just slightly lower for mothers of children younger than age six than for all women (estimations based on LFS data).

Fathers and parental leave

Paternity leave is an important mechanism for fostering active fatherhood in Slovenia (Rener et al, 2005, 2007; Hrženjak et al, 2006; Humer, 2009). In a 2010 survey (Rakar et al, 2010), more than 90% of fathers aged 20–49 with a child aged one to five declared that they were acquainted with the father's entitlement to 15 fully compensated days of paternity leave. The possibility to take an additional 75 days and to have social security contributions paid by the state was known to 80% of the fathers. Almost 45% of the fathers who knew about provisions did not seriously consider them (Stropnik and Kump, forthcoming). Sixty-three per cent of fathers took up to 15 days of paternity leave when it was introduced in 2003, and roughly four in five fathers took it in 2012. However, only one in five leave-takers took more than 15 days during 2009–12 (MoLFSAEO, 2013, own calculations; Stropnik, 2013). Using administrative data, Stropnik and Kump (2009) analysed the uptake of paternity leave between 2005 and 2009. On average, those fathers who used fully compensated paternity leave took 14.5 out of 15 days. Those who also used unpaid paternity leave took between 55 and 65 days out of the 75 days available. No impact of income on the uptake of paid paternity leave was identified, which is logical considering the full wage compensation during the first 15 days and the relatively low proportion of fathers who took more days of leave.

Rakar et al (2010) asked fathers aged 20–49 who had a child in 2003 or later about the reasons for not having taken more days of paternity leave or any at all. Two main reasons identified were that the family could not financially afford more unpaid leave and that the father had not seriously considered the provisions, although he knew about them (Rakar et al, 2010). However, giving the financial constraint reason may be an excuse for fathers who, for various reasons, such as uncertainty or not feeling able to care for a young child, did not want to stay at home with their child (Stropnik and Kump, forthcoming). In fact, about 7% of men in the sample said that they would not take any days at all (not even those that are fully compensated), and about 5% of men would not take more than 15 days even if more days were fully compensated (Stropnik and Kump, forthcoming).

Only around 1% of fathers had not taken additional days of paternity leave because of a fear that co-workers, friends and/or acquaintances would make fun of them. This low rate shows the absence of stigma and the general acceptability of father engagement in Slovenia. However, the employers' negative view of fathers' uptake of paternity leave was confirmed: about 27% of fathers did not take more leave because their employers were not in favour of it (Rakar et al, 2010). Obstacles on the employers' side were reported by Rener et al (2005), Stropnik (2005) and Rakar et al (2010), and included employers' negative reactions when fathers requested temporary absence from work due to the intended uptake of paternity or parental leave. This occurred despite the fact that the Employment Relationships Act specifies that the employer must enable the employees to reconcile their family and employment responsibilities more easily. However, the employers usually claim that the person's presence at work is indispensable, which prevents some fathers from insisting on the leave uptake, and even causes them to fear losing their job.

Stropnik and Kump (forthcoming) investigated the determinants of fathers' use of paternity leave. Their logistic regressions show that childbirth order, fathers' age at the time of birth of the youngest (or only) child, marital status, parental education and fathers' employment status did not significantly affect the likelihood that fathers would take paternity leave. However, fathers were significantly more likely to take paternity leave when mothers were employed full-time than when mothers were employed part-time. The likelihood of fathers taking paternity leave was significantly higher between 2006 and 2009 than in the time period between 2003 and 2006 (the leave was introduced in 2003); the rate was highest for partners of mothers aged 25–29. The authors explain the relative lack of significant predictors as a result of the design of the leave policy – very high coverage was achieved by making leave an entitlement with full wage compensation.

The use of paternity leave right after the birth of the child is particularly important for both partners: the father's participation is perceived as a much-needed help and support to the mother. Fathers on paternity leave tend to engage in domestic work, particularly in the care of and play with older children, but also in caring for the newborn child. However, when fathers return to work and mothers stay at home with their child(ren) on maternity/parental leave, there is a clear pattern of return to a gendered division of labour at home (Rener et al, 2005, 2007, 2008; Humer, 2009).

While fathers have only had paternity leave since 2003, their right to parental leave dates back to 1975. However, fathers have not been very eager to make use of their entitlement or to take many days of parental leave. In 2003, a little more than 2% of fathers took parental leave, which increased to nearly 7% by 2011–12 (MoLFSAEO, 2013, own calculations; Stropnik, 2013). Considering the full wage compensation during parental leave, the reasons for this low level of participation may be found in the traditional division of household labour, societal attitudes and employers' expectations and demands of their male employees (Rener et al, 2005; Stropnik, 2005; Stropnik and Šircelj, 2008). Surprisingly, in the 2010 survey, as many as 22% of the respondents aged 20–49 who had children did not know that parental leave could be shared between the parents (Rakar et al, 2010).

According to Stropnik and Kump (2009) the number of days of parental leave taken by fathers who took leave in the period from December 2005 to April 2009 increased with the number of children, which is the reverse of the finding regarding the uptake of paternity leave. Of the 260 days available, men with one child took an average of 171 days, those with two children took 161 days per child born in the observed period, those with three children took 191 days per child and those with four or more children took even more days.

Fathers also do not take leave to care for a sick child as often as mothers. Recent research shows that: in 18% of households, the sick child leave used for the youngest child was taken mostly by fathers; in 54% of households, it was taken mostly by mothers; while parents shared leave equally in 22% of households (Robnik, 2012). The main reason for the unequal sharing of sick childcare leave was financial: because the wage compensation rate is 80% of the average earnings over the preceding 12 months, the parent with the lower earnings usually takes the leave.

Fathers and childcare

The provision of parental leave and ECEC can enable parents to balance their work and parenting roles. ECEC is well-regulated and organised in Slovenia; it is also widely available and affordable due to very high public subsidies. Children are entitled to ECEC from the end of parental leave (when the child is slightly older than 11 months) on a full-time basis in preschool day-care centres, which provide nursery and kindergarten classes. Hence, there is a seamless transition from parental care to ECEC.

The act regulating ECEC (the Kindergarten Act 2005) requires that services are available to all children and directs the municipalities to open additional classes if warranted by the number of parents who express interest in enrolling their children into ECEC programmes. In the 2012/13 school year, about 56% of children up to age three were included in nurseries (Ložar, 2013). This far exceeds the EU 2020 target of 33% (EC, 2011: 2), which was already reached in Slovenia in 2003 (Čelebič, 2012). The majority of children attend all-day programmes (Ložar, 2013).

All families with children in approved ECEC programmes provided by public and private preschool day-care centres/providers are entitled to a subsidy, which amounted to an average of about 68% of the care costs per child in 2011. Currently, parents with a per capita income equal to or higher than the average income pay a maximum of 77% of the total care expenses. Families with a per capita income below 18% of the (net) average wage in Slovenia are exempt from contributing anything. The costs for a second child are 30% of the income-adjusted fee and the services are free of charge for each subsequent child.

From the mid-1980s until 2008, the supply of ECEC almost completely met the demand. The availability of free ECEC services for the second and subsequent child between 2008 and 2012 and an upturn in the birth rate in the 2000s have contributed to a growth in demand for ECEC. In response, municipalities expanded their capacities quite rapidly and many are now meeting the new demand.

According to the 2002 Eurobarometer survey, most Slovenians believe that both mothers and fathers should carry out child-rearing tasks. The overall index measuring the prevalence of that belief was almost 90 on a scale of 0 to 100, where 100 indicated the complete sharing of activities (Fahey and Spéder, 2004). This preference for equal sharing also applied to changing nappies; preferences did not vary by gender (Fahey and Spéder 2004). In both measures of task-sharing, Slovenia ranked fifth in the EU, just behind Sweden, Denmark, Estonia and Finland. Nevertheless, the actual time spent on childcare continues to be very unevenly distributed among Slovenian couples with children younger than age six: in 2000, it was 2.23 hours per day for mothers and 0.56 hours for fathers (European Communities, 2004). Among employed parents, this was negligibly reduced to 2.16 and 0.55 hours, respectively, which shows that employment status does not affect the time spent on the care of young children and reflects the parents' high labour force participation rate. According to preliminary results of the 2010 Statistics on Income and Living Conditions (SILC), men spent 11 hours per week on household work, childcare and similar activities, while women spent 24 hours per week on these activities (Inglič and Stare, 2011).

Research on father involvement

Time engaged with children

A review of the literature on fatherhood in Slovenia shows a lack of studies focusing on fathers' engagement with children. The only available research focuses on paternity leave and fathers' engagement during the time they are on paternity leave. In addition, there are several studies on the division of household labour between women and men, but the data include all women and men, regardless of whether they have children or not. Hence, there is no information available on fathers' engagement in specific childcare activities with young children.

Available time-use data show that Slovenian fathers appear to devote significantly less time than mothers to childcare. In general, roughly 16% of men and 40% of women aged 25–44 years participated in childcare. The percentages participating in other named activities involving children were roughly 20% and 30%, respectively. Around the year 2000, men aged 25–44 years who engaged in childcare spent about half an hour less per day on the physical care and direct supervision of children (0.58 hours) compared to women, who spent 1.24 hours. Men spent an additional 1.02 hours (and women 1.07 hours) on teaching, reading and talking with their children (Eurostat time-use data[4]). Furthermore, men aged 25–44 who have at least one preschool child and who work full-time spend, on average, 4.2 hours per week on childcare as a primary or secondary activity (compared to 10.2 hours for women) (OECD Family Database[5]).

Level of father engagement

There is a considerable gap between fathers' subjective perception of their fathering activities and the everyday reality of their contribution to childcare in Slovenia. In 2000, only about 25% of Slovenians aged 20–64 years agreed with the statement: 'Fathers are not engaged enough in the care of their children' (Stropnik and Šircelj, 2008: 1039). The median value on the five-point scale (1 meaning 'I strongly agree' and 5 meaning 'I strongly disagree') was 3.47 for men's answers and 3.26 for women's answers, indicating that women agreed with that statement more than men (Černič Istenič, 2001).

The fathers typically use the first part of paternity leave (15 calendar days) while the mother is on maternity leave, most often after she returns from hospital. The study by Rener et al (2005) showed that fathers' activities were mainly in support of mothers during this time. Fathers engaged in care for and play with older children, as well as doing the shopping, but they also cared for and fed the newborn child. Cradling the newborn was the activity that engaged the highest percentage of fathers: 60% stated that they did so to the same extent as the mother, 33% reported sometimes cradling the baby and 5% stated that they cradled the newborn more often than the mother. A small percentage of fathers (2%) reported that they never cradled the baby during the first 15 days of paternity leave.

The second most common activity of fathers on paternity leave was comforting the newborn child. In 44% of cases, fathers estimated that they comforted the baby just as often as the mother, 50% did it often, 4% more often than the mother and 2% of fathers responded that they had never comforted the baby. Changing nappies and clothing for the baby was an activity that 53% of fathers participated in sometimes, 38% engaged in just as much as the mothers and 4% reported doing more often than the mothers. In terms of bathing and washing the baby, 34% of fathers participated sometimes, 46% just as often as the mother and 8% more often than the mother. The activity fathers engaged in least often was getting up at night because of the child: a third of them did it just as frequently as the mother, 48% reported sometimes getting up and 9% responded that they never got up at night because of the newborn. Fathers of two or more children reported getting up during the night less often than fathers for whom it was their first child (Rener et al, 2005).

Information on fathers' engagement in childcare tasks, which is based on two comparable surveys – the 2000 survey by Stropnik and Černič Istenič (2001) and the 2010 survey by Rakar and colleagues (2010) – is presented in Table 4.2. The data come from fathers and mothers who were not from the same families, who were aged 20–49 years with at least one child aged under 10. The first two columns in Table 4.2 refer to the percentages of fathers who were the first and the second main performers, respectively, of individual activities and the third column provides the sum. Although the fathers' and the mothers' answers are not directly comparable because they are not part of couples, they are presented separately in the last two columns. There clearly is a difference between the fathers' evaluation of their own engagement and the mothers' perception of the engagement of their male partners.

Obviously, fathers are less likely than mothers to be either first or second main performers of childcare activities in both surveys. Overall, while fathers' engagement in performing childcare tasks was similar in 2000 and 2010, they were somewhat more engaged in 2010 (see column 3). They were more frequently named as being the first main performers of particular tasks (see column 1). For instance, 16% of fathers were those persons who were most frequently preparing meals for their children aged 0–10 years in 2010, compared to 13% of fathers in 2000. However, there is a perception gap by gender: fathers' engagement was perceived higher in their own rating than in the rating of mothers (columns 4–5). For instance, in 2010, 37% of mothers reported that fathers were first or second main persons arranging administrative affairs for the child(ren) while 57% of fathers were of the same opinion (please note that mothers and fathers belonged to different families).

As a rule, the more a task involves direct childcare activities, the less frequently it was performed by men: fathers were much less engaged in preparing meals for the children and dressing the children than in playing with them, performing indirect tasks for them or jointly undertaking some activities (like sports activities, trips, gardening, etc). The distribution of childcare tasks between the partners is significantly more equal among younger (25–29 years) than older parents (30–39 and 40–49 years) (Černič Istenič, 2001), particularly in the case of dressing the children.

Determinants of father engagement with young children

Unfortunately, no research has been done in Slovenia on what factors increase or decrease father engagement with young children. Neither an in-depth review of the literature nor direct contact with colleagues engaged with fatherhood research have produced any information about studies on this topic. Slovenia is a small and relatively young

Table 4.2: Father engagement in childcare activities (fathers with children aged 0–10 years)

	Father is the first main performer (%)	Father is the second main performer (%)	Father is the first or second main performer combined		
	Fathers' and mothers' answers	Fathers' and mothers' answers	All answers (sum 1 + 2)	Fathers' own answers	Mothers' answers about fathers
	1	2	3	4	5
Year 2000 (N = 340: 175 fathers and 165 mothers)					
Preparing the meals for the child(ren)	12.9	13.8	26.7	36.0	17.0
Dressing the child(ren)	13.2	18.8	32.0	37.1	26.7
Visiting a doctor with the child(ren)	21.2	20.3	41.5	50.3	32.1
Arranging administrative affairs for the child(ren)	29.1	17.9	47.0	56.6	37.0
Organising childcare service in case of emergency	21.8	16.5	38.3	49.1	26.7
Choosing day-care facilities/school	21.8	32.6	54.4	59.4	49.1
Playing with child(ren) or undertaking something with the child(ren)	28.8	36.5	65.3	73.7	56.4
Year 2010 (N = 319: 144 fathers and 175 mothers)					
Preparing the meals for the child(ren)	15.9	7.8	23.7	32.6	16.6
Dressing the child(ren)	17.5	10.3	27.8	33.3	23.4
Visiting a doctor with the child(ren)	28.4	14.1	42.5	56.9	30.9
Arranging administrative affairs for the child(ren)	34.1	20.6	54.7	84.7	30.3
Organising childcare service in case of emergency	28.4	13.4	41.8	55.6	30.9
Choosing day-care facilities/school	26.6	28.8	55.4	56.9	54.3
Playing with child(ren) or undertaking something with the child(ren)	40.9	27.5	68.4	76.4	62.3

Note: The term 'father' includes the biological father and the mother's partner who is not the child's biological father. Data for the year 2000. N = 340 (175 fathers and 165 mothers).

Source: Rakar et al (2010: Table 6.11), own calculations.

country; therefore, resources for data collection and analysis in the social sciences are generally quite scarce. Clearly, this is a research gap that needs to be addressed by future endeavours.

Research on father involvement and father well-being

In recent decades, several studies have focused on Slovenian trends in parenting, fatherhood in the context of the division of work at home, the impact of paternity leave on fathering and the impact of employers on fostering care masculinities in organisations (see Rener et al, 2005, 2008; Hrženjak et al, 2006; Kanjuo Mrčela and Černigoj Sadar, 2007; Stropnik and Kump, 2009; Robnik, 2012; Švab and Humer, 2013). Studies of new fatherhood were also brought about by legislative changes, such as the introduction of paternity leave in 2003 and the accompanying activities that promoted active involvement of fathers in family life (eg activities of the former Office for Equal Opportunities, TV advertisements and 'Daddies courses'). However, there has not been any comprehensive research on fatherhood or fathers' engagement in childcare activities, nor has there been any comprehensive effort to study the effects of new fatherhood on the fathers themselves, on children or on couple relationships.

In the framework of the national research project on 'Prospects of New Fatherhood in Slovenia: The Influence of Paternity Leave on Active Fatherhood', fathers were interviewed about their informal social networks, the household division of family work and childcare, and their activities during their partner's pregnancy and the first 15 days of paternity leave (Rener et al, 2005). The results show that the men's activities, such as attending the partner's ultrasound and other examinations, preparing the child's room during their partner's pregnancy, and their presence at the birth of the child, have affected the development of fathers' identity positively, which is a crucial condition for active fatherhood.

The 'School for Parents' – a short course for future fathers that is a prerequisite for fathers' presence at childbirth – was attended by more than three quarters of fathers (69% of fathers attended the course of their own will and 8% on their partner's request). Those fathers who had not participated in the course generally declared that they wanted to participate but had not had the opportunity, or that they simply had not found it necessary. The attendance of courses was positively associated with the father's educational level: more educated fathers were more likely to attend the course (Rener et al, 2005).

The majority of fathers surveyed attended the ultrasound examination during their partner's pregnancy: 70% of fathers of their own accord and 10% at their partner's request. A lower percentage of fathers accompanied their partner to regular gynaecological examinations: 29% of the fathers in the sample did so of their own accord, while 14% did it at their partner's request. It appears that education plays an important role in fathers' decision-making as fathers with higher levels of education were more likely to attend gynaecological examinations. More than 80% of fathers were present at the birth of their child; all visited their partner and newborn child in the hospital, 90% participated in preparing the room for the baby, and 86% shopped for the newborn (Rener et al, 2005).

Work-related behaviour

Holter (2007) showed a shift in male gender norms from men as primary family providers to alternative masculinity identities that include active fatherhood and a greater involvement of men in family life. Generally, Slovenian men increasingly strive to transcend the traditional gendered division of labour in favour of more egalitarian partnerships, especially by way of active fatherhood. However, a considerable proportion of employers in the private sector, in particular, do not actively support them in their efforts (Hrženjak et al, 2006; Rener et al, 2007, 2008). Men's reconciliation of work and family life depends on various formal workplace mechanisms, such as the ease with which men can take various types of leave, work reduced hours, use flexitime and work from home (Hrženjak et al, 2006). Informal mechanisms include positive employer attitudes towards active fatherhood and various arrangements made with co-workers and management.

Father involvement is supported by the possibility of varying the start and end of the workday for family reasons by at least one hour. In 2010, about a quarter of employees in Slovenia had flexitime, while almost 10% determined their own work schedule (Lah and Svetin, 2011). Full-day absence for family reasons was generally possible for fewer than half of all employees and rarely possible for a fifth of employees. However, research shows that men do not make use of reconciliation provisions as frequently as do women (Kanjuo Mrčela and Černigoj Sadar, 2007).

While paternity leave is an important mechanism for fostering father involvement, there is considerable return to the traditional division of domestic work between the partners when fathers return to work and mothers stay at home using maternity/parental leave (Rener et al,

2005). The right to paternity leave itself does not guarantee fathers' use of it; nor does it guarantee their continued involvement with children because of possible workplace demands. One third of fathers surveyed had to deal with workplace obligations while they were on paternity leave (Rener et al, 2005), and in a 2012 survey on gender equality in family life, about 9% of fathers reported that they had not taken leave to care for a sick child because their employer was not in favour of them doing so (Robnik, 2012).

Research also demonstrates that Slovenian managers do not regard balancing work and family as a relevant issue in the workplace. Rather, it is considered a private matter that employers should not have to deal with (Kanjuo Mrčela and Černigoj Sadar, 2007). However, young employees appear not to expect much understanding for their family issues from employers. The results of a 2005 survey of 22- to 35-year-old employees show that only 12% of male respondents thought that their employer did not understand the needs of parents of young children; 56% replied that the employer showed (a lot of) understanding (Kanjuo Mrčela and Černigoj Sadar, 2007). In 2012, three quarters of both men and women were satisfied or very satisfied with their work–family balance (Robnik, 2012).

Fatherhood programmes

Fatherhood programmes in Slovenia mainly involve activities for future fathers, such as the 'School for Parents', rather than focusing on fathers of young children. The 'School for Parents', led by medical staff in health-care centres and hospitals, consists of courses for future mothers and fathers before the child is born. There are nine thematic lectures: the introductory lecture is followed by lectures on anatomy, physiology, pregnancy, delivery, care in the post-natal period, breastfeeding and infant nutrition, birth planning, and, finally, the changes that pregnancy brings to the family, partners and children. There is also a short course for fathers who wish to be present at childbirth (Grum, 2014).

Another set of activities, under the banner 'Daddy, be active', supports father involvement and was organised by the former Office for Equal Opportunities in the mid-2000s. Awareness-raising activities focused on fathers included TV and radio messaging, radio shows, an educational documentary film, 'Daddies courses', and a one-year project in which ministries registered the fathers taking paternity and parental leave ('fathers-on-paternity-leave counter'). The TV spots were broadcast during sporting events, and the 'Daddies courses' were popular sporting and socialising events where fathers ran with their children (hand in hand, with prams, etc) (OEO, 2005/2006). Unfortunately, these programmes did not continue after the end of the project, which may be seen as a step backward in promoting active fatherhood in Slovenia.

The Slovenian fatherhood regime

Coltrane and Galt (2000) argue that there were several waves of 'new fatherhood' over the last centuries. The first wave dates back to the 19th century, when middle-class fathers in the US began being present at the birth of the child, which was not established as a common practice until the early 20th century (Coltrane and Galt, 2000). The second wave of new fatherhood followed the second wave of the feminist movement of the 1970s and 1980s and was characterised by studies on the role of men in family life and the introduction of paternity and parental leave and other forms of promoting father involvement. Today, presence at childbirth is considered to be a transformative moment in fathers' identity formation, which significantly affects future father involvement (Rener et al, 2005; Seidler, 2006). In 2011, in Slovenia, fathers were present at 80% of first child births and at 72% of later births (Žnidaršič, 2013), compared to only about 25% of births in 1995 (Žnidaršič, 2012).

Research (Rener et al, 2005, 2007, 2008; Švab and Humer, 2013) confirms the existence of two dominant models of fatherhood in Slovenia: the complementary and the supportive model. In the complementary model, fathers only rarely participate in childcare and other family work and they mainly perform traditionally male tasks. Among childcare tasks, they usually engage in playing with children. The second model, which is becoming more popular, is the supportive model. Here, fathers' participation in both childcare and household work is perceived as a support/help function to their female partners. This help can also come from kinship support networks, mainly grandmothers and grandfathers, as well as paid help (nannies and domestic workers) (Rener et al, 2005, 2008; Humer, 2009).

The general historical shift from the male-breadwinner model towards the new fatherhood model occurred in Slovenia as well, but it never conformed to the classical breadwinner model. The reason for this is that both men and women provide financially for the family, particularly in the post-Second World War period, when women's employment was promoted by the state as a result of the demand for labour. The new fatherhood is mainly characterised by fathers' increased emotional involvement and participation in care activities, which go beyond the provision of material and financial support to the family (Švab, 2001). New fatherhood in Slovenia is primarily described as a greater emotional attachment between fathers and children and increased father engagement in care rather than an increased participation in other household work (Švab, 2001; Rener et al, 2008; Humer, 2009; Humer and Kuhar, 2010; Švab and Humer, 2013). For individual fathers, changes in the direction of new fatherhood are mostly evident at the symbolic level: in men's desire to be involved with their children and in the increasing value attached to fathers' caring role (Švab, 2000; Ule and Kuhar, 2003; Rener et al, 2005; Humer, 2009). While fathers support the idea of a more active role for men in the family and they have more egalitarian attitudes towards the division of labour between women and men in the public and the private sphere (Rener et al, 2008; Humer, 2009), an unequal division of domestic and care work between the partners persists.

Although, today, Slovenian fathers spend more time with their children compared to the previous generations of fathers, they still spend disproportionately less time with their children than do mothers (Humer, 2009). The version of new fatherhood in Slovenia – unlike the ideal type of involved fatherhood or Holter's 'new man' – is limited to supportive fathering activities, which strengthens and maintains the position of the mother as the primary care provider and the father as the secondary care provider. Švab and Humer (2013) show that men engage in more pleasant, less routine and more time-flexible childcare activities. Fathers usually take care of children when mothers are at work or otherwise occupied with housework. They are also more able than mothers to negotiate the timing of their involvement, such as spending more time with their children on weekends. In addition, fathers are less likely than mothers to plan and organise the childcare tasks, even when both parents share the care work relatively evenly (Švab and Humer, 2013). This enables men to more readily reconcile their childcare responsibilities with their professional lives than women, who experience the stress associated with the daily coordination of paid work with family life (Humer, 2009).

Holter (2007) suggests two models of change in fatherhood: the 'new men' and the 'new circumstances'. In Slovenia, a mix of these two models exists, with the 'new circumstances' model being more common. Slovenian families have traditionally been dual-earner families, and the pattern of both parents being engaged in the labour force is not a new circumstance. However, the added expectation that in addition to being providers, men should also engage actively with their children, as reflected in paternity leave policies, is relatively new.

Men are also experiencing new circumstances at work, where higher demands are made on their time. The main incentive for change is the father's relationship with his child (Holter, 2007). Fathers in Slovenia do take basic paternity leave and make some adjustments to their working life in order to accommodate family demands, such as a flexible working schedule or taking the annual leave during school holidays. However, there are only a minority of Slovenian men who would qualify as 'superdads' (Kaufman, 2013) or as 'working fathers' (Ranson, 2012), significantly reorganising their lives due to family needs.

Conclusions and recommendations for policy

Due to the fact that Slovenian women usually work full-time and remain attached to the labour market when they become mothers, the dual-earner model is, and has been, the norm in Slovenia. As breadwinning financial responsibility is typically shared between parents, relevant policies do not differentiate between fathers and mothers when it comes to rights related to the reconciliation of work and family. In practice, however, the traditional division of labour by gender has been changing only slowly, with younger fathers taking on an increased share of childcare responsibilities. Fatherhood in Slovenia mainly occurs in a supporting parental role that strengthens and maintains the position of motherhood and mothering and reduces the role of fathering to a secondary, supportive parenting role (Humer, 2009).

All fathers covered by social security insurance are eligible for the paternity and parental leave and benefits. Normally, there is full earning compensation for parental leave and for the first 15 days of paternity leave. A high proportion of fathers, disregarding their social characteristics, take the initial paid paternity leave before the child is six months old. The fact that paternity leave is taken among all social strata is a consequence of the design of this policy: its high eligibility and full earnings compensation. In addition, one can presume that a considerable proportion of fathers in Slovenia would most likely take more than 15 days of paternity leave if full earnings compensation were available (Stropnik and Kump, forthcoming). For reluctant leave-takers, an attractive and repeated awareness-raising campaign might be effective: a campaign that would follow Nordic countries' practice of positively correlating care for an infant with masculinity.

Time-use surveys confirm a mismatch between fathers' egalitarian attitudes and their traditional behaviour in daily practice. When it comes to daily childcare tasks and responsibilities, fathers are not equal partners. They prefer to play a supportive role, which translates into less care work and responsibility. Men's participation in childcare appears to be optional: fathers can choose which work they prefer to do and when they prefer to do it (Švab and Humer, 2013). The basic care for babies remains mothers' work, while fathers become more involved with somewhat older children. Men are more involved in enjoyable, less routine childcare, such as conversation, reading, listening, playing and educational activities (Humer, 2009; Švab and Humer, 2013).

Gaps in research

More in-depth research is needed in Slovenia on the structural and perceived barriers to fathers taking more parental leave. One important issue is how parents come to an agreement on the division of the parental leave. Sundstrom and Duvander (2002) and Lappegard (2008) argue that fathers' parental leave is residual to mothers' in Sweden and Norway, respectively. Consequently, the father is allowed or persuaded to use some leave when the mother chooses to return to work. There is no information on how many mothers in Slovenia were indeed willing to share the leave with the child's father, on the one hand, and how many have unsuccessfully negotiated the sharing of the parental leave with their partners, on the other. An insight into the couple's decision-making process would help understand why only 7% of fathers take all or some of the 260 fully compensated days of parental leave available.

Research on father involvement with children, and father well-being in particular, is missing. Occasional surveys provide some basic data, but the analyses have remained at a descriptive level, or do not differentiate between all persons/men and parents/fathers. Multivariate research on the determinants of fathers' engagement in specific childcare activities, such as changing nappies, preparing meals for children or playing with them, has not been performed. The financing of research is usually related to the revisions of relevant acts, like the introduction of paternity leave, so there is enough information (including multivariate analysis results) on fathers' uptake of the paternity leave.

Promising initiatives and suggestions for changes

A positive model of active fatherhood needs to be promoted in Slovenia. National surveys pointing to the link between father involvement and healthy child development, as well as fathers' well-being, may help to achieve this goal. It has been generally accepted that an emotional bond between father and baby increases the quality of the future father–child relationship. Hence, it is alarming that one in four Slovenian fathers has never, and one in five fathers has almost never, been alone with a child younger than one year (Robnik, 2012). This was especially predominant among fathers with only elementary or vocational education. One in five fathers was very often alone with the baby, and one in six was alone with the baby often. This was most common for fathers with secondary education.

The statutory provisions for fathers in Slovenia are quite comprehensive and well-designed, but employers have to offer more flexibility and understanding for increased father involvement. Many men strive to transcend traditional gender roles and to achieve greater equality in partnership, especially through active fatherhood. However, men do not necessarily always enjoy support by the wider society in general, and more particularly by their employers.

Reconciliation policies and activities should thus be promoted widely among employers. The 'Family-Friendly Enterprise' certificate, implemented in Slovenia in 2007, is a good example of such an effort. Its objective is to provide businesses with the tools to implement human resource policies that improve work–life balance and the quality of life of employees. The employers' responsibility towards their employees is part of the framework of corporate social responsibility (Stropnik, 2010). So far, the certificate has been awarded to 175 enterprises (with 11 more included in the current evaluation). These companies have adopted and implemented at least three measures from a catalogue of work–family reconciliation measures, such as flexible working hours, company childcare services, job sharing, adoption leave and part-time work.

Traditionally, there have been positive attitudes towards gender equality in Slovenian society. This is reflected in many national policies. The Resolution on the National Programme for Equal Opportunities of Women and Men of 2005–13 specifies the elimination of gender stereotypes in families and partnerships, and calls for an equal division of work and parental responsibilities within families. The proposed measures include programmes and projects aimed at encouraging active fatherhood (including incentives for fathers to take the paternity and parental leave), a more equal use of leave to care for a sick family member and the elimination of stereotypes and the change of behavioural patterns regarding the division of labour in families. Specified responsible bodies and follow-up indicators promised to lead to some positive shifts. In fact, the uptake of paternity leave will be stimulated by the longer period of fully compensated leave that was adopted in 2014, albeit with a delayed implementation. It will take much longer for other positive shifts to occur as they depend on changes in people's perceptions, attitudes and practices that can only partially be influenced by legislation.

Notes

[1] See: www.oecd.org/social/family/database

[2] See: http://stats.oecd.org/

[3] See: http://stats.oecd.org/

[4] See: http://epp.eurostat.ec.europa.eu/portal/page/portal/statistics/search_database

[5] See: www.oecd.org/social/family/database

References

Boh, K. (1966) *Časovni budžeti: Kako zaposlena žena troši prosti čas* [*Time budgets: how employed woman uses her time*], Ljubljana: Inštitut za sociologijo in filozofijo pri Univerzi v Ljubljani.

Čelebič, T. (2012) *Pre-school education in Slovenia and its international comparison with the EU countries. Summary*, IMAD Working Paper Series, XXI(4), Ljubljana: Institute of Macroeconomic Analysis and Development. Available at: http://www.umar.gov.si/fileadmin/user_upload/publikacije/dz/2012/DZ_04-2012_Summary.pdf

Černič Istenič, M. (2001) 'Vloge med spoloma' ['Gender roles'], in N. Stropnik and M. Černič Istenič (eds) *Prebivalstvo, družina in blaginja: stališča do politike in ukrepov* [*Population, family and welfare: attitudes towards policy and measures*], Ljubljana: Institute for Economic Research, pp 75–104.

Coltrane, S. and Galt, J. (2000) 'The history of men's caring', in M. Meyer Harrington (ed) *Care work. Gender, class and the welfare state*, New York, NY, and London: Routledge, pp 15–37.

Dienhart, A. (1998) *Reshaping fatherhood: the social construction of shared parenting*, Thousand Oaks, CA, London and New Delhi: SAGE.

EC (European Commission) (2010) *Indicators for monitoring the employment guidelines including indicators for additional employment analysis: 2010 compendium*, 20 July, Brussels: European Commission, DG Employment, Social Affairs and Equal Opportunities. Available at: http://www.arhiv.uem.gov.si/fileadmin/uem.gov.si/pageuploads/Compendium2010.pdf

EC (2011) *Early childhood education and care: providing all our children with the best start for the world of tomorrow*, 17 February, Brussels: European Commission. Available at: http://register.consilium.europa.eu/doc/srv?l=EN&f=ST%206264%202011%20INIT

Eurofound (2009) *Second European quality of life survey. Overview*, Dublin: European Foundation for the Improvement of Living and Working Conditions. Available at: http://www.eurofound.europa.eu/pubdocs/2009/02/en/2/EF0902EN.pdf

European Communities (2004) *How Europeans spend their time: everyday life of women and men; data 1998–2002*, Luxembourg: Publications Office of the European Communities.

Eurostat (2011) 'Tables, graphs and maps interface (TGM) table. Employment rate by gender, age group 15–64'. Available at: http://epp.eurostat.ec.europa.eu/tgm/table.do?tab=table&init=1&plugin=1&language=en&pcode=t2020_10

Fahey, T. and Spéder, Z. (2004) *Fertility and family issues in an enlarged Europe*, Luxembourg: Office for Official Publications of the European Communities.

Grum, B. (2014) 'Starševska šola' ['School for parents']. Available at: http://www.mojmalcek.si/teme/nosecnost/87/sola_za_starse.html

Holter, Ø.G. (2007) 'Men's work and family reconciliation in Europe', *Men and Masculinities*, 9(4): 425–56.

Humer, Ž. (2009) *Etika skrbi, spol in družina: procesi relokacije skrbi med zasebno in javno sfero* [*Ethics of care, gender, and family: processes of relocation of care between the private and the public sphere*], PhD thesis, Ljubljana: Fakulteta za družbene vede.

Humer, Ž. and Kuhar, M. (2010) 'Domače in skrbstveno delo ter odnosi med spoloma: stare zgodbe v novih preoblekah?' ['Domestic and care work and gender relationships: old stories in new format?'], *Družboslovne razprave*, XXVI(64): 81–99.

Hrženjak, M., Humer, Ž. and Kuhar, R. (2006) *Fostering caring masculinities: Slovenian national report*, Ljubljana: Mirovni inštitut.

Inglič, R. and Stare, M. (2011) *Survey on living conditions, Slovenia, 2010 – provisional data*, First Release, 16 September, Ljubljana: Statistical Office of the Republic of Slovenia. Available at: http://www.stat.si/StatWeb/en/mainnavigation/data/show-first-release-old?IdNovice=4178

Jacović, A. (2012) *Expenditure and receipt of social protection schemes, Slovenia, 2010 – provisional data?*, First Release, Demography and Social Statistics, Social Protection, 23 July, Ljubljana: Statistical Office of the Republic of Slovenia. Available at: http://www.stat.si/StatWeb/en/mainnavigation/data/show-first-release-old?IdNovice=4864

Jalušič, V. (1999) 'Women in post-socialist Slovenia: socially adapted, politically marginalized', in S.P. Ramet (ed) *Gender politics in the Western Balkans: women and society in Yugoslavia and the Yugoslav successor states*, University Park, PA: The Pennsylvania State University Press, pp 109–31.

Kanjuo Mrčela, A. and Černigoj Sadar, N. (eds) (2007) *Delo in družina – s partnerstvom do družini prijaznega delovnega okolja [Work and family – with partnership towards a family-friendly work environment]*, Ljubljana: University of Ljubljana, Faculty of Social Sciences.

Kaufman, G. (2013) *Superdads: how fathers balance work and family in the 21st century*, New York, NY, and London: New York University Press.

Korintus, M. and Stropnik, N. (2009) 'Hungary and Slovenia: long leave or short?', in S.B. Kamerman and P. Moss (eds) *The politics of parental leave policies*, Bristol: The Policy Press, pp 135–57.

Lah, L. and Svetin, I. (2011) *Reconciliation between work and family life, Slovenia, 2nd quarter 2010 – final data*, First Release, Demography and Social Statistics, Labour Market, 31 March, Ljubljana: Statistical Office of the Republic of Slovenia. Available at: http://www.stat.si/StatWeb/en/mainnavigation/data/show-first-release-old?IdNovice=3821

Lappegard, T. (2008) 'Changing the gender balance in caring: fatherhood and the division of parental leave in Norway', *Population Research and Policy Review*, 27(2): 139–59.

Ložar, B. (2013) *Kindergartens, Slovenia, school year 2012/13 – final data*, First Release, Demography and Social Statistics, Education, 26 March, Ljubljana: Statistical Office of the Republic of Slovenia. Available at: http://www.stat.si/StatWeb/en/mainnavigation/data/show-first-release-old?IdNovice=5386

MoLFSAEO (Ministry of Labour, Family, Social Affairs and Equal Opportunities) (2013) *Družinski prejemki, zavarovanje za starševsko varstvo [Family benefits, parental protection insurance]*, Ljubljana: Ministry of Labour, Family, Social Assistance and Equal Opportunities. Available at: http://www.mddsz.gov.si/si/uveljavljanje_pravic/statistika/druz_prejemki_zavarovanje_sv/

OEO (Office for Equal Opportunities) (2005/2006) 'Projects. Daddy, be active!', Ljubljana: Office for Equal Opportunities. Available at: http://www.arhiv.uem.gov.si/en/index.html

Rakar, T., Stropnik, N., Boškić, R., Dremelj, P., Nagode, M. and Kovač, N. (2010) *Raziskava o vplivih veljavnih ukrepov družinske politike na odločanje za otroke* [*Research on the impact of family policy measures on deciding to have children*], Ljubljana: Social Protection Institute of the Republic of Slovenia. Available at: http://www.mddsz.gov.si/fileadmin/mddsz.gov.si/pageuploads/dokumenti__pdf/rodnost-koncno_porocilo.pdf

Ranson, G. (2012) 'Men, paid employment and family responsibilities: conceptualizing the "working father"', *Gender, Work and Organization*, 19(6): 741–61.

Rener, T. (1993) 'Politika materinjenja ali "Father knows the best: for him the play, for her the rest"' ['Mothering policy or "Father knows the best: for him the play, for her the rest"'], *Časopis za kritiko znanosti, domišljijo in novo antropologijo*, XXI(162/3): 15–22.

Rener, T., Švab, A., Žakelj, T. and Humer, Ž. (2005) *Perspektive novega očetovstva v Sloveniji: vpliv mehanizma očetovskega dopusta na aktivno očetovanje* [*Perspectives of new fatherhood in Slovenia: influence of the paternity leave mechanism on active fathering*], Ljubljana: Univerza v Ljubljani, Fakulteta za družbene vede.

Rener, T., Švab, A., Žakelj, T. and Humer Ž. (2007) *Novi trendi v starševstvu – analiza očetovstva in predlogi za izboljšave družinske politike na tem področju* [*New trends in parenthood – the analysis of fatherhood and recommendations for the improvements of family policy in this field*], research report, Ljubljana: Fakulteta za družbene vede, Center za socialno psihologijo.

Rener, T., Švab, A., Žakelj, T., Humer, Ž. and Vezovnik, A. (2008) *Novi trendi v starševstvu: analiza očetovstva ter predlogi za izboljšave družinske politike na tem področju* [*New trends in parenthood: analysis of fatherhood and proposals for respective improvements in the family policy*], research report, Ljubljana: Fakulteta za družbene vede, Center za socialno psihologijo.

Robnik, S. (2012) *Enakost spolov v družinskem* življenju *in v partnerskih odnosih* [*Gender equality in family life and partners' relations*], Ljubljana: Ministry of Labour, Family and Social Affairs, Office for Equal Opportunities and European Coordination. Available at: http://www.mddsz.gov.si/fileadmin/mddsz.gov.si/pageuploads/dokumenti__pdf/enake_moznosti/RaziskavaEnakostSpolovPartnerstvo.pdf

Scambor, E., Wojnicka, K. and Bergmann, N. (eds) (2013) *The role of men in gender equality: European strategies & insights: study on the role of men in gender equality*, Luxemburg: European Commission Directorate – General for Justice. Available at: http://ec.europa.eu/justice/gender-equality/files/gender_pay_gap/130424_final_report_role_of_men_en.pdf

Sedmak, M. and Medarič, Z. (2007) 'Vpliv zaposlitve na družinske odločitve in družinsko življenje ['Influence of employment on family decisions and family life'], in M. Sedmak and Z. Medarič (eds) *Med javnim in zasebnim: ženske na trgu dela [Between the public and the private: women in the labour market]*, Koper: Annales, pp 75–100.

Segal, L. (1997) *Slow motion: changing masculinities, changing men*, London: Virago.

Seidler, J.V. (2006) 'Masculinities and work/life balance', opening lecture at the international conference 'Fostering Caring Masculinities' (FOCUS), 20–22 October, Girona, Spain.

Silva, E.B. (1999) *The new family?*, London, Thousand Oaks, CA, and New Delhi: Sage Publications.

Šircelj, M. (2006) *Rodnost v Sloveniji od 18. do 21. stoletja [Fertility in Slovenia from 18th to 21st century]*, Posebne publikacije, 5, Ljubljana: Statistical Office of the Republic of Slovenia. Available at: http://www.stat.si/doc/pub/rodnostvsloveniji.pdf

SI-Stat Data Portal (2013) Ljubljana: Statistical Office of the Republic of Slovenia. Available at: http://pxweb.stat.si/pxweb/Database/Demographics/Demographics.asp#05

SORS (Statistical Office of the Republic of Slovenia) (2002) 'Families by the number of children, type of family and type of settlement, Slovenia, Census 2002', in SORS, *Census of population, households and housing 2002*, Ljubljana: Statistical Office of the Republic of Slovenia. Available at: https://www.stat.si/popis2002/en/rezultati/rezultati_red.asp?ter=SLO&st=22

Stacey, J. (1996) *In the name of the family: rethinking family values in the postmodern age*, Boston, MA: Beacon Press.

Stropnik, N. (2005) *Stališča prebivalstva kot odraz novih trendov v starševstvu in podlaga za preoblikovanje družinske politike v Sloveniji [People's attitudes as a reflection of new trends in parenthood and the basis for reshaping of family policy in Slovenia]*, Ljubljana: Institute for Economic Research.

Stropnik, N. (2010) 'How can corporate social responsibility contribute to gender equality and work–life balance: example of the "Family-Friendly Enterprise" certificate in Slovenia', *Naše gospodarstvo*, 56(5/6): 11–20.

Stropnik, N. (2013) 'Slovenia', in P. Moss (ed) *International review of leave policies and related research 2013*, International Network on Leave Policies and Research, pp 240–5. Available at: http://www.leavenetwork.org/fileadmin/Leavenetwork/Country_notes/2013/Slovenia.FINALcitation.pdf

Stropnik, N. and Černič Istenič, M. (2001) *Prebivalstvo, družina in blaginja: stališča do politike in ukrepov* [*Population, family and welfare: attitudes towards policy and measures*], Ljubljana: Institute for Economic Research.

Stropnik, N. and Kump, N. (2009) 'What kind of men take parental leave?', XXVI International Population Conference, Marrakech, Morocco, 27 September–2 October.

Stropnik, N. and Kump, N. (forthcoming) 'Paternity leave practices by fathers in Slovenia and assessment of determinants'.

Stropnik, N. and Šircelj, M. (2008) 'Slovenia: generous family policy without evidence of any fertility impact', in T. Freyka, T. Sobotka, J.M. Hoem and L. Toulemon (eds) *Childbearing trends and policies in Europe*, Demographic Research, vol 19, Special Collection 7, Rostock: Max Planck Institute for Demographic Research, pp 1019–58. Available at: www.demographic-research.org/volumes/vol19/26/19-26.pdf

Sundström, M. and Duvander, A.Z. (2002) 'Gender division of child care and the sharing of parental leave among new parents in Sweden', *European Sociological Review*, 18(4): 433–47.

Švab, A. (2000) 'Poti in stranpoti novih očetovskih identitet: nekaj misli o sociološki interpretaciji novega (postmodernega) očetovstva' ['Ways and side-ways of new fathers' identities: some thoughts on the sociological interpretation of a new (post-modern) fatherhood'], *Teorija in praksa*, 37(2): 248–63.

Švab, A. (2001) *Družina: od modernosti k postmodernosti* [*Family: from modernity to postmodernity*], Ljubljana: Znanstveno in publicistično središče.

Švab, A. and Humer, Ž. (2013) '"I only have to ask him and he does it …" Active fatherhood and (perceptions of) division of family labour in Slovenia', *Journal of Comparative Family Studies*, 44(1): 57–79.

Ule, M. (1977) *Družbeno uveljavljanje* [*Women's emancipation in the society*], Ljubljana: Fakulteta za družbene vede.

Ule, M. and Kuhar, M. (2003) *Mladi, družina, starševstvo. Spremembe življenjskih potekov v pozni moderni* [*Youth, family, parenthood. Changes in life courses in late modernity*], Ljubljana: Univerza v Ljubljani, Fakulteta za družbene vede, Center za socialno psihologijo.

UNICEF (United Nations Children's Fund) (2012) 'Measuring child poverty: new league tables of child poverty in the world's rich countries', Innocenti Report Card 10, UNICEF Innocenti Research Centre. Available at: http://www.unicef-irc.org/publications/pdf/rc10_eng.pdf

Žnidaršič, T. (2012) *Fathers' Day 2012*, Special Release, Demography and Social Statistics, Population, 15 June, Ljubljana: Statistical Office of the Republic of Slovenia. Available at: http://www.stat.si/StatWeb/en/mainnavigation/data/show-first-release-old?IdNovice=4781

Žnidaršič, T. (2013) *Fathers' Day 2013*, Special Release, Demography and Social Statistics, Population, 13 June, Ljubljana: Statistical Office of the Republic of Slovenia. Available at: http://www.stat.si/StatWeb/en/mainnavigation/data/show-first-release-old?IdNovice=5558

FIVE

The United Kingdom

*Margaret O'Brien, Sara Connolly, Svetlana Speight,
Matthew Aldrich and Eloise Poole*

The cultural and policy context of fatherhood

The family and work policy context of fatherhood in the UK occupies a midway position between continental Europe's social investment and solidarity model and the USA's private, market-oriented model. There is cultural endorsement that the government and citizens should work together to ensure the welfare of families and children, particularly those deemed 'deserving', through taxation and voluntary action (Daly, 2010). It is notable that public spending on family benefits is 4% of gross domestic product (GDP), above the Organisation for Economic Co-operation and Development (OECD) average of 2.6% of GDP (OECD, 2009). However, unlike its Nordic neighbours, the UK is more likely to spend in terms of child-related cash and tax transfers to parents than in public infrastructure, such as nurseries and centre-based facilities.

Historically, British contemporary family and work policies influencing fathers need to be set against two evolving societal processes and structures. First, the post-Second World War national welfare state provision of universal health and social security underpinned a male-breadwinner and female-homemaker division of family labour in a stable married family unit. Second, the inclusion (since 1973) in a pan-European governmental arrangement – first the European Economic Community (EEC) of six countries and now the European Union (EU) of 29 countries – has, despite its diversity, promoted female employment and work–family reconciliation policy measures in the UK. The politics and policies of both the UK and the EU have witnessed significant changes influencing families over the last 60 years (Lewis, 2009). However, two common features have been a move towards: (1) a mixed economy of welfare, incorporating private and public provisions, especially since the economic downturn of 2008; and (2) a dual-earner/dual-carer family model and increased parental separation and divorce, away from the strong male-breadwinner model (Lewis, 1992).

Like other countries across the world, Britain has been expanding programmes to promote the stronger engagement of men in family care activities throughout the life course. Part of the motivation has been to help modernise work–family policies and to catch up with the changing position of women. Today, fathers in Britain are expected to be accessible to and nurturing of, as well as economically supportive of, their children. They are more self-conscious about juggling the different characteristics of 'the good father', particularly in terms of how they manage conflicts between having a job and looking after the children (Dermott, 2008; Finn and Henwood, 2009). Caring fathers are now an integral part of overall culture through advertising images and media depictions of sporting icons. However, such changes are challenging to implement in everyday life in the context of combining the British neoliberal flexible labour market framework with the more holistic work–family reconciliation offered by the EU model. The global economic crisis since 2008 further unsettled economic conditions for British families, and men's behaviour as fathers, partners and workers is affected by rising job insecurity and stagnant wages.

Leave provisions

The British legacy of the father-breadwinner/mother-homemaker model is, in part, responsible for the late arrival, by European standards, of statutory paternity leave in 2003 (Kamerman and Moss, 2009). It also explains why, despite cultural endorsements of active and nurturing fatherhood models since the 1980s (McKee and O'Brien, 1982), the UK has one of the longest maternity leave entitlements in the world – 52 weeks (Moss, 2014). This mother-focused employment policy has its origin in the original framing of the Labour government's legislation in the Employment Protection Act of 1975. This law, which first introduced statutory maternity leave in the UK, adopted a model that combines a long leave of 40 weeks with a short period of payment of six weeks rather than the EEC 'best practice' model at the time of short leave of 12–14 weeks with full payment (Fonda, 1980). Subsequent UK governments of all political orientations have attempted to respond to the changing nature of work and family circumstances for fathers and mothers while juggling these contradictory national and pan-European policy pathways.

A focus on fathers has been part of, but not central to, work–family policy development in Britain. Interest in fathers has ebbed and flowed and cross-departmental policy initiatives have not always been integrated into a coherent framework. During the 1990s, across mainstream political parties, rhetoric stressed both the economic and caring responsibilities of fathers. This policy turn had its roots in the Labour Party's first family policy Green Paper (Home Office, 1999: 26), which declared an intention 'to extend choice for both mothers and fathers by giving them the chance to spend more time at home, as well as support their children financially'. The key government minister, Patricia Hewitt, Secretary of State for Trade and Industry and Minister for Women, had a great interest in developing work–family policy that was father-inclusive (Hewitt, 2004). Similarly, since 2010, the recent Coalition government has continued to emphasise the parental sharing of family responsibilities and the balance of work and family commitments: 'making it easier for parents to share caring responsibilities; giving families more choice and control' (Children and Families Bill, 2013: 22). However, boosting maternal employment has received the most active policy attention, with less attention devoted to explicit policy measures to encourage paternal caring.

Nonetheless, there is a gradual enhancement of British fathers' rights in the workplace and support to engage separated fathers in the lives of their children. Since April 2003, for the first time, British fathers have a legal right to take a two-week paid paternity leave after the birth of a child (Employment Act 2002[1]), building on a three-month unpaid parental leave entitlement available since 1999. A new element to the employment legislation has been a provision to support flexible working hours (eg flexitime or a compressed work week) for fathers, as well as mothers, of children younger than six years of age or for parents of older disabled children. Subsequent legislation has extended fathers' entitlements to both leave and flexible working hours. In April 2011, a new right to allow fathers to take up to six months Additional Paternity Leave (APL) during the child's first year, if the mother returns to work before the end of her maternity leave, was introduced (HM Government, 2010). Fathers taking APL can be paid for a maximum of 19 weeks at the flat rate or 90% of their average earnings, whichever is the lower figure; such payment – the Additional Statutory Paternity Pay (ASPP) – is only available during the period that the mother would be entitled to payment for maternity leave (O'Brien et al, 2014).

In terms of separated and divorced fathers, an emphasis on 'relationship support' and mediation has developed over the decade. This policy approach contrasts with the 1990s' discourse of 'feckless' or 'deadbeat' dads failing to financially support their children (Collier, 1995). For example, the Child Support Agency, formed in 1991, focused purely on economic and not caring fatherhood, narrowly concentrating on enforcing the financial maintenance of children after divorce. The language of more recent legislation has attempted to integrate the financial and care responsibilities of fathers and mothers, using terminology such as 'co-operative parenting' and 'shared parental responsibility' (Department for Education and Ministry of Justice, 2012; Department for Work and Pensions, 2012). This approach suggests that a cultural transition towards the family man ideals of 'intimate fatherhood' (Dermott, 2008) is gaining potency in family policy formulation.

Contextual demographic and family trends related to fatherhood

After providing information on the cultural and policy context in which British father involvement occurs, this section describes the relevant demographic trends, features of family structure and labour force participation (LFP) patterns that affect fathers. As seen in Table 5.1, crude marriage rates have continued to decline in the UK over the decade from 4.9 to 4.4, but have decreased at a slower rate than over previous decades. Divorce rates have also declined somewhat, from 2.6 to 2.1 (crude rates), as fewer people formally marry. In 2013, the average age at marriage (including remarriage) for women was 37.0 years, slightly younger than the male mean age of 38.6 years (ONS, 2013). However, the greatest number of men and women marry between ages 30 to 34; cohabitation tends to happen earlier in the life course, and for a growing number, is becoming an alternative to formal marriage. Marriage rates are higher for Asian British, who also have lower divorce rates. Same-sex marriage was legalised in 2013 by the Marriages (Same Sex Couples) Act. In the first year after legislation, there were more female than male marriages: of the 1,500 marriages between 29 March and 30 June 2014, 56% of marriages were female couples.

The growth in cohabitation mirrors wider European demographic trends: in EU countries, between 25% and 50% of all children are born outside marriage (European Commission, 2009). Although divorce rates are stabilising, divorce, the separation of consensual unions and re-partnering have changed the nature of fathers' families. Fathers are now more likely than in previous generations to experience more than one family type (serial fathering), and in the process, fathers typically cease to reside with the children of their first relationship.

Table 5.1: Selected indicators related to parenting for the UK, circa 2000 and circa 2012

Indicator	2000	2012
Crude marriage rate (persons marrying per 1,000 total population)	4.9	4.4 (2011)
Crude divorce rate (persons divorcing per 1,000 total population	2.6	2.1 (2011)
Total fertility rate	1.6	1.9
Crude birth rate (live births per 1,000 population)	11.5	12.8
Mothers' mean age (standardised) at first birth	26.5	28.1
Standardised mean age of mother	28.5	29.8
% non-marital births	39.5	47.5
Births per 1,000 men	23.7	26.1
% of one-family households that are:		
Couple no children	40.8 (2001)	43.6 (2010)
Husband/wife with dependent children	28.3 (2001)	25.8 (2010)
Unmarried couple with dependent children	4.8 (2001)	6.0 (2010)
Lone parent with dependent children	10.3 (2001)	11.0 (2010)
Mother only with children	12.7 (2001)	14.1 (2010)
Father only with children	2.1 (2001)	2.1 (2010)
% of children < 5 living with:		
Two parents	75.8	71.5 (< 6 years)
Father only	1.3	2.6 (< 6 years)
Mother only	22.8	22.9 (< 6 years)
% of married-couple families that are:		
Dual-earner families	63 (2001)	60 (2011)
Male-provider families	23	22
Labour force participation (LFP)		
LFP rate, men (aged 15–64)	76.9	73.9
Fathers (≥ 15) of kids < 19	78.1	75.0
Fathers (≥ 15) of kids < 5	87.9	85.6
Men, % full-time (% of all those in employment)	91.7	88.3
Men, mean number of hours/week	44.7 (FT)	44.4 (FT)
(actual including overtime)	20.8 (PT)	23.2 (PT)
Fathers, mean number of hours/week	45.4 (FT)	44.7 (FT)
(actual including overtime)	18.5 (PT)	23.2 (PT)
LFP rate, women (16–64)	64.4	64.4
Mothers (≥ 15) of kids < 19	61.4	60.7
Mothers (≥ 15) of < 5	54.1	56.7
Women, % full-time	55.8	56.8
Women, mean number of hours/week	40.6 (FT)	41.0 (FT)
(actual including overtime)	21.3 (PT)	22.9 (PT)
Mothers, mean number of hours/week	40.2 (FT)	40.1 (FT)
(actual including overtime)	20.7 (PT)	22.8 (PT)

Sources: ONS (2011, 2012a, 2012b,2013) and author's own calculations using data from the UK General Household Survey (GHS), UK Labour Force Survey (LFS) and EU Labour Force Survey (EU-LFS). The GHS and LFS data are available from the UK Data Archive - http://www.dataarchive.ac.uk and the EU-LFS data are available from Eurostat http://ec.europa.eu/eurostat/web/microdata/european-union-labour-force-survey.

Marriage and partnership delay has, in turn, influenced childbearing. By 2012, 47.5% of births were to women in non-married unions. The age at first childbirth increased for British women from 28.5 in 2000 to 29.8 in 2012. Similarly, the mean age of all fathers at the birth of their first child has increased by nearly two years over the last two decades – from 31.1 years in 1993 to 32.9 in 2013 (ONS, 2013). Despite the trend to later onset of parenthood, the UK has one of the higher birth rates in Europe, reaching 1.9 Total Period Fertility Rate (TFR) in 2012, a rise from 1.6 in 2000, driven in part by higher birth rates for non-UK-born women (2.19 in 2012). Pakistan was the most common country of birth for non-UK-born fathers between the years of 2008 and 2013, followed by Poland and India (ONS, 2014).

Despite an increase in cohabiting-couple families over the past decade, married-couple families are still the most common family type in the UK, both with and without dependent children, forming more than 69% of family households (see Table 5.1). British Asian fathers are more likely to live in married-couple households with dependent children than either white or British Afro-Caribbean fathers. The proportion of children living in lone-mother households has increased from 13% in 2001 to 14% in 2010, and is more common for Afro-Caribbean British. While the proportion of lone-father households has remained stable, at 2.1%, there has been some growth (1.3% to 2.6%) for households with young children throughout this period.

There are two important recent trends in UK LFP: delayed entry to the labour market for both men and women due to increasing enrolment in higher education and a continued growth in female, mostly part-time, employment. By 2011, women's LFP had stabilised at 64%, though the participation rate and hours worked by mothers, especially those with young children, was lower. At the same time, men's LFP has declined from 77% to 74%. The LFP of fathers with young children is higher than that of men in general (86% versus 74%) and, overall, when full-time workers are compared, fathers work slightly more hours than men in general. However, average hours for both fathers and men in general have fallen over the past decade; between 2000 and 2011, for fathers average hours have fallen from 45.4 to 44.7 and for non-fathers hours have fallen from 44.7 to 44.4. Over the past decade, the male-breadwinner model has stabilised as a minority form in Britain (22%), and the dual-earner regime has become the most common model for couple families with dependent children (60% in 2011) (Connolly et al, 2013). However, within the dual-earner group, slightly more than half of mothers usually work only part-time, with the number of hours per week rising since 2000 from 21 to 23. While it may be the case that part-time employment can help to ease work–family conflict for mothers and fathers and simultaneously contribute to the household income, British evidence shows that it has negative effects on women's career and economic benefits (Connolly and Gregory, 2008).

Fathers and parental leave

Since the late 1990s, strategies to enhance the visibility of fathers' leave entitlements have accelerated in many countries across the world (ILO, 2014). There has been experimentation with a range of policy instruments based on incentives, penalty and even compulsion. Leave provision for British fathers occupies a midway position between the generosity of Nordic Europe and its total absence in the US. In 2015, the statutory leave available for British fathers is as follows: (1) paternity leave is an individual entitlement, two weeks in duration after birth at a flat-rate payment of £138.18 (€160) a week, or 90% of average weekly earnings if that is less (HM Government, 2015); (2) parental leave was initiated in 1999 as part of the EU Parental Leave Directive (an individual entitlement, 18 weeks, unpaid) up to the child's fifth birthday, with a maximum of four weeks leave to be taken in any one calendar year; and (3) shared parental leave (Children and Families Act 2014[2]), a new provision from April 2015. Under this provision, after the first two weeks of maternity leave (four weeks for manual workers), the mother is able to transfer maternity leave *without returning to work* to her partner, provided he also meets specific employment requirements. Shared parental leave can be taken with more flexibility than maternity leave, in week-long blocks, and some days are available so that parents can share leave – for example, each parent working different days in a particular week. However, the fact that shared parental leave is transferred from the mother means that, according to the government's own estimates, fewer than one in three couples will be eligible. Further, if the mother ends her maternity leave in favour of shared parental leave before six weeks, she forfeits the higher rate of pay (90% of earnings) that applies to those weeks.

Male employees have to meet three conditions in order to be eligible for all forms of leave: (1) they are the biological or joint adoptive father of the child or they are the mother's husband, partner or civil partner (fathers in same-sex relationships are also included in this condition); (2) they expect to have shared responsibility for the child's upbringing; and (3) they have worked continuously for their employer for 26 weeks, ending with the 15th week before the baby is due, and remain employed at the time of the child's birth. For shared parental leave, the parent must also be employed by the same employer while they take the leave. In terms of paternity leave, some employers – particularly those from large private and public sector organisations – go beyond the statutory minimum and supplement paternity leave payments, and even duration, as part of employee benefit and retention awards (Chanfreau et al, 2011). Small- and medium-sized private sector employers have less financial capacity to be generous and are more likely to pay the minimum statutory rate.

Evidence from Chanfreau et al's (2011) analysis of the 'Maternity and paternity rights and women returners survey 2009/10' shows that, nationally, 39% of British fathers received full pay for less than two weeks, 33% received full pay for exactly two weeks and 9% received full pay for more than two weeks. Data were collected from telephone interviews with a nationally representative sample of 2,031 mothers and 1,253 fathers who had worked in the 12 months prior to the birth of their child, and for 12 to 18 months after the birth. Overall, 91% of fathers took time off around the time of their baby's birth. Of those taking time off, 49% took statutory paternity leave only, 25% took statutory leave plus other paid leave, 18% took other paid leave only and 5% took unpaid leave. Those taking statutory paternity leave were most likely to take the statutory two weeks (50%), 34% took less than two weeks and 16% took more than two weeks. Statutory paternity leave can be taken in a single block of either one or two weeks and must be taken within 56 days of the birth.

The odds of taking paternity leave were significantly higher for men working in the public sector and other workplaces where there were family-friendly arrangements. As shown in other countries, local workplace norms can facilitate or hinder fathers taking statutory paternity leave or any leave after the child's birth. Where there were no family-friendly arrangements available, the take-up of time off work following the birth was lowest (only 88% of fathers took time off compared with 93% taking time off where there were between one or two family-friendly arrangements available). In a UK qualitative study of fathers' experience of working flexibly, Gatrell et al (2014) show how British fathers can feel marginalised from the possibilities of flexible work if line managers focus only on their economic provider roles.

In addition, 66% of men in Chanfreau et al's (2011) sample took time off work before the baby was born for child-related reasons, such as antenatal appointments. The most common number of days taken off was one to two days (27%), but 20% of fathers took between three and four days, and 19% took five or more days off work. Professionals were the most likely to take time off during the antenatal period (76%), followed by fathers in skilled trades (75%). Fathers who worked in administrative, secretarial, sales and customer service jobs were least likely to take time off (53%). In terms of hourly pay, fathers earning less than £6 per hour were much more likely to take no time off (18%) compared to fathers in the top two earning brackets (7% and 3%).

The 'Maternity and paternity rights and women returners survey 2009/10' did not collect systematic data on the exact timing of women's return to work, but by 12–18 months after childbirth, three out of four mothers (77%) had returned to employment. As in previous surveys, mothers' decision to return to work was mainly motivated by economic considerations. The factors with the strongest association to returning to work included: employer size and sector; the duration of pre-birth job; the type of maternity pay received; family structure; and mothers' educational level.

Although there is still surprisingly little international research on what parents 'do' during parental leave and even less on what fathers 'do', a body of knowledge is developing on the implementation of leave and its impact (Huerta et al, 2013). The logic has been that giving fathers the opportunity to spend more time at home through leave after childbirth should result in them being more involved in childcare. This hypothesis has had some support from a study using the UK Millennium Cohort Study (MCS) (Tanaka and Waldfogel, 2007). The data show that policies affect taking leave and working shorter hours, and that these are related to fathers being more involved with the baby. Fathers' involvement was examined in four specific types of activities: being the main carer, changing nappies, feeding the baby and getting up during the night. Analysis showed that fathers who took (any) leave after the birth were 25% more likely to change nappies and 19% more likely to feed and to get up at night when the child was aged 8–12 months. In addition, increased working hours for fathers were associated with lower levels of father involvement. Tanaka and Waldfogel (2007) conclude that policies providing parental leave and/ or shorter working hours could promote greater father involvement with infants, but they caution against definitive causality claims.

Fathers and childcare

Although publically funded nurseries were available in the UK during the Second World War to support mothers' engagement in the war effort, it was not until the late 1990s that government interest in childcare was reactivated. The Labour Party introduced a National

Childcare Strategy (DfEE, 1998), signalling attention to early childcare services. The two key overarching aims of the childcare strategy were to improve child outcomes directly by giving children the opportunity to attain a high-quality early education, and to reduce child poverty by enabling low-income mothers (and particularly single mothers) to go out to work (Speight et al, 2009). Fathers have not been an explicit focus of governmental childcare investment, but the rhetoric is increasingly one of supporting 'hard-working parents' or providing family-friendly support, which includes fathers.

A range of early education and care services have been introduced, with the aim of increasing the availability, flexibility and quality, and reducing the cost, of childcare (DCSF, 2004; DfE, 2014b). In the UK context, early education and care services are devolved to the four jurisdictions that is, England, Northern Ireland, Scotland and Wales. Since 1998, all four-year-old children in England (and since 2004, all three year olds as well) are entitled to a funded, part-time early education place. Currently, all three and four year olds are entitled to 570 hours of government-funded early education per year (equating to 15 hours a week over 38 weeks). Two year olds in low-income families are also entitled to funded, part-time placements: starting in September 2014, funded places have been made available to nearly 40% of families (DfE, 2014a, 2014b).

All jurisdictions in the UK are committed to the mixed economy of childcare, where both demand-side and supply-side subsidies are used to stimulate and shape the childcare market. However, private individuals paying for their use of childcare services accounted for approximately 60% of day nurseries' total fee income in 2010 (Blackburn, 2013). Support with relatively high childcare costs at the demand side is limited and is linked with parents' working status (eg through employer-supported, tax-free, childcare vouchers), and is means-tested (DfE, 2014b).

In 2011, 36% of under two year olds and 87% of three to four year olds were in formal childcare arrangements, such as nurseries, play groups or childminders.[3] These rates of take-up of formal childcare by these age groups were remarkably higher than in 2001. It is also notable that significant proportions of preschool children (about a third) receive regular childcare from informal providers such as grandparents (see Table 5.2).[4]

Other evidence from the UK MCS, which covers a large cohort of children born in 2000, gives more information on father involvement in childcare while the partner is at work. It shows that father/partner care is provided to 24.8% of nine month olds, 10.6% of two year olds and 18.2% of three to four year olds. That makes childcare by fathers the second most frequent form of informal care after grandparents for British children under the age of five years.

Table 5.2: UK rates of childcare use, by age of child, 2001 and 2011

	2001		2011	
	Aged 0–2	Aged 3–4	Aged 0–2	Aged 3–4
	%	%	%	%
Any childcare	54	80	57	90
Formal providers	29	67	36	87
Nursery school	1	20	5	14
Nursery class	NA	NA	1	17
Reception class	NA	NA	0	29
Day nursery	18	27	17	13
Playgroup or preschool	5	20	7	15
Childminder	6	5	5	4
Nanny or au pair	1	1	1	1
Informal childcare	33	33	34	30

Sources: Adapted from Bryson et al (2006), Huskinson et al (2013) and Speight et al (2009).

Research on father involvement

This section focuses on what is known about how much time British fathers spend with their children using time-use studies and other research evidence on fathers' family relationships and care of young children. Time-budget diaries typically measure the amount of time spent on child-related activities as the 'main activity', which relates to Lamb et al's (1987) classic paternal involvement construct of 'engagement'.

Time engaged with children

As seen in Table 5.3, the average daily time that men spent interacting with a child aged under four as their main activity rose from 54 minutes in 2000 to 84 minutes by 2005. This trend shows a substantial increase from the mid-1970s, where fathers of children under the age of five years devoted less than a quarter of an hour per day to child-related activities as their main activity (Fisher et al, 1999; Sullivan et al, 2009). A similar upward trend in men's childcare has been found in comparative studies across industrialised societies (Smith and Williams, 2007; Gimenez-Nadel and Seville, 2012). In 2005, paternal engagement was higher among those who were aged 25 to 34, had pre-degree-level qualifications and were married (see Table 5.3).

Table 5.3: Trends in UK fathers' engagement with children younger than five years, 2000 and 2005

	Average number of minutes per person per day		% of fathers participating in activity	
	2000	2005	2000	2005
Childcare of own co-residential children: main activity (total)	54	84	57	63
Fathers, aged 16–24	46	60	49	33
Aged 25–34	70	91	72	63
Aged 35–44	70	81	75	68
No qualifications	56	76	66	48
Below degree-level qualifications	71	90	72	66
Degree or equivalent	76	74	72	61
Married	59	90	63	66
Cohabiting	55	· 74	58	60

Source: Adapted from Lader, Short and Gershuny (2006).

Level of father engagement

Analysis of the data collected as part of the 'Understanding Society' panel survey during 2009–11 (Poole et al, 2014) shows that 64–65% of fathers with a child younger than age four eat an evening meal with their children six or seven times a week; 94–95% give cuddles or hugs very often; and 63–67% talk with their children about things that matter on a regular basis (see Table 5.4). Other analysis using data collected from 'Understanding Society' 2009–11 (Poole et al, 2014) has found that both fathers and mothers who report better-quality relationships with their partners are more involved with their children, when controlling for other factors. This supports the 'spillover model' that marital conflict affects parenting behaviour, which, in turn, affects children, rather than the 'compensatory' model, which suggests that parents try to compensate for poor partner relationships with good child relationships.

Increased father involvement in the care of children, through preference, unemployment, underemployment or non-employment, is also manifested in a growing family type, where fathers are the primary carers and stay at home while their partners go outside the home to work. There are now 62,000 British men classified as economically inactive while their partner works outside the home – a rise from 21,000 in 1996 (ONS, 2011).

Table 5.4: Father involvement with preschool children, % reporting activity on a daily or regular basis, 2009–11

Type of involvement	Children aged 0–2 (%)	Children aged 3–4 (%)
How many evening meals eaten with children in last week: 6 or 7	65	64
How often cuddles or hugs children: very often	95	94
How often praises children	90	88
How often talks to children about things that matter to them: most days	63	67

Source: Poole et al (2014).

During the late 20th century, it became more socially acceptable, indeed, normative, for British fathers to be present at the birth of children. For instance, Lewis (1987) showed that rates in Nottingham increased from 10% of 1950s' births to 70% of births in the early 1980s. With the advent of new technologies to monitor pregnancy confirmation and foetal development, such as ultrasound and screening tests, fathers are being drawn into the pregnancy experience at even earlier stages (Draper, 2002).

Fathers' care of infants and their experience of the transition to parenthood has been examined in qualitative case studies (eg Miller, 2010, 2011), which build on the early work of Lewis (1987) and McKee (1982), and in larger national surveys and cohort studies (Redshaw and Henderson, 2013). In her longitudinal qualitative study of a group of 17 men as they anticipate and then experience fatherhood for the first time, Miller (2011) portrays their daily individual lives and everyday practices of caring. Her participants described highly emotional encounters with their infant using the language of caring and conveying tender and caring masculinities. Their accounts illuminate the tensions that fathers face when they return to work after paternity leave and then find it difficult to keep connected to daily baby routines – they are 'returning to a new normal' (Miller, 2011: 11). Other evidence of this life-course phase draws on nationally representative survey data on English fathers, as reported by their 4,616 partners (Redshaw and Henderson, 2013). According to the mothers, 80% of fathers were 'pleased' or 'overjoyed' in response to their partner's pregnancy. In the infancy period, more than 75% reported that fathers engaged by changing nappies, bathing the infant, helping or supporting feeding, helping when the baby cried, playing with the baby, and looking after the baby when the mother was out. The most common activity reported for all fathers during infancy was playing with the baby (96%). This study measured antenatal and post-natal paternal engagement by a range of factors, including: presence or absence at antenatal classes, as well as at the birth; involvement in pregnancy; and involvement in later infant care activities. It found that paternal engagement was highest in partners of white first-time mothers, in those living in less deprived areas, and in those whose pregnancy was planned. Greater paternal engagement was positively associated with first contact with health professionals before 12 weeks of gestation and higher rates of breastfeeding. This trend for first-time fathers to be more involved in infant care than fathers of subsequent children has also been found in the UK MCS (Calderwood et al, 2005).

Determinants of father engagement with young children

In terms of examining the determinants of father engagement with young children, few British studies have included both psychological factors, such as paternal sensitivity or individual motivation, and structural factors (Lamb and Lewis, 2010; Lewis, 2013). Writers drawing on psychodynamic theory (eg Trowell and Etchegoyen, 2002), point to the significance of men's own early childhood relationships in shaping their capacity to care and emotionally invest in their own children. From an analysis of clinical case studies, Emanuel (2002: 144) suggests that 'It is something that is highly determined by the quality of the man's internalised mother and father and his relationship with them, as well as the external environment he finds himself in'. Indeed, researchers have found that men who report 'loving and secure relationships' with their own parents, also display more attuned and sensitive involvement with their children, in contrast to fathers with problematic family histories (Lamb and Lewis, 2010: 98). Childhood family structure is also a relevant factor in shaping father involvement: men who grow up in families experiencing parental separation are more likely to be non-resident fathers themselves (Poole et al, 2014).

Increasing awareness of the significance of fathers to children's lives has led some clinicians in Britain to investigate paternal mental health, particularly post-natal depression, and how it influences engagement with young children (eg Ramchandani and McConachie, 2005; Ramchandani et al, 2005; Ramchandani and Psychogiou, 2009). Such studies have shown that depressed fathers are typically less responsive and sensitive to their babies and more likely to have difficulties in couple relationships.

Men's parenting cannot be seen in isolation from the quality of couple relationships. Evidence for the UK shows that fathers who report high 'couple stress' factors are more likely to shout at their children and those who report high 'couple bliss' factors are more likely to praise their children, with similar associations being present for mothers (Poole et al, 2014). These studies support the findings by Pleck and Masciadrelli (2004) and Jones' (2010) analysis of the UK MCS, which suggest that high father involvement with children is associated with a positive couple relationship.

The influence of parental employment patterns on the amount of time fathers spend with their children has received significant attention in the UK. In general, increases in paternal responsibility and direct engagement tend to occur in households where both partners are in full-time employment. Ferri and Smith (1996) examined British fathers' involvement in childcare and household tasks using the 1958 'National Child Development Study' (NCDS) birth cohort. Marked variation in the employment situation of cohort mothers and fathers was found by the age of 33, although the majority (59% of mothers and 53% of fathers) were in dual-earner households, primarily where the mother worked part-time. When mothers worked, more than a third cited fathers as the main child carer, followed by grandparents or other kin. The most egalitarian sharing of childcare tasks (mainly cooking for children, bathing and dressing) was found in dual-earner families where both parents worked full-time: two thirds of cohort mothers and three quarters of cohort fathers reported sharing these tasks. The same pattern was found in the more recent birth cohort MCS (Dex and Joshi, 2004), which also suggested that joint parental working hours were significant predictors of more paternal engagement in care. Sixty-three percent of full-time working mothers in dual-earner households reported the equal sharing of the care of the cohort baby when their working hours were 90% or more of male hours. In contrast, 59% reported equal sharing when maternal working hours were less than 90% of male hours. In general, the average working week was eight hours longer for fathers than for mothers (47 versus

39). The importance of maternal working hours in influencing paternal involvement, both when the child is younger than age one and at age three, has also been shown in Norman, Elliot and Fagan's (2014) longitudinal analysis of MCS families. They found that both fathers' and mothers' employment hours when the child was nine months old have a longitudinal influence on paternal involvement when the child reaches age three. However, it is the hours worked by the mother when the child is aged nine months that has the stronger association with paternal involvement at age three.

Fathers, constrained by economic considerations or a preference to work long weekly hours, can feel disappointed in missing out on time with their children and not having space for a satisfying family or personal life: 57% of fathers and 59% of mothers who worked full-time did not feel that they spent enough time with their nine- to 10-month-old child (Dex and Ward, 2007).

There is some evidence that fathers attempt to compensate for a long working week by spending more time with children at weekends. In a cross-sectional study of fathers' time with children (co-resident and younger than 15 years), Hook and Wolfe (2012) found that UK fathers spend more interactive care time (talking, reading, teaching and playing as a primary activity) with their children on weekends than on weekdays. More time alone with the child is also reported at weekends, but no compensatory increase in physical childcare was found. However, making up for 'lost time' with children has been found to be more difficult for fathers who routinely work Saturdays or Sundays or atypical hours (La Valle et al, 2002; Barnes et al, 2006). Using the UK's 2000 'Survey of Time Use', Hook (2012) found that 45% of fathers with a resident child under the age of 15 reported working on Saturday or Sunday, and that this pattern of work had the greatest impact on fathers employed in non-professional occupations. Weekend-working non-professional fathers spent three hours less with their children than similar men not working weekends (5 hours 20 minutes versus 8 hours). By contrast, there was only a two-hour reduction for comparable fathers in professional occupations who also tended to spend more time with their children at weekends, irrespective of work scheduling. Multivariate analysis showed that non-professional fathers in occupations with less status and control were at higher risk of weekend work (51% versus 38%) and overwork (48 versus 45 hours), and had less time with children anyway.

Research on father involvement and well-being

Despite the growing body of research showing the positive effects of father involvement on maternal and child mental health (Flouri, 2005; Flouri and Malmberg, 2012; Twamley et al, 2013), there is very little UK research exploring the impact of fatherhood or father involvement on men's own well-being, except in the field of the transition to fatherhood considered earlier. However, recent evidence is suggestive of an association between subjective happiness and the primary care of an infant. A study compared father–infant interaction during play and mealtimes for 25 fathers who took a primary caring role – providing more than 20 waking hours per week to their 11-month-old infants – and for 75 fathers that did not (Lewis et al, 2009). 'Paternal mood' was rated on a five-point scale (1 = unhappy/angry; 2 = not unhappy/angry for whole time period; 3 = moderately positive/a mix of positive and negative or neutral; 4 = mostly happy and positive; 5 = very happy, animated) with an inter-rater agreement of $\kappa = .86$. Primary-caring fathers and their infants showed a more positive emotional tone during play than non-primary-caring fathers, although there were no differences between the groups during mealtimes. Of note was the finding of a trend towards increased paternal happiness with increased hours of childcare, which the authors suggest may indicate a gain for fathers who are more involved in the care of their infants. Primary-caring fathers did not differ in educational level or gender role attitudes compared with non-primary-caring fathers; neither were there differences between the partners of the two groups of fathers on any variables and/or differences in temperament. However, primary-caring fathers had a lower occupational status and earned a smaller proportion of the family income.

A further study suggesting an impact on men's well-being from their fatherhood status arises from the limited attention that demographers have given to fathers. In a large nationally representative record linkage study of men in England and Wales, Grundy and Tomassini (2006) examined the long-term consequences of particular paternity pathways. They analysed associations between aspects of paternity history and subsequent mortality and health in a sample of 20,260 mature men in long-term first marriages over a 23-year period (1981–2004). Using multivariate analysis, findings show some negative health outcomes for youthful fatherhood and for fathers who have large families. Notably, men who had a child before the age of 23 had higher mortality and higher odds of poor health in 1991 and 2001 than other fathers, while men who had a child at age 40 or older had lower mortality and lower risks of long-term illness. Men who had had four or more children also appeared to have worse health in later life. The authors suggest that more research is needed on the mechanisms underlying these patterns, but since this study, no further British epidemiological research on fatherhood and paternity effects on health has been reported.

Work-related behaviour

Although work hours for British men and fathers may have fallen somewhat recently and women's and mothers' paid work time has increased (Connolly et al, 2013), the levels of work–family conflict reported by UK fathers are still among the highest in Europe (Speight et al, 2014). In 2010, 35% of UK fathers with dependent children reported that they often or always worried about work problems when not working, 37% said that they often or always felt too tired after work to enjoy the things they would like to do at home, and 34% said that their job often or always prevented them from giving the time they wanted to their partner and family (Speight et al, 2014). Similarly, qualitative studies of British employed fathers point to tensions in accommodating work and care commitments (Dermott, 2008; Miller, 2011; Yarwood, 2011). Yarwood (2011) describes the ways working fathers of children younger than age five typically adopt a 'pick and mix' approach in their 'father talk' and juggle fathering identities as workers and carers.

Cross-national research shows that the well-being of men and women in the UK is among the lowest in Europe (Scott et al, 2012), and the high levels of work–family conflict are a contributory factor. The global economic downturn and the economic recession are key contextual factors, and evidence shows that work–family conflict is higher for those who struggle to live on their current income (McGinnity and Russell, 2013).

In terms of other work-related behaviours, there have been several UK studies exploring the effect of fatherhood on working hours (Dermott, 2006; Biggart and O'Brien, 2010; Kanji, 2013), but less on its income impact (Smith Koslowski, 2011). While British fathers tend to work longer weekly hours than men in general, Dermott's (2006) study shows that once other factors are taken into account, the significance of fatherhood in relation to hours of paid work disappears. She argues against a causal relationship between work effort and fatherhood, suggesting instead that fatherhood tends to occur in the same life-course period that often coincides with longer working hours for men. Other evidence points to the importance of the female partner's earning power in attenuating paternal work effort. Thus, using panel data from the MCS, Kanji (2013) finds that fathers with a female partner who is the main earner work considerably fewer hours than other fathers.

The importance of situating men's working hours and transition to fatherhood in a longitudinal context has been demonstrated in Smith Koslowski's (2011) analysis of British and other European men as they move status between 1994 and 2001. She uses data from the European Community Household Panel and finds that fathers earn more than men who do not become fathers, but this is explained by a build-up in income prior to fatherhood. Also, when compared to non-fathers, they earn more per hour but do not work longer hours. A further significant finding in this study is that fathers who spend more time with their children earn more per hour and work fewer hours per week on average than those who spend less time with their children. Smith Koslowski (2011) has been able to find variability within employed fathers, with an emergent category of men who endeavour to both care and earn – they spend as much time with their children as is possible (though rarely more than mothers), while also developing the most favourable labour market outcome. This study has led to a reassessment of the fatherhood premium thesis that fathers operate as a homogeneous group to accrue wealth though work effort (Killewalda, 2013). Other evidence shows the importance of social class in shaping both fatherhood premiums and penalties. In a study of the effect of parenthood on the earnings distribution in Australia, the UK and the US, Cooke (2014) shows that the lowest-earning men in all three countries face small, but significant, fatherhood penalties. By contrast, high-earning British and US fathers generate significant premiums as compared to childless men.

Fatherhood programmes

Over the past two decades, there has been research interest in supporting father involvement in children's lives, especially when families undergo adverse experiences or stressful transitions. Educators, as well as child and family practitioners, are attempting to be less mother-focused in their practice and approach (eg Maxwell et al, 2012). However, as McBride and Lutz (2004: 468) argue, US parenting programmes, which give attention to fathers and father figures, are in 'an infancy stage of development'. This pattern is just as true of the UK.

In the UK, preschool children's centres are a primary site for educators and child and family practitioners wishing to engage with fathers from diverse backgrounds. The centres originated in the late 1990s as part of the Labour government's Sure Start programme, a geographic area-based initiative aimed at supporting children younger than age five and their families in disadvantaged neighbourhoods (Anning and Hall, 2008). By 2014, the purpose of children's centres continues to be one of providing access to a range of early childhood services, as well as advice and support for parents and carers. On 30 November 2013, there were 3,055 children's centres, an increase from 2004, when there were only 524 centres (Directgov, 2013).

A baseline assessment of Sure Start local programmes found that the importance of engaging men had got lost in the pressure to provide services for women and children (Lloyd et al, 2003). Of the 128 Sure Start programmes initially started, 36% were classified as having 'low' provision for fathers, 52% as having 'moderate/intermediate' provision and 12% as having 'high' levels of provision (Lloyd et al, 2003). In the original guidance to practitioners, fathers were not specifically targeted, but rather a more generalised approach was utilised, involving parents, grandparents and other carers (Potter and Carpenter, 2008). Professionals and agencies that involved fathers had decided on this approach early in the planning process and had developed an agreed-upon plan to contact fathers with clear rules of engagement (Lloyd et al, 2003). A report commissioned by the Department for Children, Schools and Families in 2008 commented that 'father inclusive practice was not seen to be routine or mainstream in family services', but that where it did occur in national policy, it was focused on a small number of services, which included Sure Start (Page et al, 2008: 99).

The Coalition government, which was formed in 2010, acknowledged that fathers have a role in their children's early years:

> Government and the [family service] sector have a role to play in setting the right tone and expectation, and helping professionals to think about how to better engage fathers in all aspects of their child's development and decisions affecting their child. (Department for Education, 2011: 37)

In particular, this policy report focused on involving fathers during pregnancy and childbirth, providing relationship support to prevent relationship breakdown, using family support and outreach services to engage with fathers, and including non-resident fathers and strategies to increase father involvement in children's centres. Legislation through the Children and Families Act 2014[5] has provided an enabling framework for some of these ambitions, for example, the new offer of unpaid leave of absence for fathers-to-be to attend an antenatal appointment.

However, in terms of children's centres, there has been a gradual weakening of the requirement to engage with fathers, which was at its height in the mid-1990s. While 56% of children's centre leaders report fathers being a high-priority target group (Poole et al, forthcoming), this is a drop from higher levels just a few years previous (Tanner et al, 2012). More recently, the Office for Standards in Education, Children's Services and Skills (Ofsted, 2013) *Framework for children's centre inspection* identified the need for centres to focus services on target groups, defined as those that may require 'perceptive intervention and/or additional support', which includes fathers and those from minority ethnic groups (Ofsted, 2013: 25). However, this aspiration may not necessarily happen in practice.

Since the economic downturn, there have been substantial reductions in financial support from central government to local authorities to fund children's centres and their services. In response, local authorities have merged some centres to create centre clusters that are all under one management team. Between April 2010 and November 2012, the number of children's centres in England fell from 3,631 to 3,230 (Truss, 2013). The statutory nature of the services provided by children's centres does offer some protection against government funding reductions as the Child Care Act 2006 requires that there is sufficient provision of early childhood services and that there are consultations before services are changed or children's centres are closed.

In terms of government programmes to encourage fathers' leave-taking or use of flexible work options once legal entitlements are in place, there has only been a limited provision, primarily through technical advice to employees and employers on government websites, and a national (undocumented) advertising campaign to coincide with the launch of paternity leave in April 2003, but no formal programmes. Recent evidence suggests that national awareness of flexible work options has increased from a low baseline of 42% of employees mid-decade to 79% in 2011 (Fourth Work–Life Balance Employee Survey of 2012[6]), but that there is some confusion among employers and employees about men's parental leave options and how they interface with maternity leave. The gap in information has led the Advisory, Conciliation and Arbitration Service (ACAS), an independent and impartial dispute resolution organisation, to produce a user-friendly website.

Awareness of new masculinities and active fatherhoods has increased in the UK. There are an increasing number of organisations with websites, such as the Fatherhood Institute[7] and Working with Men,[8] which disseminate research on fathering and provide training, consulting and educational opportunities to practitioners and to fathers and mothers in community settings and workplaces. These organisations provide not only resources, but also networking opportunities and groups for new fathers. Specific programmes, like The Babyfather Initiative[9] and the Expectant Fathers Programme,[10] make special efforts to also include 'hard-to-reach' fathers and have an Internet presence to offer parenting training and consultation to fathers. Other initiatives, such as the Daddy Cool Project,[11] target young men with events and workshops around male role models and positive fatherhood. In addition, programmes for specific father groups are increasing, such as Fathers Inside,[12] which is a parenting programme specifically for fathers in prison. Programmes targeting couples, often across the transition to parenthood, have been delivered and evaluated by the Fatherhood Institute, the Tavistock Centre for Couple Relationships and the National Society for the Prevention of Cruelty to Children (NSPCC).

The British fatherhood regime

As this chapter has shown, 'involved' fatherhood is now embedded in the cultural, political and public discourses of the British fatherhood regime (Gregory and Milner, 2008). There has been a gradual development of national policies and programmes framed as services to promote a stronger engagement of men in family care activities through the life course. The beginnings of the 'new father' rhetoric were observed in the 1980s, supported by first-wave discoveries of male nurturance (eg Lamb, 1976; McKee and O'Brien, 1982), and these views have now become mainstream (Collier and Sheldon, 2008; Gregory and Milner, 2011a, 2011b). More recently, in response to the rise in dual-earner families, the importance of female employment 'activation' and the political imperative of being 'modern and contemporary', political parties – Left and Right – rhetorically promote policies for a *modern working family*, where parents share the care of children and fathers are engaged. Even employer organisations, such as the Confederation of British Industry, are calling for more government-subsidised childcare so that families 'can make an even bigger contribution to the world of work' (BBC, 2014).

However, formal institutional support for involved fatherhood is rather weak. In terms of leave, the UK does have a national statutory father-care-sensitive parental leave package, unlike, for example, the US, but it is short or minimalist, with low/no income replacement

(O'Brien, 2009; Baird and O'Brien, 2015). Paternity leave has existed since 2003, but it is paid at a low flat rate and there are no father-targeted leave entitlements, which are known to create incentives for paternal uptake. Instead, successive governments have adopted designs based on maternal transfer, which are known to not encourage paternal uptake, and relabelled new measures as shared parental leave. Over the past decade, governments have shown caution in restructuring or reforming the parental leave architecture – in part, not wishing to breach the UK's rather long, albeit low-paid, maternity leave.

In addition, Britain's formal childcare provision is costly, with low investment in both high-quality nurseries (supply side) and few early education opportunities for two to four year olds before school commences. This weak parenting support infrastructure is one factor holding back greater levels of full-time maternal employment in families with preschool children. While the dual-carer worker model is ascending, it is not yet a dominant form of parental working arrangement for British couples with young children. Thus, a *modified breadwinner/carer* or one-and-a half-earner model appears more normative.

Conclusion and recommendations for policy

This chapter has presented British father involvement with young children as situated in a unique policy and demographic context. British fathers started the decade with the longest working hours in Europe, no statutory access to paternity leave and no statutory right to flexible working arrangements to care for their children. Today, fathers can take two weeks paid leave after the birth of a child, and evidence shows that by the end of the decade, more than 90% of fathers did take some time off work (Chanfreau et al, 2011). They also have a statutory entitlement to a widening range of flexible working arrangements, measures important in encouraging greater male involvement in the care of children. In terms of political vision, an active father, responsible for all aspects of a child's life (emotional, social, educational and economic), has been promoted, although not always in a consistent manner (Featherstone, 2009).

The evidence showing an increase in British fathers' care time and reduction in paid work time suggests that a dichotomy between 'good provider' and 'active carer' is an inaccurate depiction of British fatherhood (Smith Koslowski, 2011) and that both practices are embedded in contemporary fathering. Indeed, qualitative studies of fatherhood in Britain are most likely to portray diversity: commitment to the labour market can occur alongside expressive caring practices (Brannen et al, 2004) in a 'pick and mix' style (Yarwood, 2011).

Gaps in research

Research into men and work, and men and families, has been ongoing for many decades in the UK. There is a renewed policy emphasis and concern about men's relationship with their children, parenting, economic and social support for children when relationships break down, and how parenting arrangements impact long-term outcomes for children. As non-residential fatherhood becomes more common, even in the early years of children's lives, further mixed-methods studies need to incorporate fathers' perspectives. Poole et al's (2014) analysis shows that non-residential fathers are not a homogeneous group, although the majority try to keep in contact with their children. More research is needed on the quality and type of contact between fathers and their children who live apart and the meanings of parenting at a distance (Kiernan, 2005; Skinner, 2013). Increasingly, scholars are aware that if research is focused only on fathers who are co-resident, married and presumed biological, theory and concepts will not reflect the diversity of fathers and father figures in contemporary society (Sigle-Rushton, 2010; Henz, 2014).

Another gap in British research is the exploration of minority ethnic, faith and migration identities, and their impact on fathering practices. A body of work is developing, for example, Salway et al's (2009) study of the negotiation of tradition and modernity within the diverse ethnicities of British Asian fathers from different backgrounds, including Bangladeshi Muslim, Pakistani Muslim, Gujarati Hindu and Punjabi Sikh, and Brannen et al's (2014) project on intergenerational fathering practices across British, Irish and Polish men. Also, there is Kilkey, Plomien and Perrons's (2014) project on Polish migrant men's fathering narratives, which challenge the construction of male migrants as independent and non-relational. However, a greater critical mass of work is needed in this area, particularly as Britain becomes increasingly multicultural.

It is clear that a further gap in research is fathers' well-being. Most research explores the impact of fathers on children rather than the reverse. Longitudinal data are essential for this topic, and Britain's set of cohort studies can provide a rich source of quantitative data on family members. Supplementation with qualitative data through sub-studies would help further illuminate the relationship between caring and fathers' well-being.

A further research gap is in the area of older fathers, grandfathers and intergenerational aspects of fathering (Brannen et al, 2004). Men are becoming fathers to their first child at older ages and are also fathers of subsequent children at an older age, especially those men in new partnerships after separation and divorce. Increased longevity and lower mortality rates have extended men's reproductive and caring lives and provide a further dimension for understanding fathering.

Finally, in order to make fatherhood more visible, there needs to be improvement in data collection about British fathers. For example, a key challenge in responding to the needs of fathers and men in vulnerable family contexts is the lack of comprehensive and systematic data collection on fathers. Basic demographic information on the parental status of men, male fertility and family formation is not routinely collected. When British men are admitted into public institutions, such as prisons, there is typically no registration of parental status or parenting responsibilities.

Promising initiatives and suggestions for change

Since Britain is at an early stage of development in terms of leave policy, the next step should be a non-transferable daddy week or longer. The evidence in this chapter suggests that British fathers would be receptive to such a measure and that it could operate to further engage fathers in the early years of their children's lives. Economic modelling of such a four-week daddy quota has been carried out by a leading think tank in the UK (Thompson and Ben-Galim, 2014), suggesting an annual cost of £150 million.

Investment in high-quality extensions to universal early years care and education would also support a dual-earner/carer family model and address structural gender differences in career and income development for parents. The UK's membership of the EU in terms of a social investment welfare approach has had some impact on ensuring that universal early years education and well-compensated leave for both mothers and fathers remains on the policy agenda. This policy influence signifies the vital role of intergovernmental bodies, such as the EU, in promoting work–family reconciliation measures, minimally adopted even in countries such as the UK, with underlying resilient maternalist and male-breadwinner cultures.

Notes

[1] See: http://www.legislation.gov.uk/ukpga/2002/22/contents

[2] See: http://www.legislation.gov.uk/ukpga/2014/6/contents/enacted

[3] We do not report here figures for children aged five and older as, in the UK, compulsory schooling starts the first school term after the child turns five. In practice, most children start attending a full-time reception class attached to a primary school once they turn four.

[4] Childcare provided by parents (including step-parents) who are co-resident with the child is not included in informal childcare. However, time the child spends with their non-resident parent (away from the resident parent) is included in the definition of informal childcare (alongside any time the child spends with grandparents, other family members and friends of the parents).

[5] See: http://www.legislation.gov.uk/ukpga/2014/6/contents/enacted

[6] See: http://www.esds.ac.uk/doc/7112/mrdoc/pdf/7112_employee_survey.pdf

[7] See: http://www.fatherhoodinstitute.org/

[8] See: http://www.workingwithmen.org/

[9] See: http://www.barnardos.org.uk/babyfather/babyfather_fatherhood_program.htm

[10] See: http://www.efprogramme.co.uk/=68

[11] See: http://www.daddycoolproject.org.uk/

[12] See: http://www.safeground.org.uk/programmes-services/fathers-inside/

References

Anning, A. and Hall, D. (2008) 'What was Sure Start and why did it matter?', in A. Anning and M. Ball (eds) *Improving services for young children: from Sure Start to children's centres*, London: SAGE Publications.

Baird, M. and O'Brien, M. (2015) 'Dynamics of parental leave in Anglophone countries: the paradox of state expansion in the liberal welfare regime', *Community, Work and Family*, 18(2): 198–217.

Barnes, M., Bryson, C. and Smith, R. (2006) *Working atypical hours: what happens to family life?*, London: NatCen and Relationships Foundation.

BBC (British Broadcasting Corporation) (2014) 'Report on Confederation of British Industry conference speeches'. Available at: http://www.bbc.co.uk/news/business-29983051

Biggart, L. and O'Brien, M. (2010) 'UK fathers' long work hours: career stage or fatherhood?', *Journal of Fathering*, 8: 341–61.

Blackburn, P. (2013) 'Future directions for a mature UK childcare market', in E. Lloyd and H. Penn (eds) *Childcare markets: can they deliver an equitable service?*, Bristol: The Policy Press, pp 43–59.

Brannen, J., Moss, P. and Mooney, A. (2004) *Working and caring over the twentieth century: change and continuity in four generation families*, London: Palgrave.

Brannen, J., Mooney, A., Wigfall, V. and Parutis, V. (2014) 'Fatherhood and transmission in the context of migration: an Irish and a Polish case', *International Migration*, 52: 165–77.

Bryson, C., Kazimirski, A. and Southwood, H. (2006) 'Childcare and early years provision: a study of parents' use, views and experience', Department for Education and Skills, Research Report RR723.

Calderwood, L., Kiernan, K., Joshi, H., Smith, K. and Ward, K. (2005) 'Parenthood and parenting', in S. Dex and H. Joshi (eds) *Children of the 21st century: from birth to nine months*, Bristol: The Policy Press.

Chanfreau, J., Gowland, S., Lancaster, Z., Poole, E., Tipping, L. and Toomse, M. (2011) 'Maternity and paternity rights and women returners survey 2009/10', Department for Work and Pensions, Research Report No 777.

Children and Families Bill (2013) *Contextual information and responses to pre-legislative scrutiny*, London: Crown Copyright.

Chowbey, P., Salway, S. and Clarke, L. (2013) 'Supporting fathers in multi-ethnic societies: insights from British Asian fathers', *Journal of Social Policy*, 42(2): 391–408.

Collier, R. (1995) *Masculinity, law and the family*, London: Routledge.

Collier, R. and Sheldon, S. (2008) *Fragmenting fatherhood: a socio-legal approach*, Oxford: Hart Publishing.

Connolly, S. and Gregory, M. (2008) 'Moving down: women's part-time work and occupational change in Britain 1991–2001', *The Economic Journal*, 118(526): F52–F76.

Connolly, S., Aldrich, M., O'Brien, M., Speight, S. and Poole, E. (2013) 'Fathers and work', ESRC Briefing Paper. Available at: http://www.modernfatherhood.org/wp-content/uploads/2013/06/Fathers-and-work.pdf

Cooke, L.P. (2014) 'Gendered parenthood penalties and premiums across the earnings distribution in Australia, the United Kingdom, and the United States', *European Sociological Review*, 30(3): 360–72.

Daly, M. (2010) 'Shifts in family policy in the UK under New Labour', *Journal of European Social Policy*, 20(5): 433–43.

DCSF (Department for Children, Schools and Families) (2004) *Choice for parents, the best start for children: a ten year strategy for childcare*, London: The Stationery Office.

Department for Education (2011) *Supporting families in the Foundation years*. Available at https://www.gov.uk/government/uploads/system/uploads/attachment_data/file/184868/DFE-01001-2011_supporting_families_in_the_foundation_years.pdf

Department for Education and Ministry of Justice (2012) 'Co-operative parenting following family separation: proposed legislation on the involvement of both parents in a child's life'.

Department for Work and Pensions (2012) *Public consultation – supporting separated families; securing children's futures*, London: DWP. Available at: www.dwp.gov.uk/consultations/2012/childrens-futures.shtml

Dermott, E. (2006) 'What's parenthood got to do with it? Men's hours of paid work', *British Journal of Sociology*, 57(4): 619–34.

Dermott, E. (2008) *Intimate fatherhood*, London: Routledge.

Dex, S. and Joshi, H. (eds) (2004) *Children of the 21st century: from birth to nine months*, Bristol: The Policy Press.

Dex, S. and Ward, K. (2007) *Parental care and employment in early childhood: analysis of the Millennium Cohort Study (MCS) sweeps 1 and 2*, Working Paper No. 57, London: Equal Opportunities Commission.

DfE (Department for Education) (2014a) 'Provision for children under five years of age in England: January 2014'.

DfE (2014b) 'Childcare and early years survey of parents 2012–2013'.

DfEE (Department for Education and Employment) (1998) *Meeting the childcare challenge, Green Paper*, London: The Stationery Office.

Directgov (2013) 'Current distribution of children centres across the country'. Available at: http://childrenscentresfinder.direct.gov.uk/snapshot-childrens-centre/#LambethDirect

Draper, J. (2002) '"It's the first scientific evidence": men's experience of pregnancy confirmation', *Journal of Advanced Nursing*, 39(6): 563–70.

Emanuel, R. (2002) 'On becoming a father – reflections from infant observation', in J. Trowell, and A. Etchegoyen (eds) *The importance of fathers: a psychoanalytic re-evaluation*, London: Institute of Psychoanalysis.

European Commission (2009) *The Social Situation in the European Union 2009*, Luxembourg: Office for Official Publications of the European Communities, doi 10.2767/30749.

Featherstone, B. (2009) *Contemporary fathering, theory, policy and practice*, Bristol: The Policy Press.

Ferri, E. and Smith, K. (1996) *Parenting in the 1990s*, London: Family Policy Studies Centre.

Finn, M. and Henwood, K. (2009) 'Exploring masculinities within men's identificatory imaginings of first time fatherhood', *British Journal of Social Psychology*, 48(3): 547–62.

Fisher, K., McCulloch, A. and Gershuny, J. (1999) 'British fathers and children: a report for channel 4 "dispatches"', University of Essex, Institute for Social and Economic Research.

Flouri, E. (2005) *Fathering and child outcomes*, London: Wiley.

Flouri, E. and Malmberg, L.-E. (2012) 'Father involvement, family poverty and adversity, and young children's behaviour in stable two-parent families', *Longitudinal and Life Course Studies*, 3(2): 254–67.

Fonda, N. (1980) 'Statutory maternity leave in the United Kingdom: a case study', in P. Moss and N. Fonda (eds) *Work and the family*, London: Maurice Temple Smith.

Gatrell, C.J., Burnett, S.B., Cooper, C.L. and Sparrow, P. (2014) 'Parents, perceptions and belonging: exploring flexible working among UK fathers and mothers', *British Journal of Management*, 25(3): 473–87.

Gimenez-Nadal, J.I. and Seville, A. (2012) 'Trends in time allocation: a cross-country analysis', *The European Economic Review*, 56(6): 1338–59.

Gregory, A. and Milner, S. (2008) 'Fatherhood regimes and father involvement in France and the UK', *Community, Work and Family*, 11(1): 61–84.

Gregory, A. and Milner, S. (2011a) 'Fathers and work–life balance in France and the UK: policy and practice', *International Journal of Sociology and Social Policy*, 31(1): 34–52.

Gregory, A. and Milner, S. (2011b) 'What is "new" about fatherhood? The social construction of fatherhood in France and the UK', *Men and Masculinities*, 14(5): 588–606.

Grundy, E. and Tomassini, C. (2006) 'Fatherhood history and later life health and mortality in England and Wales: a record linkage study', *Biodemography and Social Biology*, 53(3/4): 189–205.

Henz, U. (2014) 'Long-term trends of men's co-residence with children in England and Wales', *Demographic Research*, 30(1): 671–702.

Hewitt, P. (2004) 'Keynote speech, Fathers Direct', Working with Fathers Conference, London, 5 April.

HM Government (2010) 'Additional Paternity Leave impact assessment'. Available at: http://www.legislation.gov.uk/uksi/2010/1055/impacts/2010/32

HM Government (2015) 'Paternity pay and leave'. Available at: https://www.gov.uk/paternity-pay-leave/pay (accessed 5 February 2015).

Home Office (1999) *Supporting families*, London: Home Office.

Hook, J.L. (2012) 'Working at the weekend: fathers' time with family in the United Kingdom', *Journal of Marriage & Family*, 74(4): 631–42.

Hook, J.L. and Wolfe, C.M. (2012) 'New fathers? Residential fathers' time with children in four countries', *Journal of Family Issues*, 33: 415.

Huerta, M., Adema, W., Baxter, J., Han, W., Lausten, M., Lee, R. and Waldfogel, J. (2013) 'Fathers' leave, fathers' involvement and child development: are they related? Evidence from four OECD countries', OECD Social, Employment and Migration Working Papers No 140. Available at: www.oecd.org/els/workingpapers

Huskinson T., Pye, J., Medien, K., Dobie, S., Ferguson, C. and Gardner, C. (with Gilby, N., Littlewood, M. and D'Souza, J.) (2013) 'Childcare and early years survey of parents 2011', Department for Education Research Report SFR08/2013. Available at: https://www. gov.uk/government/statistics/childcare-and-early-years-survey-of-parents-2011

ILO (International Labor Organization) (2014) *Maternity and paternity at work: law and practice across the world*, Geneva: ILO.

Jones, E. (2010) 'Parental relationships and parenting', in K. Hansen, H. Joshi and S. Dex (eds) *Children of the 21st century: the first 5 years*, London: IOE.

Kamerman, S.B. and Moss, P. (eds) (2009) *The politics of parental leave policies. Children, parenting, gender and the labour market*, Bristol: The Policy Press.

Kanji, S. (2013) 'Do fathers work fewer paid hours when their female partner is the main or equal earner?', *Work, Employment and Society*, 27(2): 326–42.

Kiernan, K.E. (2005) 'Parenthood and parenting', in S. Dex and H. Joshi (eds) *Children of the 21st century: from birth to nine months*, Bristol: The Policy Press.

Kilkey, M., Plomien, A. and Perrons, D. (2014) 'Migrant men's fathering narratives, practices and projects in national and transnational spaces: recent Polish male migrants to London', *International Migration*, 52(1): 178–91.

Killewalda, A. (2013) 'A reconsideration of the fatherhood premium: marriage, coresidence, biology, and fathers' wages', *American Sociological Review*, 78(1): 96–116.

Lader, D., Short, S. and Gershuny, J. (2006) *The time use survey 2005: how we spend our time*, London: Office for National Statistics.

Lamb, M.E. (ed) (1976) *The role of the father in child development*, New York, NY: Wiley.

Lamb, M.E. and Lewis, C. (2010) 'The development and significance of father–child relationships in two-parent families', in M.E. Lamb (ed) *The role of the father in child development* (5th edn), Hoboken, NJ: Wiley.

Lamb, M.E., Pleck, J.H., Charnov, E.L. and Levine, J.A. (1987) 'A biosocial perspective on paternal behavior and involvement', in J. Lancaster, J. Altmann, A.S. Rossi and L.R. Sherrod (eds) *Parenting across the lifespan: biosocial dimensions*, Hawthorne, NY: Aldine de Gruyter.

La Valle, I., Arthur, S., Millward, C., Scott, J. and Clayden, M. (2002) *Happy families? A typical work and its influence on family life*, Bristol: The Policy Press.

Lewis, C. (1987) *Becoming a father*, Buckingham: Open University Press.

Lewis, C. (2013) 'Fatherhood and fathering research in the UK: cultural change and diversity', in D. Shwalb, B. Shwalb and M.E. Lamb (eds) *Fathers in cultural context*, New York, NY: Routledge.

Lewis, J. (1992) 'Gender and the development of welfare regimes', *Journal of European Social Policy*, 2(3): 159–73.

Lewis, J. (2009) *Work–family balance, gender and policy*, Cheltenham: Edward Elgar.

Lewis, S.N., West, A.F., Stein, A., Malmberg, L.-E., Bethell, K., Barnes, J., Sylva, K., Leach, P. and Families, Children and Child Care (FCCC) project team (2009) 'A comparison of father–infant interaction between primary and non-primary caregiving fathers', *Child: Care, Health and Development*, 35: 199–207.

Lloyd, N., O'Brien, M. and Lewis, C. (2003) *Fathers in Sure Start*, London: National Evaluation of Sure Start, University of London.

Maxwell, N., Scourfield, J., Featherstone, B., Holland, S. and Tolman, R. (2012) 'Engaging fathers in child welfare services: a narrative review of recent research evidence', *Child and Family Social Work*, 17: 160–9.

McBride, B.A. and Lutz, M. (2004) 'Intervention: changing the nature and extent of father involvement', in M.E. Lamb (ed) *The role of father involvement in child development* (4th edn), Hoboken, NJ: John Wiley and Sons.

McGinnity, F. and Russell, H. (2013) 'Work–family conflict and economic change', in D. Gallie (ed) *Economic crisis, quality of work, and social integration: the European experience*, Oxon: Oxford university press, p 169.

McKee, L. (1982) 'Fathers' participation in infant care: a critique', in L. McKee and M. O'Brien (eds) *The father figure*, London: Tavistock.

McKee, L. and O'Brien, M. (eds) (1982) *The father figure*, London: Tavistock.

Miller, T. (2010) 'It's a triangle that's difficult to square: men's intentions and practices around caring. Work and first-time fatherhood', *Fathering* 8(3): 362–78.

Miller, T. (2011) *Making sense of fatherhood: gender, caring and work*, Cambridge: Cambridge University Press.

Moss, P. (ed) (2014) 'International review of leave policies and related research'. Available at: http://www.leavenetwork.org/

Norman, H., Elliot, M. and Fagan, C. (2014) 'Which fathers are the most involved in taking care of their toddlers in the UK? An investigation of the predictors of paternal involvement', *Community, Work & Family*, 17(2): 163–80.

O'Brien, M. (2009) 'Fathers, parental leave policies and infant quality of life: international perspectives and policy impact', *The Annals of the American Academy of Political & Social Science*, 624: 190–213.

O'Brien, M., Moss, P., Koslowski, A. and Daly, M. (2014) 'United Kingdom country note', in P. Moss (ed) *International review of leave policies and research*. Available at: http://www.leavenetwork.org/lp_and_r_reports/

OECD (Organisation for Economic Co-operation and Development) (2009) 'Family database', Paris. Available at: http://www.oecd.org/social/family/database.htm

Ofsted (Office for Standards in Education, Children's Services and Skills) (2013) *The framework for children's centre inspection*, Manchester: Ofsted.

ONS (Office for National Statistics) (2011) *Social Trends: Households and families and Labour market*, (ST number 41). Available at: http://www.ons.gov.uk/ons/rel/social-trends-rd/social-trends/social-trends-41/index.html

ONS (2012a) *Measuring National Well-being, Social Trends 42 – Population*. Available at http://www.ons.gov.uk/ons/dcp171766_224403.pdf

ONS (2012b) *Characteristics of Mother 1, England and Wales, 2012*. Available at: http://www.ons.gov.uk/ons/rel/vsob1/characteristics-of-Mother-1--england-and-wales/2012/index.html

ONS (2013) *Vital Statistics: Population and Health Reference Tables, Winter 2013 update*, London: Office for National Statistics. Available at http://www.ons.gov.uk/ons/rel/vsob1/vital-statistics--population-and-health-reference-tables/winter-2013-update/index.html

ONS (2014) *Births in England and Wales by Parents' Country of Birth, 2013*, London: Office for National Statistics. Available at: http://www.ons.gov.uk/ons/dcp171778_375070.pdf

Page, J., Whitting, G. and Mclean, C. (2008) 'A review of how fathers can be better recognised and supported through DCSF policy', Department for Children, Schools, and Families.

Pleck, J.H. and Masciadrelli, B.P. (2004) 'Paternal involvement by U.S. residential fathers: levels, sources and consequences', in M.E. Lamb (ed) *The role of the father in child development* (4th edn), Hoboken, NJ: John Wiley and Sons.

Poole, E., Speight, S., O'Brien, M., Connolly, S. and Aldrich, M. (2013) 'What do we know about non-resident fathers?', ESRC Briefing Paper. Available at: http://www.modernfatherhood.org/wp-content/uploads/2013/11/Briefing-paper-Non-resident-fathers.pdf

Poole, E., Speight, S., O'Brien, M., Connolly, S. and Aldrich, M. (2014) 'Father involvement with children and couple relationships'. Available at: http://www.modernfatherhood.org/wp-content/uploads/2014/10/Fathers-relationships-briefing-paper.pdf

Poole, E., Fry, A. and Tanner, E. (forthcoming) 'Evaluation of children's centres in England: follow-up survey of centre leaders', DfE Research Report, Department of Education.

Potter, C. and Carpenter, J. (2008) '"Something in it for dads": getting fathers involved with Sure Start', *Child Development and Care*, 178(7): 761–72.

Ramchandani, P. and McConachie, H. (2005) 'Mothers, fathers and their children's health', *Child: Care, Health and Development*, 31: 5–6.

Ramchandani, P.G. and Psychogiou, L. (2009) 'Paternal psychiatric disorders and children's psychosocial development', *The Lancet*, 374(9690): 646–53.

Ramchandani, P., Stein, A., Evans, J., O'Connor, T.G. and ALSPAC (Avon Longitudinal Study of Parents and Children) (2005) 'Paternal depression in the postnatal period and child development: a prospective population study', *The Lancet*, 365: 2201–5.

Redshaw, M. and Henderson, J. (2013) 'Fathers' engagement in pregnancy and childbirth: evidence from a national survey BMC', *Pregnancy and Childbirth*, 13: 70. Available at: http://www.biomedcentral.com/1471-2393/13/70

Salway, S., Chowbey, P. and Clarke, L. (2009) *Understanding the experiences of Asian fathers in Britain*, York: Joseph Rowntree Foundation.

Scott, J., Dex, S. and Plagnol, A. (2012) *Gendered lives: gender inequalities in production and reproduction*, Cheltenham: Edward Elgar.

Sigle-Rushton, W. (2010) 'Men's unpaid work and divorce: reassessing specialization and trade in British families', *Feminist Economics*, 16(2): 1–26.

Skinner, C. (2013) 'Child maintenance reforms: understanding fathers' expressive agency and the power of reciprocity', *International Journal of Law, Policy & the Family*, 27(2): 242–65.

Smith, A.J. and Williams, D. (2007) 'Father friendly legislation and paternal time across Western Europe', *Journal of Comparative Policy Analysis*, 9(3): 175–92.

Smith Koslowski, A. (2011) 'Working fathers in Europe: earning and caring', *European Sociological Review*, 27(2): 230–45.

Speight, S., Smith, R., La Valle, I., Schneider, V., Perry, J., Coshall, C. and Tipping, S. (2009) 'Childcare and early years survey of parents 2008', Department for Children, Schools, and Families Research Report DCSF–RR136.

Speight, S., O'Brien, M., Connolly, S., Poole, E. and Aldrich, M. (2014) 'Work–family conflict: how do UK fathers compare to other European fathers?', presentation at the 'Modern Fatherhood Conference', July, London. Available at: http://www.modernfatherhood.org/publications/work-family-conflict-how-do-uk-fathers-compare-to-other-european-fathers/

Sullivan, O., Coltrane, S., McAnnally, L. and Altintas, E. (2009) 'Father-friendly policies and time-use data in a cross-national context: potential and prospects for future research', *The Annals of the American Academy of Political & Social Science*, 624(1): 234–54.

Tanaka, S. and Waldfogel, J. (2007) 'Effects of parental leave and work hours on fathers' involvement with their babies: evidence from the Millennium Cohort Study', *Community, Work & Family*, 10: 409–26.

Tanner, E., Agur, M., Hussey, D., Hall, J., Sammons, P., Sylva, K., Smith, T., Evangelou, M. and Flint, A. (2012) 'Evaluation of Children's Centres in England (ECCE). Strand 1: first survey of children's centre leaders in the most deprived areas', DfE Research Report DFE–RR230.

Thompson, S. and Ben-Galim, D. (2014) *2014 Childmind the gap: reforming childcare to support mothers into work*, London: IPPR.

Trowell, J. and Etchegoyen, A. (2002) (eds) *The importance of fathers: a psychoanalytic re-evaluation*, London: Institute of Psychoanalysis.

Truss, E. (2013) 'House of Commons written answer [128769]', 7 January. Available at: http://www.publications.parliament.uk/pa/cm201213/cmhansrd/cm130107/text/130107w0003.htm

Twamley, K., Brunton, G., Sutcliffe, K., Hinds, K. and Thomas, J. (2013) 'Fathers' involvement and the impact on family mental health: evidence from Millennium Cohort Study analyses', *Community, Work & Family*, 16(2): 212–24.

Yarwood, G. (2011) 'The pick and mix of fathering identities', *Fathering: A Journal of Theory, Research, & Practice about Men as Fathers*, 9(2): 150–68.

SIX

The United States

Marina A. Adler

The cultural and policy context of fatherhood

The US occupies a rather unique position among advanced countries when it comes to family policy in general, and policies directed at fathers in particular. It has neither a coherent set of family policies nor a federal administrative body, such as a 'Department of Families and Youth', to implement such policies, and the term 'family policy' is not used in public discourse (Bogenscheider and Corbett, 2010; Coltrane and Behnke, 2013). This may be due to the dominant cultural belief that the family is a private domain that should not be part of public policy. Hence, most working parents do not receive public social protections and rely on the workplace for family leave and on the market for childcare provision (Orloff and Monson, 2002). For example, the US is the only advanced country, as well as one of only four nations in the world, that has no statutory rights to paid maternity leave for employees (Hara and Hegewisch, 2013). The lack of statutory laws on paid family-related leave and public childcare reflects the reluctance of the government to pursue coherent family policies such as those found in European countries. Even among liberal welfare states, which are characterised by low social spending and very limited means-tested social benefits, this is an exceptional position. The US's public spending in 2009 for social expenditures was 19.2% (Organisation for Economic Co-operation and Development [OECD] = 22.1%) and spending on family benefits is the lowest (besides Korea and Mexico) in the OECD – 1.22% of gross domestic product (GDP) (OECD average = 2.61%). The proportion of public social spending on early childhood was 12%, much lower than the other OECD countries (OECD, 2012). In place of providing support for all parents via paid leave and child allowances, the US government relies on the tax system and employers to help middle-class families. The tax credit against owed taxes for employed parents with dependent children covers only part of the annual costs incurred by children. In addition, the Earned Income Tax Credit (EITC) for low-income workers with children can lift working poor parents above the poverty line.

Due to the special circumstances surrounding US family-related policies, this chapter begins by describing how the government uses social policy to shape programmes that are intended to affect parents in general, and fathers in particular (Orloff and Monson, 2002; Coltrane and Behnke, 2013). Policy provisions offered by workplaces in terms of paternal leave and flexitime will be discussed later in the chapter, as will specific fatherhood programmes.

Leave provisions

The Family and Medical Leave Act 1993 (FMLA) entitles eligible employees, who have worked for at least one year in firms with at least 50 employees, to 12 weeks of *unpaid* leave to accommodate the birth or adoption of a child (Hara and Hegewisch, 2013). While it applies to mothers and fathers and to biological and adoptive parents, this Act only covers about 60% of all employees and its unpaid provisions make it economically unfeasible for most families. It is up to the states and employers to provide paid family leave, flexible hours and childcare to fill in the gap left behind by the FMLA. In 2004, California was the first state to offer paid family leave: eligible mothers and fathers are entitled to up to six weeks of partially paid leave (California Work and Family Coalition and Next Generation, 2014). Since then, only two additional states (Washington in 2007 and New Jersey in 2009) and the District of Columbia (in 2008) have passed some form of paid family leave law (Guerin, no date).

In all other states, employers decide whether or not to provide paid leave to parents, as well as how much to provide. According to the 2012 FMLA Survey (Klerman et al, 2013), only about one third (35%) of employees work for a company that offers paid maternity leave and only one fifth (20%) are entitled to paid paternity leave. Access to paid leave is a social class issue because paid leave is mainly provided to higher-paid employees in white-collar professional and managerial positions in larger companies. A recent survey of the 100 most 'family-friendly' companies (Hara and Hegewisch, 2013) shows that only 14% offer more than 12 weeks of paid maternity benefits, 60% offer between five and 12 weeks, and 26% offer less than five weeks. Hence, Hara and Hegewisch (2013: 5) conclude that 'voluntary employer provisions are not bridging the gap left by the lack of a federal mandate for paid leave and that the majority of new parents remain without paid parental leave'.

Rather than developing policies in support of all working parents, the US government has focused its efforts mainly on poor families, particularly on unmarried mothers and the fathers of their children (Geva, 2011). Interventions targeting fathers emerged as a response to trends in non-marital childbearing and divorce that were considered 'threatening' to traditional family values (Cabrera, 2010). In particular, the US addresses poor fathers as a problem in the context of welfare policy targeting low-income families (Marsiglio and Roy, 2012): 'Although in many countries the idea of new fatherhood has been the driver of new laws and policy initiatives, in the United States a policy "silence" surrounds breadwinning fathers who already live up to cultural expectations as "good" fathers' (Marsiglio and Roy, 2012: 7).

Unlike in other countries where policies are directed at fathers so they can be more involved in the care of their children, the US is primarily concerned with fathers who fail to live up to the normative expectations surrounding their provider role (Marsiglio and Roy, 2012). Hence, the focus is on paternity establishment, child support payments and marriage promotion. Federal and state initiatives for fathers are generally short-term programmes involving job training or marriage education rather than efforts that lead to sustained improvements in father involvement (Marsiglio and Roy, 2012; McFadden and Tamis-LeMonda, 2013). What is lacking, then, is general societal support for fathers in the positive sense or public incentives for father involvement.

US ideas of masculinity are linked much more to men's economic self-support, their independence from public assistance and their capacity to head a household as breadwinner and father than in other advanced countries (Orloff and Monson, 2002). From a policy perspective, 'being a man' means being a self-sustaining employee and married family wage-earner (a wage that sustains the entire family) rather than a 'citizen' who is entitled to social support (Orloff and Monson, 2002). By constructing fatherhood through the lens of male breadwinning and marital commitment, policymakers are engaging in a 'masculinity politics' (Curran and Abrams, 2000; Randles, 2013) that produces policies emphasising 'marital masculinity' for poor and disadvantaged fathers. These men's identities are reduced to being 'responsible' husbands and fathers who are expected to work harder and increase their earnings (Randles, 2013). Their success as men and fathers is tied to economic providing in the context of marriage rather than to nurturing and caring for children. It appears that in terms of social rights to public resources to help sustain a family, US fathers are less 'decommodified' than men in the other advanced countries covered in this book (see Esping-Andersen, 1990). In other words, because the

US government does not have policies supporting citizens as parents, men (and poor women) are less insulated from pressures to participate in the labour market for survival (Orloff and Monson, 2002).

When fathers fail to conform to expectations of being self-supporting, wage-earning family providers, social service institutions respond in a punitive manner (Curran and Abrams, 2000). This negative side of fathering – absent fathers, 'deadbeat dads' and the lack of father involvement in terms of legal responsibility, financial support or co-residence – has been part of the welfare policy debate since the early 1980s. Initially, the priority was paternity establishment in order to ensure that fathers take legal (and financial) responsibility for their biological children – inside and outside of marriage. Thus, in 1984, the guidelines for legally establishing paternity in parental disputes and as a basis for child support payments were passed by Congress (Curran, 2003). By the 1990s, findings from large-scale projects like Early Head Start and Fragile Families again raised concerns over 'welfare dependency', 'missing men' and 'absent fathers'. The Clinton administration enacted the Personal Responsibilities and Work Opportunity Act 1996 (PRWOA) in part to deal with 'missing fathers' in welfare recipients' families. To encourage voluntary acknowledgement of paternity, this federal law required hospitals to provide the opportunity for fathers to record their legal paternity when their child is born (McFadden and Tamis-LeMonda, 2013).

Thus, the PRWOA laid the groundwork for a voluntary acknowledgement of paternity at the time of childbirth. Less voluntary, however, is the requirement that unmarried mothers have to reveal the name of their child's father in order to apply for welfare. This is a prerequisite of the Temporary Assistance to Needy Families (TANF) provision of the Welfare Reform Act, which enables state governments to sanction fathers who do not provide child support by garnishing their pay checks, suspending their drivers licences or arresting them (Cabrera, 2010; Sorensen, 2010). Designed as a cost-saving feature of welfare reform, fathers' financial provisions are considered a cornerstone of 'responsible fatherhood' and 'healthy families'. Nevertheless, some criticise these policies because they marginalise fathers' position in families and thus actually reinforce stereotypical notions of masculinity. Research on low-income families also shows that fathers' voluntary direct payments or in-kind contributions are usually preferred to official child support (Edin and Kefalas, 2005; Bronte-Tinkew et al, 2006).

Policies that include fathers are mainly directed at supporting fragile families and encouraging traditional marriage in cases of unmarried parents. They are based on the assumption that there is a 'marriage crisis' among lower-income Americans and they are subsumed under the heading of the 'The Healthy Marriage Initiative'. They include grants for research on marriage education and promotion programmes. In the forefront of this marriage promotion campaign are various conservative and/or faith-based organisations. Nevertheless, Skolnick (2003) argues that the claims justifying marriage promotion policies are not supported by social science research. Thus, most low-income women remain poor even after marriage and most unmarried poor women remain single because of a shortage of men with stable incomes. Hence, it is not marriage itself, but successful relationships, that are important. In addition, these programmes reinforce gender stereotypes by encouraging 'marital masculinity' (Randles, 2013) and the 'provide-and-reside model' of responsible fatherhood (Marsiglio and Roy, 2012). Marriage promotion policies have also been critiqued as problematic in relationships involving domestic violence, instability or substance abuse (Cabrera et al, 2004; Edin and Kefalas, 2005).

Since the Clinton administration created the Fatherhood Research Initiative, fatherhood itself has become part of the policy agenda (Doherty et al, 1998). In 1994, the non-profit organisation National Fatherhood Initiative (NFI) began to advocate for involved, 'responsible' and committed fatherhood (Holmes et al, 2013). This 'pro-father involvement' shift in academia and practice led to a definition of 'responsible fathering' that includes establishing legal paternity, providing economic and emotional support for the child and mother, and directly interacting with and caring for the child (Doherty et al, 1998). In 2001, the Department of Health and Human Services (DHHS) and, later, the National Responsible Fatherhood Clearinghouse provided guidelines for practitioners and policymakers involved with fatherhood initiatives that encourage responsible fathering. In these guidelines for father programming, holistic approaches to dealing with diverse families (as opposed to marriage promotion) and respect for the varied experiences of fathers are emphasised (rather than 'one size fits all' programmes). However, Bush's Healthy Marriage and Responsible Fatherhood Initiative and the Responsible Fatherhood and Healthy Families Act 2007 continued to prioritise 'healthy marriage' education and a focus on child support enforcement. In 2011, the Obama administration modified this act by replacing marriage promotion with increased training and employment opportunities for fathers and an emphasis on developing their parenting skills. Most fatherhood programmes try to address disadvantaged fathers' prospects of becoming financial providers for their children and some involve increasing fathers' caring skills.

Contextual demographic and family trends related to fatherhood

The US is not only exceptional in terms of its policy context, it also has higher marriage and divorce rates than other advanced countries. In addition, compared to Europeans, Americans have children earlier and have higher fertility rates. As Table 6.1 shows, the current marriage rate is around 6.8 and the divorce rate is around 3.6. While both marriage and divorce have become less popular over last decade, cohabitation has increased. At the same time, family formation has been postponed – the average age at first birth for women increased from 24.9 to 25.8. These data disguise major differences by ethnic group. For example, African-American women have their first child much earlier (23.6) than white women (25.9). While the percentage of births to unmarried women has increased from 33% to 41%, African-American women are much more likely to have children outside of marriage (72%) than white women (36%).[1] Interestingly, the trend in non-marital childbearing also shows that the difference between African-American and white women is shrinking.

Although the crude birth rate (CBR) has been reduced from 14.4 to 12.6, the total fertility rate (TFR) is 1.9 and thus remains higher than those in Europe. As a decade ago, the CBR for African Americans is significantly higher (14.6) than that for Whites (10.7). The number of births per 1,000 men has declined from 50 to 46.1 and the reduction is larger among black men (66.2 to 58.2) than white men (47.6 to 44). Overall, the demographic trends echo Europe's: fewer people are getting married and divorced, more cohabit, fewer have children, they have children later, and fewer men become fathers.

Recent trends in what Hofferth et al (2013) call the 'father family structure' show that the percentage of husband–wife–children families has been reduced from around 24% to around 20%. Solo-father families are increasing somewhat, but overall remain quite rare (2.6%). Whereas, overall, most children younger than age five are today living with two parents (about 70%), among African Americans this percentage is only about 35% for younger than 18 year olds.[2] Table 6.1 also shows that while there was a slight reduction of dual-earner families over the last decade, they are still the majority of family forms (54%). Thus, in 2010, about 62% of American children lived with two parents who were in the labour force and 36% lived with one parent who was in the labour force (OECD, 2012).

The labour force participation (LFP) of fathers of children under age six is higher (95%) than that of men in general (79%), who work an average of 40.6 hours a week. Mothers of under six year olds (64%) have a similar LFP rate as women in general (68%), who work an average of 35.6 hours a week. About 82% of employed women

Table 6.1: Selected indicators related to parenting for the US, circa 2000 and circa 2012

Indicator	2000	2012
Crude marriage rate (per 1,000 population)	8.2	6.8 (2011)
Crude divorce rate	4.0	3.6 (2011)
Total fertility rate	2.6	1.9
Crude birth rate	14.4	12.6
Mothers' mean age at first birth	24.9	25.8
% non-marital births	33.2	40.7
	(Black: 68.5; White: 27.1)	(Black: 71.6; White: 35.9)
Births per 1,000 men	50.0	46.1
% of family households that are:		
Husband/wife	51.7	48.4 (2010)
Unmarried couple	5.2	6.6 (2010)
Husband/wife with children	23.5	20.2 (2010)
Mother only with children	7.2	7.2 (2010)
Father only with children	2.1	2.6 (2010)
% of children < 5 living with:		
Two parents	68.6	71.5 (< 6 years)
Father only	6.4	2.6 (< 6 years)
Mother only	19.8	22.9 (< 6 years)
% of married-couple families that are:		
Dual-earner families	59.8	54.1
Male-provider families	16.8	18.7
Labour force participation (LFP)		
LFP rate, men (age 15–64)	83.9	78.8
Fathers (15+) of kids < 18	NA	93.8 (2011)
Fathers of < 6 year olds	NA	95.1 (2011)
Men, % full-time	92.3	91.3
Men, % part-time	7.7	8.7
Men, mean number of hours/week	42.5	40.6 (2011)
LFP rate, women (15–64)	70.7	67.6
Mothers (15+) of kids < 18	72.9	70.9 (2011)
Mothers of < 6 year olds	65.3	64.2 (2011)
Women, % full-time	82.0	81.7
Women, % part-time	18.0	18.3
Women, mean number of hours/week	36.4	35.6 (2011)

Sources: CDC/NCHS National Vital Statistics System, available at: http://www.cdc.gov/nchs/nvss/marriage_divorce_tables.htm; Martin et al (2002, 2013); Vespa et al (2013); Laughlin (2013); BLS (2003, 2012, 2013); OECD (2014); Parker and Wang (2013); and Lofquist et al (2012).

older than age 15 worked full-time compared to 91% of men, which is unchanged since 2000. Only 9% of men and 18% of women work part-time. Together, these statistics show that the US is a dual-earner regime with high working hours.

Fathers and parental leave

As the US does not provide statutory paid family leave, workplaces decide whether to provide such benefits to their employees. According to Wallen (2001), benefits by 'family-friendly' employers can include the following, mainly for mothers: time flexibility (including job sharing) and telecommuting, financial assistance, employee services (childcare), formal family policies, and community programmes. Lovell and Helmuth (2009) reviewed a number of promising paid parental leave policies. Some state legislatures use insurance-type programmes like Temporary Disability Insurance (TDI) or Family Care Insurance (FCI), and some employers have implemented paid benefit plans that: (1) allow employees to combine vacation, sick, parental and family leave; (2) provide partially paid leave; or (3) increase paid disability leave for parents around the birth of a child. In addition, there are a number of employee-funded plans based on payroll deductions, matching funds or future leave, or sick leave donation plans. Several companies provide one to six weeks of paid job-guaranteed leave to new fathers and allow telecommuting, part-time scheduling and flexitime for new parents (Lovell and Helmuth, 2009). A recent study (Hara and Hegewisch, 2013) shows that, in 2012, only about 74% of *Working Mother* magazine's 'best' US companies provided any paid paternity leave, and those who did (53%) provided only one to two weeks.

American fathers have traditionally taken very little time off at the time of the birth of a child, mainly because this is not supported by policies and not encouraged by employers. Few men are entitled to any paternity leave, which is usually unpaid, and involves a week or less (Kaufman et al, 2010). Estimates show that the majority of fathers (89%) take some paid or unpaid leave, but this leave is very short: 64% took one week or less and 36% took two or more weeks (Nepomnyaschy and Waldfogel, 2007). Overall, 70% of new fathers took less than 10 days leave, 24% took between 10 and 60 days, and only 6% took more than 60 days leave (Klerman et al, 2013).

White men, higher-earning, higher-educated and fathers in their 30s are the most likely to take leave (Nepomnyaschy and Waldfogel, 2007), mainly because they have more access to paid leave than other groups of men. Harrington et al (2013) found that only about 20%

of professional fathers in their 2011 sample took off more than two weeks after the birth of their most recent child, and only 10% left their job for more than four weeks. This short initial leave time taken by fathers to bond with and care for the newborn reinforces the idea that mothers are the primary carers of infants.

It is reasonable to assume that fathers who spend more time with their newborns would be able to better bond with them, learn how to care for them and, thus, become more involved fathers in the long term. Indeed, several studies show that taking paternal leave, especially taking longer leave, is associated with higher, more sustained levels of father involvement (Pleck, 1993; Nepomnyaschy and Waldfogel, 2007; Tanaka and Waldfogel, 2007; Huerta et al, 2013). Specifically, fathers who took any paternity leave were more likely to routinely care for their infants. In addition, taking two or more weeks of leave increased fathers' involvement in daily direct caring activities, such as changing nappies, bathing and feeding nine months after birth, even when controlling for other characteristics (Nepomnyaschy and Waldfogel, 2007; Huerta et al, 2013). Huerta et al (2013) found that for children younger than one year, fathers who took leave were statistically significantly more likely to change nappies and help their infant get dressed at least once a day than those who did not take leave. For two to three year olds, the leave-taking fathers were more likely to read to their children.

Nevertheless, another study by Meteyer and Perry-Jenkins (2010) found that among working-class fathers, the average length of paternity leave taken was less than eight days, and that the length of the leave taken did not predict levels of father involvement with their one-year-old infants. Their measure of father involvement was relative: the proportion of 15 direct infant care tasks like feeding, changing nappies or bathing performed by fathers. The authors speculate that the effect of leave on father involvement may be more pronounced for higher-earning fathers.

Fathers and childcare

A substantial body of literature has documented that American working parents experience problems and high levels of stress related to finding reliable and quality day-care arrangements for their infants and preschool children during working hours (Wallen, 2001; Jacobs and Gerson, 2004). In 2010, 43% of children aged under three were in formal childcare or preschool and, on average, they attended about 31 hours per week in those formal arrangements (OECD, 2012). In 2011, 33% of under five year olds were in non-relative care for about

33 hours a week (Laughlin, 2013). Among those aged three to five, 67% were in preschool programmes.

Fathers provide a significant amount of childcare for young children as a primary, secondary or tertiary carer, which means that they are the sole or partial provider of childcare during or after the mothers' work hours or are responsible for shorter time periods as children are moved to other childcare arrangements. Unlike in the other countries covered in this book, the US does not provide easy access to affordable formal childcare, and, thus, parents are more often the childcare provider for preschool children. Based on data from the Current Population Report (CPR) and Survey of Income and Programme Participation (SIPP), in 2011, about 61% of American younger than five year olds were in some form of regular childcare arrangement. For 20% of them, their fathers were the primary carer. Thus, these children spent more time in father care than in any other arrangement (Laughlin, 2013). This percentage was even higher for married couples (23%), when the mother was employed part-time rather than full-time (28%), and when the mother worked a non–day shift (31%) (US Census Bureau, 2011). Another analysis estimates that for about 18% of all children younger than five, their fathers are a 'regular care arrangement', that is, they provide care at least once in a typical week when their mothers are at work or in school (Laughlin, 2013). Among fathers with employed wives, 21% were primary carers and 34% were a regular carer for their preschool children (Laughlin, 2013). In 2011, the most widely used regular care arrangements for preschool children of white employed mothers were fathers (31%) and grandparents (32%). African-American children with employed mothers were more likely to be cared for by their grandparents (31%) than their fathers (23%).

Recent Census data also show that there were about 189,000 'stay-at-home fathers' in 2012, who are defined as married fathers with children younger than age 15 who stayed at home for at least a year to take care of their children while their wives were employed. Another 87,000 fathers stayed at home for a year while their wives were not in the labour force. Among these 276,000 fathers, 180,000 (65%) cared for children younger than age six (US Census Bureau, 2012).

Research on father involvement

This section focuses on what is known about how much time American fathers spend with their children and what they do with and for their young children. The emphasis is on empirical studies that assess fathers' direct care activities with their children, usually called 'engagement'.

Studies reviewed here focus on positive affective and instrumental engagement, such as playing with, physically caring for and reading to the child under age five.

Time engaged with children

The amount of time fathers spend with their children is considered an indication of accessibility and availability. A review of available studies is difficult because relatively few studies specifically focus on children under age five, the time reported can be hours per day or per week, these hours can be based on self-reports or partner reports, and time or the percentage of time can refer to solo involvement or co-parenting. However, the general message of the available data is that mothers spend, on average, about two to three times as much time with their young children as fathers do. Data based on time-use surveys reveal that, in 2006, the percentage of time dedicated to care work (as primary or secondary activity) for American men aged 25–44 was 2% for childless men, 7% for fathers of one preschool child and 8% for fathers with two or more preschool children (OECD, 2012). While childless women also only spend about 2% of their time on care work, mothers spend 11% when they have one preschool child and 13% if they have two or more preschool children. According to the American Time Use Survey (ATUS) 2003–06, married full-time employed fathers aged 25–54 with at least one child younger than five spent about 1.3 hours in primary childcare on an average workday, compared to 1.5 hours on a weekend day (Allard and Janes, 2008). The amount of time fathers spend with their children decreases dramatically when the child is older than age six. The most recent ATUS data show that, in 2012, on a typical weekday, men spend an average of about 1.58 hours or 17% of their time with primary childcare for children, and 2.07 hours or 14% of their time on a weekend (BLS, 2012).

According to a recent research report (Pew Research Center, 2013), in 2011, fathers of children of all ages self-reported spending, on average, 7.3 hours per week with their children. While women reported spending about 30.2 hours per week performing solo childcare, fathers only report spending an average of 10.7 hours per week on solo childcare (Raley et al, 2012). This distribution of father care depends on mothers' employment status: fathers with stay-at-home partners care approximately eight hours per week for children, and those with employed partners provide care for 11–15 hours per week. In dual-earner families, fathers are more time-involved, but less so in absolute terms than in proportional terms: because employed mothers contribute less, fathers contribute proportionately more (Pleck and Masciadrelli, 2004). According to Harrington et al's (2013) study, professional fathers spent about 2.7 hours per 'typical working day' caring for their children and 77% of the fathers want to spend more time with their children on an average workday.

Various studies (Bianchi et al, 2006; Gray and Anderson, 2010) suggest that the amount of time that married fathers spend with their children has increased over the last few decades. This paternal care time occurs more on weekends than during the week and includes few of the caring tasks associated with mothers. The types of activities that fathers engage in with their young children are highly gendered in that fathers engage in affective playing and companionship activities rather than in routine instrumental care (Gray and Anderson, 2010; Yoshida, 2012).

Level of father engagement

Two recent reports published by the DHHS in 2012 and 2013 provide information on the direct care activities that fathers engage in with their young children based on data from the National Survey of Family Growth (NSFG) (2002, 2006–10). The first is by Martinez et al (2012, see also Martinez et al, 2006) and presents data collected in 2002 from a nationally representative sample of men aged 15–44 years. The second report is by Jones and Mosher (2013), who examined a nationally representative sample of 1,790 co-residential fathers (aged 15–44) of under five year olds and combined data for 2006 through 2010. In both data sets, fathers indicated which of the following direct interaction activities they engaged in with any of their children (no focal child specified) over the previous four weeks: (1) eating meals with or feeding the children; (2) bathing, changing nappies or dressing the children, or helping the children do so; (3) playing with the children; and (4) reading to the children (see Table 6.2). They also indicated whether they engaged in the activities 'not at all or less than once a week', 'about once a week', 'several times a week' or 'every day (at least once a day)'. In addition, the fathers rated their competency as a father on a scale of 'a very good job', 'a good job', 'an okay job', 'not a very good job' or 'a bad job'. Unfortunately, these latter data were not provided by the age of the child.

Not surprisingly, the analysis of the NSFG data finds that co-residential fathers generally report being more engaged in childcare activities with their preschool children than non-residential fathers. Unfortunately, some measures are not available (marital status in 2002) or directly comparable (age). The data for the various care activities are examined by fathers' marital status, age, education and race/ethnicity, and the focus is on the most involved fathers – those who engage in an activity every day.

Table 6.2: Percentage of co-residential fathers of children younger than age five who performed these activities every day (2002, left panel, and 2006–10, right panel)

Father characteristic	Feed/eat with 2002	Bathe, change nappy 2002	Play with 2002	Read to 2002	Feed/eat with 2006–10	Bathe, change nappy 2006–10	Play with 2006–10	Read to 2006–10
All	73.8	52.5	81.1	25.3	71.8	57.6	80.7	28.9
Age								
15–24	< 30: 71.9	< 30: 47.9	< 30: 79.8	< 30:	68.5	61.1	81.1	20.4
25–34	> 30: 74.9	> 30: 55.0	> 30: 81.8	21.3	71.6	59.1	82.0	27.2
35–44				> 30: 27.6	73.0	54.7	79.0	33.5
Marital status								
Married	NA	NA	NA	NA	72.6	57.3	81.6	30.8
Cohabiting					69.9	60.1	80.7	23.3
Neither					66.9	52.6	68.3	22.5
Education								
High school or less	70.3	41.6	75.8	19.5	70.3	53.6	79.7	24.3
Some college or more	78.6	65.4	87.1	32.0	73.3	60.5	81.4	33.3
Ethnicity/race								
Hispanic/ Latino	64.1	31.8	71.9	14.8	63.9	45.0	74.1	21.9
African-American	62.7	53.9	77.8	25.9	78.2	70.4	82.2	34.9
White	78.1	61.1	86.1	30.2	73.9	60.0	82.7	30.2

Sources: CDC/NCHS, NSFG, 2002 and 2006–10.

During 2006–10, 72% of the fathers fed or ate with their preschool children every day, compared to 74% in 2002. There is very little variation in terms of fathers' age, marital status or education for the two time periods. However, in 2006–10, African-American men were most likely to eat with their children every day (78%) when compared to white (75%) and Hispanic (64%) men. In terms of bathing, changing nappies or dressing young children, the data show that during 2006–10, 58% of fathers did so every day, compared to 53% in 2002. Interestingly, it is the youngest fathers and those with higher education who did so most often (61% and 65%, respectively) during 2006–10. Men of all backgrounds have become more involved in these activities on a daily basis between waves, albeit at different levels.

With respect to playing with their children, in both waves, 81% of fathers stated that they did so every day. This does not seem to vary much by age or education in either wave. However, men who were not married or cohabiting were less likely to play with their children every day (68%) than married (82%) or cohabiting men (81%). Fewer Hispanic men engaged in this activity every day (74%, 72%) than the other groups in both waves. Reading to children is the activity that fathers engaged in the least often during 2006–10 – only 29% every day. Older fathers (34%), those with more education (33%), married fathers (31%) and African-American fathers (35%) were more likely to read to their children on a daily basis during 2006–10. Disturbingly, during the 2006–10 wave, a full 24% of the youngest fathers, 29% of cohabiting fathers and 32% of Hispanic fathers stated that they never read to their children.

The data from 2006–10 on fathers' self-assessed competency as fathers are for those with children younger than age 18. They are revealing in that 44% consider themselves 'very good fathers' and another 44% feel that they are doing a 'good job'. Most confident in their abilities are the youngest fathers (52% 'very good'), those neither married nor cohabiting (52%) and African-American fathers (54%). The fact that 84% of Hispanic fathers think that they are doing a good or very good job while their involvement in the aforementioned activities is quite low seems to indicate that their own assessment is not based on the care activities measured here. Previous research shows that the economic provider role is very salient to the identity of immigrant Mexican and Hispanic fathers based on traditional gender roles and cultural values related to machismo (Taylor and Behnke, 2005; Tamis-LeMonda et al, 2008, 2009; Cabrera et al, 2013; Saracho, 2013). Even when controlling for background characteristics, it is found that Latino immigrant fathers' lower positive engagement with their infants is mediated by traditional gender attitudes (D'Angelo et al, 2012). Conversely, because the economic provider role of African-American fathers has been compromised due to a history of slavery and discrimination, these men may find non-economic aspects of fathering, such as caring activities, as more important to their identity as fathers. Historically, marriage prohibition and forced family separations have undermined the father role in the black community (Silverstein, 1996; Franklin, 1997). Research indicates that African-American men's parenting practices involve positive interactions with their children (Roopnarine and Hossain, 2013) and that they prioritise time with and care for children over providing money (Roy and Dyson, 2010). Overall, about 88% of American fathers consider themselves to be good or very good fathers.

It is argued here that fathers who engage in direct affective and instrumental care activities with their children on a daily basis can be considered active fathers. Overall, the data show that based on self-reported daily involvement in physical childcare, between 50% and 70% of American fathers are actively engaged with their young children. The consistently low level of father involvement in reading to their children is problematic because research shows the importance of father engagement in early literacy activities for child development (Palm, 2013). According to Palm (2013), there are several barriers that may prevent co-residential fathers from reading to their children: the pressures of long work days, insecurities based on their own school failures, a lack of experience and lower interest in reading children's books.

In specifically addressing infant care, Avenilla et al (2006) present detailed results on fathers' involvement with their nine-month-old infants from a nationally representative survey of 3,106 biological fathers in the Early Childhood Longitudinal Study (ECLS-B). The data show that co-residential fathers reported doing the following care activities once or more often a day in a typical week: 38% of fathers change their infants' nappies, 42% prepare a meal/bottle for their child, 45% feed the child, 47% bathe the child, 63% dress the child and 59% put the child to bed. Hence, it appears about half of fathers are highly engaged with their infants. This is very similar to what is found for father engagement in instrumental activities with the younger than five year olds. With respect to other care activities, the fathers did the following 'always' or 'often' (Avenilla et al, 2006): getting up at night (14% and 23%), soothing the child (18% and 59%), taking the child to the doctor (18% and 16%), staying home with a sick child (12% and 13%) and taking a child to and from childcare (14% and 13%). In terms of daily play activities, 96% of the fathers tickled the child, 64% played peek-a-boo, 27% took the child outside to play and 98% held the infant. However, fewer fathers did the following every day: 8% read books with their child, 11% told stories, 35% sang songs and 24% took the child with them on errands. Overall, based on daily physical infant care, about 40–60% of American fathers appear to be active fathers. However, fathers are generally less likely to perform activities that are inconvenient or time-involved and require fathers to be the sole carer or to reduce their time at the workplace.

Determinants of father engagement with young children

As women have increasingly entered the workforce, fathers are expected to also actively engage in parenting activities. In general, fathers' participation in childcare is affected by several factors: motivation to be involved with the child; skills and self-confidence in their ability to perform fathering tasks; social supports or stresses related to that performance; and institutional conditions. Various researchers have empirically tested and expanded the original model of father involvement in a number of ways (Nangle et al, 2003; Shoppe-Sullivan et al, 2004; Jacobs and Kelley, 2006). Research examining the factors affecting the father involvement of co-residing biological or social fathers of young children takes into account marital status, age, education and race/ethnicity.

Huerta et al (2013) examined the relationship between taking parental leave and father involvement in all the childcare tasks measured in the NSFG 2002–06 data. If fathers took two or more weeks leave, the odds of their everyday involvement in all activities when their children were around nine months old increased significantly. The odds were largest for changing nappies. It appears that taking leave increases fathers' engagement in tasks that they would not do without taking leave (Huerta et al, 2013).

Hofferth et al (2013) focused on the determinants of father involvement with co-residing children younger than age 13, as measured in self-reports and as reported in mothers' diary entries. The authors performed multivariate analyses based on nationally representative data for 1997 and 2003 (Child Development Supplement of the Panel Study of Income Dynamics [PSID-CDS]) that included 1,748 families. The indicators of father involvement were: (1) father reports of activities engaged in with the child in the last month; (2) time children spent with fathers who were caring, playing or teaching in terms of weekly time; (3) how often the father expressed love (warmth) for his child in the past month; (4) how often the father sets limits and rules for the child (parental control); and (5) fathering attitudes. For fathers of children younger than age 13, the results suggest that fathers have developed a more positive attitude towards fathering and have increased their instrumental parenting, such as caring activities, while reducing warmth and play activities. In addition, while single fathers were most involved with their children and had the most positive fathering attitudes, there was no major difference between biological fathers and stepfathers in terms of engagement or attitudes. Overall, the study showed not only that fathering attitudes directly affect father involvement, but also 'that fathering attitudes mediate the effect of family structure on father involvement with children' (Hofferth et al, 2013: 77). Importantly, it was shown that 'positive mental health, part-time work hours, and greater education are associated with greater motivation for involvement' among fathers (Hofferth et al, 2013: 79).

According to a number of studies (Hofferth, 2003; Goldscheider and Kaufman, 2006; Goldscheider and Sassler, 2006; Goldscheider et al, 2009; Hofferth and Goldscheider, 2010), the experience of disrupted family structures during childhood can be linked to adult fathering trajectories. Men who grew up in unstable families and those who experienced several parental transitions as a child were more likely to become biological fathers early, to become stepfathers and to become single fathers. It is likely that childhood family structure may be an important context for explaining both attitudes towards fatherhood and subsequent levels of father involvement. In addition, men's parenting behaviour is linked to their level of education and income, their gender attitudes, and the context of their current relationship. Yoshida (2012) used data from the NSFG to examine co-residing fathers' daily involvement in the physical care of children under five. The multivariate models revealed that daily involvement in routine care was more likely among fathers with more education and an employed partner, those who were raised by their biological father, and fathers who receive public assistance. Having older children reduced fathers' participation in traditional mothers' tasks.

Raley, Bianchi and Wang (2012) assessed the effects of mothers' employment characteristics on father involvement. They found that fathers perform more solo childcare when their partners are employed, their involvement with children increases when their partners work more hours in the labour market and they engage in more routine care activities and increase their share of care work vis-a-vis their partners when their partners contribute more to family income. This suggests that men's involvement in childcare responds to women's involvement in the labour market in terms of time and income. In addition, McGill's (2014) multivariate models show that work hours reduced father involvement and that 'new father attitudes' moderate the relationship between father involvement and employment. Fathers with the most non-traditional attitudes towards childcare were able to dedicate time to their children despite spending long hours at work. The author concludes that '"new fathers" may be more likely to sacrifice their own leisure time, for example, in order to maximize child time' (McGill, 2014: 1104).

Jacobs and Kelley (2006) examined the relationship of father involvement to fathers' motivation, skills and self-confidence, social support, and institutional issues in dual-earner families with preschool children. The multivariate analyses revealed that motivational variables do not affect scores on a paternal engagement scale (eg often or always bathing the child) or scores on a paternal accessibility scale (eg monitors playing or is available). However, fathers' beliefs about their role, their skills and self-confidence, and their efficacy in childcare significantly predicted scores on a 'paternal responsibility' scale (eg buys child's clothes or determines appropriate activities for the child). In addition, the authors found that motivational variables increased the percentage of time fathers serve as the primary carer. Both parents' number of hours worked also affected paternal responsibility and time as primary carer.

Research on father involvement and father well-being

Even though fatherhood is a critical stage in men's life course, surprisingly little research has been done of the effects of father involvement on fathers' own well-being: their physical and mental health; their identity and social relationships; their satisfaction with work–life balance; and their careers and income. Thus, Settersten and Cancel-Tirado (2010) refer to fatherhood as a 'hidden variable' in men's life course. Most work in this area focuses on the transition of becoming a father rather than the time between infancy and school age.

According to Eggebeen et al (2013), the consequences of fatherhood for the well-being of fathers include challenges related to major life-course transitions, to having to live up to a societal 'code of conduct' associated with being a father and to reshaping men's identities. Today, being a 'good father' includes not only being a good provider, but also being an active carer (Settersten and Cancel-Tirado, 2010). This clearly increases the pressures on fathers to reorganise life priorities and dedicate significant amounts of time to engaging with children. It has been argued that fatherhood marks an important stage in adult development that requires long-term continued adjustments in terms of relationships, work and family responsibilities, lifestyle (Palkovitz, 2002; Palkovitz and Palm, 2009), and identity (Rane and McBride, 2000). Conversely, research suggests that:

> fathers who resist adhering to the role expectations of fatherhood, fail to assume the identity of father, show less commitment to being a father, or are less involved with their

children are significantly less likely to change in response to the transition to fatherhood. (Eggebeen et al, 2013: 348)

The effects of 'settling down' on men's physical and mental health and well-being also vary by life stage, family structure, social class and race.

According to Garfield et al (2006), men's health is affected by three factors related to fatherhood: (1) the mere presence of children; (2) the strain that children put on the couple relationship; and (3) the indirect effect of the children's own health. The mere fact of having a child may increase the desire to lead a healthier lifestyle. Research suggests that new fathers may be more aware of, and consequently avoid, potentially risky behaviours, such as smoking, substance abuse and drinking (Stettersten and Cancel-Tirado, 2010), in an effort to be a responsible role model (Palkovitz, 2002). Through engagement with their children, fathers learn about their own values and emotions, as well as develop competencies in childcare that increase their self-confidence as fathers. At the same time, the general health of fathers of newborns can be impaired by relationship strain and sleep deprivation related to the pressures of the child's needs. Having a difficult child or a child with special challenges can also have negative health consequences for fathers (Gallagher and Mechanic, 1996).

A multivariate analysis of the Fragile Families and Child Wellbeing Study, which included 3,880 fathers, showed that higher levels of fathers' time engagement and responsibility in the first five years of their children's lives are not strongly related to men's physical and mental health (Carlson and Turner, 2010). However, the authors found that increased father involvement lowered work–family stress for co-resident fathers, and Schindler (2010) found that higher levels of father engagement are related to increased psychological well-being.

The social-psychological literature shows that the effect of becoming a father on fathers' well-being varies by marital status, age and race. Fatherhood does not affect married men's general psychological well-being in terms of self-esteem, self-efficacy and depression negatively, but this is not the case for unmarried men (Nomaguchi and Milke, 2003) or single fathers (Woo and Raley, 2005). One may speculate that concerns over social legitimacy and lack of access to a larger social support network involving a partner may increase stress levels for unmarried or single fathers. While Kohler et al (2005) find that stepfathers report lower levels of life satisfaction, this effect appears to be reduced over the time of the relationship (Umbertson et al, 2010) and with the advanced age of the father (Pudrovska, 2009). According to a number of studies, non-custodial fathers and divorced fathers have higher rates of depression, and African-American fathers are more likely to be depressed than white fathers (Bronte-Tinkew et al, 2007; Gross et al, 2008; Settersten and Cancel-Tirado, 2010).

Apart from effects on men's health and identity, having young children changes their ties to family and community, encouraging them to engage in more 'kin work' and civic engagement activities. According to Eggebeen et al (2013), fathers communicate and visit more with relatives than non-fathers and begin to engage in exchange relationships with extended family, most likely because of the connection through grandchildren. Fathers of preschool children are also active in educational organisations, organised sports activates, child-oriented service organisations and religious institutions (Eggebeen et al, 2013). Carlson and Turner's (2010) analysis also found that increased father involvement improved fathers' social integration.

Work-related behaviour

In terms of fathers' work-related behaviours, becoming a father is generally associated with spending more time at work in order to increase the family income (Bianchi et al, 2006; Eggebeen et al, 2013; Stettersen and Cancel-Tirado, 2010). While this pattern reinforces the salience of the male provider role, it is not consistent across marital status, race and social class. Married, white, professional men tend to be able to increase their income based on fatherhood more than other men (Hodges and Budig, 2010). However, there is no consensus on exactly how and why fatherhood affects the work hours and earnings of men (see the debate in Eggebeen et al, 2013). Yet, because time is a finite resource, increased time spent at work is inversely correlated with time spent in fathering activities. Importantly, the attitudes of the fathers themselves about the salience of male breadwinning may determine how they divide their time at work and at home. More traditional fathers may be more committed to spending time at work and more egalitarian fathers may reduce their work hours to spend more time with their children (Eggebeen and Knoester, 2001). Graves et al (2007) found that the parental role commitment of fathers had direct positive effects on their career satisfaction and performance.

Despite some inconsistencies in the literature, several patterns along the lines of marital status, race and social class are found in the relationship between fatherhood and the work-related behaviours of men. For example, married men, especially professional ones, appear more likely to plan for fatherhood and be able to maintain a high commitment to the workplace in order to secure higher earnings (Hodges and Budig, 2010). There is an earnings premium for fatherhood even when controlling for various work-related factors (Glauber, 2008), and white, married, professional men are most likely to benefit from a 'daddy bonus' at work (Hodges and Budig, 2010). Unmarried men and African-American men are more likely to experience unplanned, early fatherhood, which may lead to attempts to rapidly increase work hours and income upon the birth of a child (Eggebeen et al, 2013). Finally, co-residential fathers' contribution to care work and engagement activities with young children may be curtailed by increased time spent at work (Eggebeen and Knoester, 2001).

The increased incidence of dual-earner couples is correlated with societal expectations of fathers to be both good providers and carers for children. This resulted in a change in fathering attitudes and perceptions of work–family conflict. For example, between 2009 and 2011, Harrington, Van Deusen and Fraone (2013) interviewed or surveyed almost 2,000 fathers of young children who were employed mainly in white-collar professional or managerial positions. Older fathers (older than age 40) were somewhat more likely to see their fathering responsibilities in terms of being traditional breadwinners than younger fathers. The authors concluded that unlike their fathers' generation, fathers today consider fatherhood neither solely nor even primarily as being about their role as economic providers for their children.

Work–family conflict is also becoming increasingly important to fathers (Winslow, 2005). The 'new male mystique' (Aumann et al, 2011: 5) refers to the phenomenon that 'men are experiencing what women experienced when they first entered the workforce in record numbers – the pressure to "do it all in order to have it all". In general, working fathers experience more work–life conflict now than they did 30 years ago: 34% reported conflict in 1977 compared to 49% in 2008 (Galinsky et al, 2008). In particular, about 60% of men in dual-earner couples reported increasing conflict because both parents have to deal with the challenges of balancing work and life. A meta-analysis by Byron (2005) confirms that working mothers and fathers experience work–family conflict almost to the same degree. However, reducing the strain of work–family conflict in the context of limited access to paid leave and unequal wages by gender often leads to mothers staying at home with the children rather than fathers (Bianchi et al, 2006). An astonishingly high 53% of the professional fathers surveyed in 2009 indicated that they would be comfortable with being an at-home father if their spouse's earnings would allow for it (Harrington et al, 2011). The young fathers in the study reported that performance expectations upon return to their job after paternity leave remained the same and that fatherhood was considered to be a positive status at work. Yet, none of them reduced their working hours to accommodate increased family demands. In fact, the majority thought that their employer would not support such requests. This indicates that workplaces do not recognise fatherhood as the major life transition that is assigned to motherhood in terms of potential changes in time commitments to work and family. The structure of workplaces still assumes that men are 'unencumbered' workers and that when they become fathers, it is the responsibility of the mother to take leave. Another indicator of father involvement is the take-up of flexitime, and in Harrington et al's studies (2011, 2013) the majority of fathers reported using formal or informal flexitime or sometimes working from home.

Fatherhood programmes

In order to encourage fathers to become more actively involved with their children, a number of direct-service fatherhood programmes have been created in the US (Curran, 2003; Bronte-Tinkew et al, 2006). Fathering initiatives can be defined as programmes 'that involve specific efforts, ideologies, and activities to shape men's parenting' (Marsiglio and Roy, 2012: 26). Most programmes include: parenting, relationship and responsible decision-making education; mentoring, conflict resolution and mediation services; peer support; child-rearing tips; and job training (Solomon-Fears, 2013). They consist of voluntary individual or couple programmes aiming to impart knowledge about childcare, building healthy relationships and increasing effective co-parenting skills. As such, they can encourage the personal commitment of fathers to their young children as economic providers through paying child support and/or as carers and teachers in terms of active engagement and nurturing behaviour. Most fatherhood initiatives focus on disadvantaged fathers or those who are considered negligent in some way, and mainly encourage responsible economic behaviour. However, there has been a recent shift from marriage promotion and child support payments to programmes helping fathers to get more education and jobs so that they can become more effective and involved fathers (Coltrane and Behnke, 2013).

Studies examining the effectiveness of federal initiatives in promoting improved fathering behaviours have mixed results (Curran, 2003; Avellar et al, 2011; Marsiglio and Roy, 2012). A number of programmes face problems at the stage of enrolling fathers and, later, at keeping them enrolled (Curran, 2003; Holmes et al, 2013). Some evidence suggests that programmes specifically tailored to the needs of particular fathers, those that involve fathers at or before the birth of the child, and those that involve both parents are most effective (Curran, 2003; Holmes et al, 2013). Avellar et al (2011) reviewed and rated evaluations of 63 fatherhood programmes that target low-income fathers. According to the authors, the majority of these programmes focus on improving fathers' training and job skills, income potential for child support payments, and child visitation, or were designed for incarcerated or immigrant fathers. Responsible fatherhood was usually measured in terms of fathers' economic provider role, that is, self-sufficiency (employment status, earnings or wages, hours worked, financial literacy, educational attainment) or fathers' financial support of children (paternity establishment, child support, compliance with court orders).

Of those programmes intending to explicitly address fathers as carers of young children and to increase fathers' active engagement with their children, several had positive effects on fathers, as measured by father involvement (frequency of contact with children, custodial status, residence with children, father–child interaction), parenting skills (treatment, cognitive stimulation, warmth, discipline, monitoring, and knowledge of developmental milestones) and fathers' well-being (substance use, physical health, mental health). The Early Head Start fatherhood programme appears to be successful in increasing fathers' complex interactions during play with their toddlers. In terms of infants, the Information and Insights about Infants programme increased the level of interaction and knowledge about infant care in the longer term and the Minnesota Early Learning Design programme moderately increased the engagement of new fathers with their infants. Dads in the Mix is an extension of the Parents as Teachers (PAT) programme that encourages more father involvement and improves fathers' nurturing and parenting skills. The Supporting Family Involvement (SFI) Preventive Intervention component for couples of young children reduces the parenting stress levels of fathers and increases father involvement (Cowan et al, 2009). Another couples-based programme, the Fathers, Relationships, and Marriage Education Study (FRAME), was found to increase fathers' time involvement, encouragement of cognitive skills and emotional warmth for their children (Holmes et al, 2013). The 24/7 Dad programme has a positive effect on fathers' attitudes about parenting knowledge and skills and the Caring Equation programme improves father–child interaction significantly.

The US fatherhood regime

Based on the information presented in this chapter, the cultural and policy context relating to masculinities and fatherhood-related demographic trends complicates the clear placement of the US into a particular 'fatherhood regime'. The increasing diversity of fathers also confounds the identification of 'typical fathers'. Differentiating 'old fathers' (traditional provider, less involved) versus 'new fathers' (less traditional and more involved), and 'good fathers' (warm and involved) versus 'bad fathers' (absent and deadbeats), American fathers have been classified in terms of how 'hands-on', nurturing, responsible and actively involved in the care of their children they are. Marks and Palkovitz (2004) even include men who are 'uninterested' in being fathers or are absent fathers as 'paternity-free' men in their typology because their ranks are increasing.

Kaufman (2013: 1–2) aptly summarises the situation for American fathers as follows:

> while expectations for father involvement have risen, the societal supports to make greater involvement possible have not kept pace. The workplace still sees men as men and not as fathers.… Fathers find themselves scrambling to take time off as their options for family leave are limited.… They do this in a variety of ways, some extreme (changing jobs) and some more tame (cutting back hours, working from home, using flex time).

Based on the evidence presented in this chapter, only relatively few American men can be considered 'superdads' (Kaufman, 2013) or even 'working fathers' (Ranson, 2012). Very few fathers significantly reduce their working hours, are stay-at-home fathers or work part-time so that they can equally share in raising their children. In terms of Holter's (2007) 'new man' versus 'new circumstances' model, most US fathers fall into the 'new circumstances' category because increased cultural expectations lead them to fit the new situation of being fathers into their lives as workers. They may take a week off at the child's birth, use flexible working hours at work when available and participate in some of the daily direct care activities. They will not (and often cannot for financial reasons) fundamentally rearrange their work lives (reduce working hours or stay at home extensively) based on aspirations that they are equally as responsible for their children as the mother. However, because American men are highly commodified, for most fathers, the question arises as to whether they can afford to be a superdad even if they wanted to.

The contextual data show that the US is a liberal welfare state with poorly developed family policy and a dual-earner gender regime. The US features high levels of full-time employment for both genders, disregarding parental status. Non-relative childcare is provided mainly through the private sector and is rather costly. This may reinforce the male provider role by encouraging women, who earn lower incomes, to reduce their employment hours when they become parents. Although fathers are relatively often the primary carer when mothers work, data on fathers' time spent with young children and details on the activities that they engage in show a continued gender division of labour. Legally, fathers have increased obligations through paternity establishment and child custody payments, but they have also gained rights in custody fights because of joint-parenting values. However, neither they nor their partners are entitled to paid parental leave and leave coverage is often sketchy at best. So, despite cultural preferences for increased father involvement, policies are not in place to support this idea, and welfare policies focusing on male provider roles are often counterproductive.

Conclusion and recommendations for policy

This chapter on American father involvement with young children has shown that a mismatch exists between the new cultural expectation requiring fathers to be both providers and carers of children and: (1) the lack of policy support and resources for fathers to live up to those expectations; and (2) the level of father engagement activities in daily practice. The weak institutional support framework impedes fathers' choices regarding what type of father they can be and is at odds with their capacity to act on the increased pressures related to dominant fatherhood values in their daily fathering practice. Overall, Silverstein's (1996) observation of a 'chilly climate' for fathers in the US still holds almost 20 years later. Consequently, American fathers remain relatively peripheral as carers and Marsiglio and Roy's (2012) 'nurturant fathering' is more of a myth than a reality.

Hence, Settersten and Cancel-Tirado (2010: 96) pose the interesting question of whether being a 'good father' is increasingly becoming a privilege in the US:

> The kind of father who is held out as an ideal – married, co-resident, actively involved in the care of children, but

also in full-time stable work with good pay and benefits – is increasingly rare. This simple fact should change the future of family research and especially family policy, for it shatters the very foundation on which it is based.

The authors suggest that social institutions and policies should be rethought so that marriage is not privileged but that any positive relationship with co-parents and children is supported via paid leave for fathers (and mothers) and affordable, quality childcare. In addition, a restructuring of the workplace so that fathers and their paternal responsibilities become more visible is necessary (Burnett et al, 2013). Hence, workplaces should offer flexibility and support for fathers' involvement with their children and encourage fathers to take their leave.

Gaps in research

While there are numerous large-scale longitudinal national surveys that include information on father involvement, such as the Early Head Start Fatherhood Study, the ECLS and Fragile Families, more consistent measures and comparable data are needed. Consistent data for children of every age should be available so that studies can specifically examine fathers' activities in the early years. This is also important for cross-national comparisons of the full range of fathering practices and attitudes in different family constellations and cultures. Sophisticated multivariate analyses can help disentangle some of the inconsistent results found in the literature. In particular, the exact mechanics of the relationship between maternal employment and father involvement found by Raley, Bianchi and Wang (2012) warrant further investigation.

There is also a need for more qualitative research using direct observations of father engagement in different contexts. Of particular relevance are culturally sensitive studies that show comparisons of the activities that co-residential and non-custodial fathers, single fathers, gay fathers, minority ethnic fathers, younger fathers and older fathers, and fathers of different social classes engage in with their children. This would include assessments of the quantity and quality of time spent with children. In addition, an examination of how to engage fathers more in early literacy activities is needed. The context and nature of the interactions with the children, the dynamics of co-parenting, and the relationship between partners in families should be investigated more directly.

Eggebeen et al (2013) point to a variety of gaps in the literature regarding research on the consequences of fatherhood over men's life course, particularly for older first-time fathers and fathers in mid-life. Further research needs to be done on minority racial and ethnic fathers, as well as immigrant fathers, in terms of the ways in which they engage with their children and how this activity is embedded in the cultural expectations within those communities. We also need to know more about how being a father affects diverse sets of men, particularly those who are not heterosexual, white professionals. Fathers outside of the mainstream, such as gay men and unemployed men, or those with various minority ethnic or racial backgrounds, face particular challenges in living up to the new fatherhood expectations.

Promising initiatives and suggestions for change

There are a number of promising interventions focusing on making fatherhood a positive experience for men. According to Bronte-Tinkew et al (2009), fathering programmes should have the following features in order to be successful: (1) culturally appropriate teaching methods and materials designed for fathers as individuals; (2) well-trained teachers and facilitators who believe in the programme and engage in one-on-one relationships with fathers; (3) high staff–participant ratios; (4) clear programme goals and a consistent curriculum; and (5) incentives to engage fathers.

Fathering programmes must also start at or before the birth of a child so that all fathers, not only low-income fathers, can develop skills. Programmes should be tailored to the needs of specific groups – teen fathers, immigrant fathers and others – and should be sensitive to the different circumstances in which fathers deal with their children (Holmes et al, 2013). Apparently, programmes that involve both parents and address co-parenting skills are more effective than those involving fathers only (Cowan et al, 2009; Holmes et al, 2013). Cowan and colleagues (2009) found greater improvements in parenting skills when couples participated in programmes together. Holmes and colleagues (2013) also make a convincing case for integrated and collaborative service delivery and policy interventions involving parenting education, relationship education and father involvement. This includes a rethinking of the location and the 'father-friendliness' design of the spaces in which fatherhood programme services are provided (Holmes et al, 2013). Holmes et al (2013: 439) argue that 'if intervention studies can demonstrate that increased father involvement is followed by increased child, father, and/or mother well-being, scholars can more persuasively argue for a causal link between father involvement and healthy development'. However, in order to have a major effect on fathers, programmes cannot merely target individual fathers' behaviour, but must deal with the structural and economic conditions that could allow more active father involvement. It is promising that there are increasing debates about the importance of fatherhood among scholars and practitioners in the media and at conferences, such as the 92Y parenting conference 'Why Fathers Matter: Creating Successful Parenting Partnerships' on 25 January 2015.[3] In addition, inspired by a White House Summit on Working Families in 2014 and starting in January 2015, President Obama has put paid family leave firmly on the US policy agenda. Policymakers, practitioners and the American public must understand the barriers to effective parenting and their relationship to the well-being of families and society in general.

In general, it is hoped that US workplaces will stop treating employed fathers as 'ghosts in the organisational machine' (Burnett et al, 2013). This means that American organisational culture needs to accommodate the family responsibilities of working parents, disregarding gender. Specific suggested policy changes in the US include that every parent should have access to paid parental leave. The 'first thousand days' in children's lives are of key importance to their own well-being, as well as to the well-being of their parents:

> Countries with healthier populations structure this formative period by making it easier for parents to parent. In practical terms, this means that in modern societies where most people work outside the home, providing paid parental leave is the single most effective social intervention that can be undertaken for improving health. (Bezruchka, 2014:194)

Notes

[1] See: http://www.childtrends.org/wp-content/uploads/2012/11/75_appendix1.pdf

[2] See: http://www.childtrends.org/wp-content/uploads/2012/11/75_appendix1.pdf

[3] See: http://www.92y.org/Parenting-Center/Resources/Parenting-Conference.aspx

References

Allard, M.D. and Janes, M. (2008) 'Time use of working parents: a visual essay', Bureau of Labor Statistics, *Monthly Labor Review*, June. Available at: http://www.bls.gov/opub/mlr/2008/06/art1full.pdf

Aumann, K., Galinsky, E. and Matos, K. (2011) *The new male mystique. National study of the changing workforce*, New York, NY: Families and Work Institute.

Avellar, S., Dion, M.R., Clarkwest, A., Zaveri, H., Asheer, S., Borradaile, K., Hague Angus, M., Novak, T., Redline, J. and Zukiewic, M. (2011) *Catalogue of research: programmes for low-income fathers*, OPRE Report 2011–20, June, Washington, DC: Office of Planning, Research, and Evaluation, Administration for Children and Families, US Department of Health and Human Services. Available at: http://www.ncdsv.org/images/OPRE-MPR_Catalog-Research-Programs-For-Low-Income-Fathers_6-2011.pdf

Avenilla, F., Rosenthal, E. and Tice, P. (2006) 'Fathers of U.S. children born in 2001: findings from the Early Childhood Longitudinal Study, birth cohort (ECLS-B)', Washington, DC: National Center for Education Statistics. Available at: http://www.researchconnections.org/childcare/resources/10013/pdf

Bezruchka, S. (2014) 'Inequality kills', in D.C. Johnston (ed) *Divided: the perils of our growing inequality*, New York, NY: The New Press, pp 190–9.

Bianchi, S.M., Robinson, J.P. and Milkie, M.A. (2006) *Changing rhythms of American family life*, New York, NY: Russell Sage Foundation.

BLS (Bureau of Labor Statistics) (2003) 'American time use survey 2003', Table A-1. Available at: http://www.bls.gov/tus/tables/a1_2003.pdf

BLS (2012) 'American time use survey 2012', Table A-2. Available at: http://www.bls.gov/tus/tables/a2_2012.pdf

BLS (2013) 'Women in the labor force: a databook', *BLS Reports*, 1040, February. Available at: http://www.bls.gov/cps/wlf-databook-2012.pdf

Bogenschneider, K. and Corbett, T.J. (2010) 'Family policy: becoming a field of inquiry and subfield of social policy', *Journal of Marriage & Family*, 72: 783–803.

Bronte-Tinkew, J., Bowie, L. and Moore, K. (2006) 'Fathers and public policy', in N. Cabrera, H.E. Fitzgerald and J.D. Shannon (eds) *Fatherhood: theory, research and practice: proceedings of the national fatherhood forum*, Hillsdale, NJ: Lawrence Erlbaum Press. Available at: http://www.childtrends.org/wp-content/uploads/2006/03/2006-28FathersandPublicPolicy.pdf

Bronte-Tinkew, J., Moore, K.A., Mathews, G. and Carrano, J. (2007) 'Symptoms of major depression in a sample of fathers of infants: sociodemographic correlates and links to father involvement', *Journal of Family Issues*, 28: 61–99.

Bronte-Tinkew, J., Horowitz, A. and Metz, A. (2009) 'What works in fatherhood programmes? Ten lessons from evidenced-based practice'. Available at: http://www.childtrends.org/?publications=what-works-in-fatherhood-programmes-ten-lessons-from-evidenced-based-practice#sthash.VfTJeWzP.dpuf

Burnett, S.B., Gatrell, C.J., Cooper, C.L. and Sparrow, P. (2013) 'Fathers at work: a ghost in the organizational machine', *Gender, Work & Organization*, 20(6): 632–46.

Byron, K. (2005) 'A meta-analytic review of work–family conflict and its antecedents', *Journal of Vocational Behaviour*, 58: 348–65.

Cabrera, N.J. (2010) 'Father involvement and public policies', in M.E. Lamb (ed) *The role of the father in child development* (5th edn), Hobokern, NJ: John Wiley, pp 517–50.

Cabrera, N.J., Ryan, R., Shannon, J.D., Brooks-Gunn, J., Vogel, C. and Raikes, H. (2004) 'Fathers in the Early Head Start National Research and Evaluation Study: how are they involved with their children?', *Fathering: A Journal of Theory, Research, & Practice about Men as Fathers*, 2: 5–30.

Cabrera, N.J., Aldoney, D. and Tamis-LeMonda, C.S. (2013) 'Latino fathers', in N.J. Cabrera and C.S. Tamis-LeMonda (eds) *Handbook of father involvement. Multidisciplinary perspectives* (2nd edn), New York, NY: Routledge, pp 244–60.

California Work and Family Coalition and Next Generation (2014) 'Paid family leave CA'. Available at: http://paidfamilyleave.org/

Carlson, M.J. and Turner, K.J. (2010) 'Fathers' involvement and fathers' well-being over children's first five years', Working Paper. Available at: http://crcw.princeton.edu/workingpapers/WP10-10-FF.pdf

Coltrane, S. and Behnke, A. (2013) 'Fatherhood and family policies', in N.J. Cabrera and C.S. Tamis-LeMonda (eds) *Handbook of father involvement. Multidisciplinary perspectives* (2nd edn), New York, NY: Routledge, pp 419–37.

Cowan, P.A., Cowan, C.P., Pruett, M.K., Pruett, K.D. and Wong, J. (2009) 'Promoting fathers' engagement with children: preventive interventions for low-income families', *Journal of Marriage & Family*, 71: 663–79.

Curran, L. (2003) 'Social work and fathers: child support and fathering programmes', *Social Work*, 48: 219–27.

Curran, L. and Abrams, L.S. (2000) 'Making men into dads. Fatherhood, the state, and welfare reform', *Gender & Society*, 14: 662–78.

D'Angelo, A.V., Palacios, N.A. and Chase-Lansdale, P.L. (2012) 'Latino immigrant differences in father involvement with infants', *Fathering: A Journal of Theory, Research, & Practice about Men as Fathers*, 10: 178–212.

Doherty, W.J., Kouneski, E.F. and Erickson, M.F. (1998) 'Responsible fathering: an overview and conceptual framework', *Journal of Marriage & Family*, 60: 277–92.

Edin, K. and Kefalas, M. (2005) *Promises I can keep. Why poor women put motherhood before marriage*, Berkeley, CA: University of California Press.

Eggebeen, D.J. and Knoester, C. (2001) 'Does fatherhood matter for men?', *Journal of Marriage & Family*, 63: 381–93.

Eggebeen, D.J., Knoester, C. and McDaniel, B. (2013) 'The implications of fatherhood for men', in N.J. Cabrera and C.S. Tamis-LeMonda (eds) *Handbook of father involvement. Multidisciplinary perspectives* (2nd edn), New York, NY: Routledge, pp 338–57.

Esping-Andersen, G. (1990) *The three worlds of welfare capitalism*, Princeton, NJ: Princeton University Press.

Franklin, D.L. (1997) *Enduring inequality: the structural transformation of the African-American family*, New York, NY: Oxford Press.

Galinsky, E., Bond, J.T., Sakai, K., Kim, S.S. and Giuntoli, N. (2008) '2008 national study of employers', Families and Work Institute. Available at: http://familiesandwork.org/site/research/reports/2008nse.pdf

Gallagher, S.K. and Mechanic, D. (1996) 'Living with the mentally ill: effects on the health and functioning of household members', *Social Science & Medicine*, 42: 1691–701.

Garfield, C.F., Clark-Kauffman, E. and Davis, M.M. (2006) 'Fatherhood as a component of men's health', *JAMA*, 296: 2365–8.

Geva, D. (2011) 'Not just maternalism: marriage and fatherhood in American welfare policy', *Social Politics*, 18: 24–51.

Glauber, R. (2008) 'Race and gender in families and at work: the fatherhood premium', *Gender & Society*, 22: 8–30.

Goldscheider, F. and Kaufman, G. (2006) 'Willingness to stepparent: attitudes towards partners who already have children', *Journal of Family Issues*, 27: 1415–36.

Goldscheider, F. and Sassler, S. (2006) 'Creating stepfamilies: integrating children into the study of union formation', *Journal of Marriage & Family*, 68: 275–91.

Goldscheider, F., Kaufman, G. and Sassler, S. (2009) 'Navigating the "new" marriage market: how attitudes towards partner characteristics shape union formation', *Journal of Family Issues*, 30: 719–37.

Graves, L.M., Ohlott, P.J. and Ruderman, M.N. (2007) 'Commitment to family roles: effects on managers' attitudes and performance', *Journal of Applied Psychology*, 92: 44–56.

Gray, P.B. and Anderson, K.G. (2010) *Fatherhood: evolution and human paternal behaviour*, Cambridge, MA: Harvard University Press.

Gross, H.F., Shaw, D.S., Dishion, T.J., Moilanen, K.L. and Wilson, M.N. (2008) 'Reciprocal models of child behaviour and depressive symptoms in mothers and fathers in a sample of children at risk for early conduct problems', *Journal of Family Psychology*, 22: 742–51.

Guerin, L. (no date) 'Paid family leave in California, New Jersey, Washington, and the District of Columbia', *NOLO Law for all*. Available at: http://www.nolo.com/legal-encyclopedia/paid-family-leave-states-29854.html

Hara, Y. and Hegewisch, A. (2013) 'Update May 2013. Maternity, paternity, and adoption leave in the United States', *IWPR #A143*, Washington, DC: Institute for Women's Policy Research.

Harrington, B., Van Deusen, F. and Humberd, B. (2011) *The new dad: caring, committed and conflicted*, Boston, MA: Boston College Center for Work & Family.

Harrington, B., Van Deusen, F. and Fraone, J.S. (2013) *The new dad: a work (and life) in progress*, Boston, MA: Boston College Center for Work & Family.

Hodges, M.J. and Budig, M.J. (2010) 'Who gets the daddy bonus?', *Gender & Society*, 24: 717–45.

Hofferth, S.L. (2003) 'Race/ethnic differences in father involvement in two-parent families: culture, context, or economy?', *Journal of Family Issues*, 24: 185–216.

Hofferth, S.L. and Goldscheider, F. (2010) 'Family structure and the transition to parenthood', *Demography*, 47: 415–37.

Hofferth, S.L., Pleck, J.H., Goldscheider, F., Curtin, S. and Hrpczynski, K. (2013) 'Family structure and men's motivation for parenthood in the United States', in N.J. Cabrera and C.S. Tamis-LeMonda (eds) *Handbook of father involvement. Multidisciplinary perspectives* (2nd edn), New York, NY: Routledge, pp 57–80.

Holmes, E.K., Cowan, P.A., Cowan, C.P. and Hawkins, A.J. (2013) 'Marriage, fatherhood, and parenting programming', in N.J. Cabrera and C.S. Tamis-LeMonda (eds) *Handbook of father involvement. Multidisciplinary perspectives* (2nd edn), New York, NY: Routledge, pp 438–54.

Holter, Ø.G. (2007) 'Men's work and family reconciliation in Europe', *Men & Masculinities*, 9(4): 425–56.

Huerta, M.C., Adema, W., Baxter, J., Han, W.-J., Lausten, M., Lee, R. and Waldfogel, J. (2013) 'Fathers' leave, fathers' involvement and child development: are they related? Evidence from four OECD countries', OECD Social, Employment and Migration Working Papers No 140.

Jacobs, J.A. and Gerson, K. (2004) *The time divide*, Boston, MA: Harvard University Press.

Jacobs, J.N. and Kelley, M. (2006) 'Predictors of paternal involvement in childcare in dual-earner families with young children', *Fathering: A Journal of Theory, Research, & Practice about Men as Fathers*, 4: 23–47.

Jones, J. and Mosher, W.D. (2013) 'Fathers' involvement with their children: United States, 2006–2010', National Health Statistic Reports, 71, US Department of Health and Human Services. Available at: http://www.cdc.gov/nchs/data/nhsr/nhsr071.pdf

Kaufman, G. (2013) *Superdads. How fathers balance work and family in the 21st century*, New York, NY: NYU Press.

Kaufman, G., Lyonett, G. and Crompton, R. (2010) 'Post-birth employment leave among fathers in Britain and United States', *Fathering: A Journal of Theory, Research, & Practice about Men as Fathers*, 8: 321–40.

Klerman, J.A., Daley, K. and Posniak, A. (2013) *Family and medical leave in 2012: technical report*, Washington, DC: US Department of Labor. Available at: http://www.dol.gov/asp/evaluation/fmla/FMLATechnicalReport.pdf

Kohler, H.P., Behrman, J.R. and Skytthe, A. (2005) 'Partner + children = happiness? The effects of partnership and fertility on well-being', *Population & Development Review*, 31: 407–45.

Laughlin, L. (2013) *Who's minding the kids? Child care arrangements: spring 2011*, Current Population Reports, Washington, DC: US Census Bureau, pp 70–135. Available at: http://www.census.gov/prod/2013pubs/p70-135.pdf

Lofquist, D., Lugaila, T., O'Connell, M. and Feliz, S. (2012) *Households and families: 2010*, 2010 Census Briefs, April, Washington, DC: US Census Bureau. Available at: http://www.census.gov/prod/cen2010/briefs/c2010br-14.pdf

Lovell, V. and Helmuth, S.A. (2009) 'Parents as child care providers: a menu of parental leave models', Institute for Women's Policy Research, IWPR Briefing Paper #A136, May.

Marks, L. and Parkovitz, R. (2004) 'American fatherhood types: the good, the bad, and the uninterested', *Fathering: A Journal of Theory, Research, & Practice about Men as Fathers*, 2: 113–29.

Marsiglio, W. and Roy, K. (2012) *Nurturing dads: social initiatives for contemporary fatherhood*, New York, NY: Russell Sage.

Martin, J.A., Hamilton, B.E., Ventura, S.J., Menacker, F. and Park, M.M. (2002) *Births: final data for 2000*, National Vital Statistics Reports, 50(5), Hyattsville, MD: National Center for Health Statistics. Available at: http://www.cdc.gov/nchs/data/nvsr/nvsr50/nvsr50_05.pdf

Martin, J.A., Hamilton, B.E., Osterman, M.J.K., Curtin, S.C. and Mathews, T.J. (2013) *Births: final data for 2012*, National Vital Statistics Report, 62(9), Hyattsville, MD: National Center for Health Statistics. Available at: http://www.cdc.gov/nchs/data/nvsr/nvsr62/nvsr62_09.pdf

Martinez, G.M., Chandra, A., Abma, J.C., Jones, C. and Mosher, W.D. (2006) 'Fertility, contraception, and fatherhood: data on men and women from cycle 6 (2002) of the National Survey of Family Growth: National Center for Health Statistics', *Vital Health Statistics*, 23(26). Available at: http://www.cdc.gov/nchs/data/series/sr_23/sr23_026.pdf

Martinez, G., Daniels, K. and Chandra, A. (2012) *Fertility of men and women aged 15–44 in the United States: National Survey of Family Growth, 2006–2010*, National Health Statistics Reports, 51, Hyattsville, MD: National Center for Health Statistics.

McFadden, K.E. and Tamis-LeMonda, C.S. (2013) 'Fathers in the US', in D.W. Shwalb, B.J. Shwalb and M.E. Lamb (eds) *Fathers in cultural context*, New York, NY: Routledge, pp 250–76.

McGill, B.S. (2014) 'Navigating new norms of involved fatherhood: employment, fathering attitudes, and father involvement', *Journal of Family Issues*, 35: 1089–106.

Meteyer, K. and Perry-Jenkins, M. (2010) 'Father involvement among working-class, dual earner couples', *Fathering: A Journal of Theory, Research, & Practice about Men as Fathers*, 8: 379–403.

Nangle, S.M., Kelley, M.L., Fals-Stewart, W. and Levant, R.L. (2003) 'Work and family variables as related to paternal engagement, responsibility, and accessibility in dual-earner couples with young children', *Fathering: A Journal of Theory, Research, & Practice about Men as Fathers*, 1: 71–90.

Nepomnyaschy, L. and Waldfogel, J. (2007) 'Paternity leave and fathers' involvement with their young children. Evidence from the American ECLS-B', *Community, Work & Family*, 10: 427–53.

Nomaguchi, K.M. and Milke, M.A. (2003) 'Costs and rewards of children: the effects of becoming a parent on adults' lives', *Journal of Marriage & Family*, 65: 356–74.

OECD (Organisation for Economic Co-operation and Development) (2012) *OECD family database*, Paris: OECD. Available at: http://www.oecd.org/els/family/database.htm

OECD (2014) *OECD StatsExtracts*. Available at: http://stats.oecd.org/

Orloff, A.S. and Monson, R.A. (2002) 'Citizens, workers or fathers? Men in the history of US social policy', in B. Hodson (ed) *Making men into fathers. Men, masculinities and the social politics of fatherhood*, Cambridge: Cambridge University Press, pp 61–91.

Palkovitz, R. (2002) *Involved fathering and men's adult development: provisional balances*, Mahwah, NJ: Erlbaum.

Palkovitz, R. and Palm, G. (2009) 'Transitions within fathering', *Fathering: A Journal of Theory, Research, & Practice about Men as Fathers*, 7: 3–22.

Palm, G. (2013) 'Fathers and early literacy', in J. Pattnaik (ed) *Father involvement in young children's lives. A global analysis*, Dordrecht: Springer, pp 13–29.

Parker, K. and Wang, W. (2013) 'Modern parenthood roles of moms and dads converge as they balance work and family', Pew Research Center Social and Demographic Trends, March 14, Washington, DC. Available at: http://www.pewsocialtrends.org/2013/03/14/modern-parenthood-roles-of-moms-and-dads-converge-as-they-balance-work-and-family/

Pew Research Center (2013) '5 facts about fathers'. Available at: http://www.pewresearch.org/fact-tank/2013/06/11/5-facts-about-fathers/

Pleck, J. (1993) 'Are "family supportive" employment policies relevant to men?', in J.C. Hood (ed) *Men, work and family*, Newbury Park, CA: Sage, pp 217–37.

Pleck, J.H. and Masciadrelli, B.P. (2004) 'Paternal involvement by US residential fathers: levels, sources, and consequences', in M.E. Lamb (ed) *The role of the father in child development* (4th edn), New York, NY: Wiley, pp 222–71.

Pudrovska, T. (2009) 'Parenthood, stress and psychological well-being in late middle life and early old age', *International Journal of Aging & Human Development*, 68: 127–47.

Raley, S., Bianchi, S. and Wang, R. (2012) 'When do fathers care? Mothers' economic contribution and fathers' involvement in childcare', *American Journal of Sociology*, 117(5): 1422–59.

Randles, J.M. (2013) 'Repackaging the "package deal". Promoting marriage for low-income families by targeting paternal identity and reframing marital masculinity', *Gender & Society*, 27: 864–88.

Rane, T.R. and McBride, B.A. (2000) 'Identity theory as a guide to understanding fathers' involvement with their children', *Journal of Family Issues*, 21: 347–66.

Ranson, G. (2012) 'Men, paid employment and family responsibilities: conceptualizing the "working father"', *Gender, Work & Organization*, 19(6): 741–61.

Roopnarine, J.L. and Hossain, Z. (2013) 'African American and African Caribbean fathers', in N.J. Cabrera and C.S. Tamis-LeMonda (eds) *Handbook of father involvement. Multidisciplinary perspectives* (2nd edn), New York, NY: Routledge, pp 223–43.

Roy, K.M. and Dyson, O. (2010) 'Making daddies into fathers: community-based fatherhood programs and the construction of masculinities for low-income African American men', *American Journal of Community Psychology*, 45: 139–54.

Saracho, O.N. (2013) 'Mexican-American father–child literacy interaction', in J. Pattnaik (ed) *Father involvement in young children's lives. A global analysis*, Dordrecht: Springer, pp 47–69.

Schindler, H.S. (2010) 'The importance of parenting and financial contributions in promoting fathers' psychological health', *Journal of Marriage & Family*, 72: 318–32.

Schoppe-Sullivan, S.J., McBride, B.A. and Ho, M. (2004) 'Father involvement: unitary versus multidimensional constructs', *Fathering: A Journal of Theory, Research & Practice*, 2: 147–64.

Settersten, R.A. and Cancel-Tirado, D. (2010) 'Fatherhood as a hidden variable in men's development and life courses', *Research in Human Development*, 7: 83–102.

Silverstein, L.B. (1996) 'Fathering is a feminist issue', *Psychology of Women Quarterly*, 20(1): 3–37.

Skolnick, A. (2003) 'Uncle Sam, matchmaker: marriage as a public policy', in W.D. Allen and L. Eiklenborg (eds) *Vision 2003: contemporary family issues*, Minneapolis, MN: National Council on Family Relations, pp 11–15.

Solomon-Fears, C. (2013) 'Fatherhood initiatives: connecting fathers to their children', Congressional Research Service Report for Congress. Available at: http://www.crs.gov

Sorensen, E. (2010) 'Rethinking public policy toward low-income fathers in the child support programme', *Journal of Policy Analysis & Management*, 29: 604–10.

Tamis-LeMonda, C.S., Niwa, E., Kahana-Kalman, R. and Yoshikawa, H. (2008) 'Immigrant fathers and families at the transition to parenthood', in S. Chuang and R. Moreno (eds) *On new shores: understanding fathers in North America*, Lanham, MD: Lexington Books, pp 229–53.

Tamis-LeMonda, C.S., Kahana-Kalman, R. and Yoshikawa, H. (2009) 'Father involvement in immigrant and ethnically diverse families from the prenatal period to the second year: predication and mediating mechanisms', *Sex Roles*, 60: 496–509.

Tanaka, S. and Waldfogel, J. (2007) 'Effects of parental leave and work hours on fathers' involvement with their babies: evidence from the Millennium Cohort Study', *Community, Work & Family*, 10: 409–26.

Taylor, B.A. and Behnke, A. (2005) 'Fathering across the border: Latino fathers in Mexico and the U.S.', *Fathering: A Journal of Theory, Research, & Practice about Men as Fathers*, 3: 99–120.

Umbertson, D., Pudrovska, T. and Reczek, C. (2010) 'Parenthood, childlessness, and well-being: a life course perspective', *Journal of Marriage & Family*, 72: 612–29.

US Census Bureau (2011) 'Who's minding the kids? Child care arrangements: 2011 – detailed tables'. Available at: http://www.census.gov/hhes/childcare/data/sipp/2011/tables.html

US Census Bureau (2012) 'America's families and living arrangements: 2012', data tables. Available at: http://www.census.gov/hhes/families/data/cps2012.html

Vespa, J., Lewis, J.M. and Kreider, R.M. (2013) *America's families and living arrangements: 2012*, Current Population Reports, Washington, DC: US Census Bureau, pp 20–570. Available at: http://www.census.gov/prod/2013pubs/p20-570.pdf

Wallen, J. (2001) *Balancing work and family. The role of the workplace*, Boston, MA: Allyn and Bacon.

Winslow, S. (2005) 'Work–family conflict, gender, and parenthood, 1977–1997', *Journal of Family Issues*, 26: 727–55.

Woo, H. and Raley, R.K. (2005) 'A small extension to costs and rewards of children: the effects of becoming a parent on adults' lives', *Journal of Marriage & Family*, 67: 216–21.

Yoshida, A. (2012) 'Dads who do diapers: factors affecting care of young children by fathers', *Journal of Family Issues*, 33(4): 451–77.

Comparative father involvement: the dynamics of gender culture, policy and practice

Marina A. Adler and Karl Lenz

The purpose of this book was to document current scholarship on the variations in father involvement with young children within the current cultural mandate of active fatherhood in several different policy contexts. The focus was on how 'hands-on' fathers are in selected countries and how their level of involvement with children occurs within the specific institutional constraints of the gender regime, family policies and workplace cultures that they live and work in. The cross-national analysis of father involvement is of particular interest to scholars and practitioners because gender-egalitarian societies require that women and men share the responsibility of providing and caring for future generations. In order to prioritise family well-being in the long run, fathers need to be empowered to participate in childcare just as mothers are empowered to participate in the labour market. With this in mind, this concluding chapter will distil the key information on the countries presented in the preceding chapters in order to find discernible patterns that may inform a new conceptual model of father involvement, as well as guide policymakers and practitioners working with fathers.

In this concluding chapter, after presenting a comparison of data from the six countries, the editors examine the extent to which the concepts of fatherhood regime, men's capability to care and agency gap are useful in understanding father involvement within the context of gendered cultures, policy regimes and individual practices. How do specific cultural norms regarding masculinity and maternalism, degrees of gender egalitarianism in family policy, and care-sensitive workplace cultures translate into specific fathering practices with young children? Based on the patterns found in the six countries, a conceptual model linking gender culture, policy and agency in terms of father involvement is presented. The interactions among national context (gender culture and policy regime), institutional context (economy, workplace culture, work time regime) and fathers' capability and agency are discussed. In addition, some 'best practices' for increasing father involvement with young children in order to promote gender egalitarianism and family well-being are included.

Comparison of the six countries

Table 1 shows that, with the exception of the US, all countries included provide generous well-compensated (above 80% of pay) maternity leave, ranging from six weeks (UK) to 20 weeks (Italy). In terms of explicit paternity leave, only Finland provides significantly more than two weeks of leave (nine weeks) at high compensation, which is generally defined as above 66% of usual pay. Slovenia and the UK provide two weeks of paternity leave, but Slovenia provides much higher compensation than the UK. While Germany offers no paternity leave, it provides two highly compensated 'bonus' months of parental leave to incentivise fathers' leave uptake. In Italy, fathers receive very short paternity leave, and while they also have the option of taking a 'bonus' as part of parental leave, that has, until recently, been poorly compensated at 30%. The US has neither statutory paid paternity nor parental leave. In fact, both the UK and US (with restrictions) only offer three months of unpaid parental leave. Finland, Germany and Slovenia provide more than six months of well-compensated shared parental leave. These family-leave-related patterns result in the following ranking of the countries regarding fathers' 'social rights to care' (availability, length and compensation of entitlements for fathers): higher rights for Finland, Germany and Slovenia, moderate rights for Italy, and lower rights for the UK and US.

In East Germany, Slovenia, the UK and the US, more than 40% of children younger than age three are in formal childcare, compared to only 22–28% in the other countries and West Germany. This suggests higher demands for childcare in countries with a high prevalence of full-time dual earners in a context of less generous leave policies (see Table 2). By contrast, in Finland, West Germany and Italy, the use of long-term maternity leave, as well as the trend by mothers to be more likely than fathers to take parental leave thereafter, lowers the demand for childcare for the very young (under two year olds). However, almost all children aged three to school age are in day care (more than 80%) in Germany, Italy, Slovenia and the UK, compared to only 73% of Finnish and 67% of American children. In the US case, this is primarily due to the lack of public childcare and the high cost of private childcare.

Table 1: Statutory leave entitlements and formal childcare coverage for six countries (most recent year available)

Country	Maternity leave (length and compensation)	Paternity leave (length and compensation)	Parental leave (length and compensation)	% children in formal childcare < age 3[c]	% Children in formal child care, age 3–school age[c]
Finland	17 weeks @ 90% of wages for first 56 days, then 70%	9 weeks @ 70% of wages	6.5 months (158 days) @ 75% for first 30 days, then @ 70%; can be shared	27.7	73.0
Germany	14 weeks @ 100% of wages	0 weeks (2 'daddy months' are part of parental leave @ 67%)	12–14 months @ 67%; can be shared; plus unpaid until child is age 3	23.1 Eastern states: 49 Western states: 22	93.9
Italy	20 weeks @ 80% (100% for public sector)	1 compulsory day + 2 days instead of mother @ 80%	6 months each parent or 10 together @ 30%[a] (100% if public sector for 30 days) If fathers take 3 months or more, parents get another month	24.2	95.7
Slovenia	15 weeks @ 100% of wages paid	2 weeks @ 100% wages, 11 weeks social security based on minimum wage (100% after economic recovery)	8.5 months (37 weeks) @ 100% of wages (130 days for each parent; father can transfer all to mother; mother can transfer 100 days to father)	41.8 (56% age 1–3 years)	85.8
UK	52 weeks; 6 weeks @ 90% of weekly income; 33 weeks at flat rate	2 weeks @ the lesser of 90% of earnings or flat rate	3 months (18 weeks per parent) @ unpaid	42.0 (36% age 0–2 years)	93.3 (87% age 3–4)
USA	0 weeks	0 weeks	3 months (12 weeks) @ unpaid; both parents[b]	43.2	66.5

Notes: [a] 2011–14, on an experimental basis, there is 80% of pay. [b] For people in companies over 50 employees, 12 weeks. [c] OECD 2010 data plus most recent additional national data in parentheses.

Table 2: Indicators of the gender regime in six countries (most recent year available)

Country	LFP fathers < age 3 or < age 6	LFP mothers < age 3 or < age 6	Men in employment, % full-time	Men emp. hours/week / Fathers hours/week	Women in employment, % full-time	Women emp. hours/week / Mothers hours/week	% of married-couple dual-earner families	% of married-couple male-breadwinner families
Finland	90.4 < age 3 / 92.8 (age 3–6)	49.2 < age 3 / 80.1 (age 3–6)	90.3	41.4 / --	83.5	38.5 / --	65.7	26.0
Germany	82.2 < age 3 / East: 78.1 West: 83.1 / 85.1 (age 3–5) / East: 83.5 West: 85.4	31.7 < age 3 / East: 38.7 West: 30.0 / 61.8 (age 3–5) / East: 66.4 West: 60.7	91.3	39.8 / 39.0	62.2	30.5 / 25.0	52.2 / East: 55.8 West: 51.6	36.6 / East: 31.0 West: 37.6
Italy	92.0 < age 6	53.2 < age 6	92.2	40.5 / 43.7	67.6	33.1 / 31.6	29.4	40.9
Slovenia	97.9 < age 6	88.5 < age 6	94.1	40.8 / 41.7	89.7	38.6 / 38.4	76.8	13.4
UK	85.6 < age 5	56.7 < age 5	88.3	44.4 (full-time only) / 44.7	56.8	41.0 (full-time only) / 40.1	60.0 (incl. unmarried)	22.0 (incl. unmarried)
US	95.1 < age 6	60.9 < age 3 / 64.2 < age 6	91.3	40.6 / --	81.7	35.6 / --	54.1	18.7

Table 2 shows that only in Germany and the UK do fewer than 90% of fathers of young children work full-time. In all countries, men tend to work around 40 hours a week on average; in Italy, Slovenia and the UK, fathers work even longer hours than non-fathers, indicating the high work time involvement of fathers. Despite some data comparability issues, it appears that Slovenia has the highest labour force participation (LFP) rate of mothers of children younger than age six, followed by Finland, the US and the UK. Italy and Germany are in the lower range, but there are variations by child age and region. In addition, Finland, Slovenia and the US clearly have the highest percentage of women working full-time (more than 80%); Finland and Slovenia also have the highest proportion of dual-earner couples. For those countries and the US, dual-earner couples mostly include two full-time earners. In Germany and the UK, however, dual-earner couples mainly involve one part-time earner; in West Germany particularly, this means that women are working relatively few hours. In Italy, the male-breadwinner model is still quite prevalent, and when women are employed, they tend to work relatively few hours. Due to time poverty, fathers in full-time dual-earner families encounter more pressure to do childcare than fathers in other arrangements, particularly in those where women stay at home. Hence, based on these patterns, one would expect fathers' time with children 'by necessity' to be highest in Finland, Slovenia and the US, and lower in the UK, Germany and Italy. Taking into account the lower use of formal childcare, fathers in Finland and the US should spend the most time with childcare. However, the capability to care is facilitated most in Finland because fathers' agency gap is reduced by well-compensated leave.

The data displayed in Table 3 relate to fathers' practice involving their young children. In general, disregarding paternity leave provisions in the countries, few fathers take a month or more of paternity and/or parental leave. Finnish and Slovenian fathers lead, taking about two to three weeks (80%), followed by the UK and the US, with one to two weeks (50–70%), Germany (29% take parental leave) and Italy (7%). Thus, there is a gap between entitlements and uptake in all countries – in all policy contexts, when fathers do take leave, it is typically for less than three weeks. Furthermore, cross-nationally, fathers generally spend between 1.0 to 1.5 hours per day with primary childcare; US fathers spend nearly two hours. Overall, fathers do about one third of total childcare, ranging from 22% (West Germany) to 42% (Finland), disregarding the policy context. However, these indicators do not reflect the nature of the tasks performed – typically everyday routine activities or pleasant playtime. For fathers in all countries, playing and recreational tasks rather than routine tasks are the more popular childcare activities.

Table 3: Indicators of father involvement in six countries (most recent year available)

Country	% Fathers taking leave	Fathers' hours in primary childcare/day	Fathers, % of total childcare	Primary care activities most often performed	% active fathers: 'substantial amount of time'[a] % perform care tasks every day[b]
Finland	3 weeks paternity leave (83%); father's month (27%); parental leave (29.6%); 42 days average overall any leave	1 hour 23 minutes	42%	Caring and monitoring, reading and playing	31% about 50%
Germany	Parental leave (29%); 3.2 months on average; 78% only take 2 months	1 hour on weekdays; more than 1 hour on Sundays	West: 22% on weekdays; 32% on weekends East: 28% and 36%	Physical care and playing	20% about 20%[e]
Italy	Any leave (6.9%); 1 month or more (20%)	1 hour 28 minutes on weekday, primary or secondary	38%	Feeding and putting to bed; relational activities	11% about 7%
Slovenia	Paternity leave (80% up to 15 days); parental leave (7%)	About 1 hour (fathers aged 25–44 who did childcare)	30%	Playing, relational activities, outdoor and organisational activities	NA about 18%
UK	Leave at birth (91%); paternity leave only (49%); additional paid leave (25%); 50% took the 2 weeks; 34% took less than 2 weeks	63% spend 1 hour 24 minutes	30%	Playing, praising, talking	24% 25% high level of involvement
US	Any leave (89%); less than 1 week (24%); 1 week (43%); 10–60 days (24%); 2 months or more (6%)	1 hour 58 minutes on weekdays; 2 hours 7 minutes on weekends	36% 43%[d]	Playing, feeding/eating with child	NA 32% high level of involvement[c]

Sources: Country chapters, also http://www.leavenetwork.org/fileadmin/Leavenetwork/Country_notes/ and http://www.oecd.org/social/family/43199641.pdf

Notes: [a] Koslowski Smith (2007) defines 'substantial amount of time' with children younger than age 6 as 28 hours a week. [b] From time-use studies: % of fathers who perform direct physical tasks every day, such as eating with/feeding, bathing, changing nappies. [c] Huerta et al (2013) use a standardised summary measure of child-related activities, ranging from 0 to 100. High father involvement is defined as doing 66.7% to 100% of activities frequently (every day or several times a week). This is only available for the UK and the US. [d] See Kaufman (2013: 15). [e] See Pfahl and Reuyß (2009).

It appears that using time as the only indicator of father involvement does not capture the degree of father involvement in essential routine care activities. This is particularly relevant in the US, where lack of paid leave for parents, lack of affordable formal childcare and a relatively high number of work hours for both parents increase time poverty among fathers and mothers. Similarly, in the UK, low financial support for families may also make more demands of fathers to do routine care. While in Slovenia, full-time dual-earner couples predominate, paid leave and highly affordable childcare accessibility may reduce these time pressures. Thus, American men may have to perform more routine tasks and a higher percentage of necessary childcare tasks than Slovenian fathers, disregarding overall time involvement in childcare. British couples solve the time dilemma by having higher part-time employment of mothers, though they do not have the benefits of well-compensated leave that Slovenian parents have. In Italy and Germany, the predominant maternalist and familist culture makes it possible for fathers to avoid both high time involvement and the performance of routine tasks. In both countries, mothers often work part-time and, thus, men can focus on employment. In addition, high maternal childcare and the high availability of public childcare may take pressure off fathers to spend time with their young children. Only in Finland do culture and policy provide couples with a real choice in sharing provider and carer tasks.

With respect to daily practice, the ranking of fathers as more or less 'active fathers' (level of father involvement) is complicated by the lack of directly comparable data for the six countries. However, using Koslowski Smith's (2007) 'substantial amount of time' spent with childcare more than a decade ago, Finland ranked highest and Italy and Germany lowest. The other countries fell somewhere in-between. The pattern for Italy and Germany is consistent with the findings in Tables 1 and 2 regarding paternity leave, the low percentage of children under age three in childcare, low mothers' LFP and the high percentage of male-breadwinner couples. Using the percentage of fathers performing direct care tasks every day as the indicator of father involvement also ranks Italy and Germany with Slovenia lowest, but moves the UK and US up, closer to Finland. Again, this is likely the result of policy and work time constraints on working parents in the liberal welfare states.

Putting it all together

Using the information presented in Tables 1–3 and the patterns found regarding father involvement in the country chapters, Table 4 presents a summary classification of the six countries. Leitner (2003) and Javornik (2014) introduced the concept 'varieties of familialism' to classify the cultural underpinnings of the countries' family policies. In addition, their level of maternalism, that is, to what extent there is a mother-centred culture that considers women the only appropriate carers of children, is included. As demonstrated by previous authors, workplace characteristics are also extremely important for understanding fatherhood regimes and fathers' agency (Gregory and Milner, 2008, 2011; Hobson and Fahlén, 2009, 2012). With respect to workplace culture, Mutari and Figart's (2001) concept of 'work time regime' allows the classification according to the degree of flexibility in work hours and gender equity. According to the authors, the expansion of work time flexibility was part of neoliberal labour market policies that included increased low-paid contractual work, part-time work and chronically long hours for full-time workers. These working time practices increased flexibility for employers but reduced sovereignty over the working time of employees. The authors arrive at several clusters in terms of work time regimes. (1) Solidaristic gender-equity countries strive for gender equity in working time through a shorter work week and high women's LFP, but do not rank high in flexibility. Finland is a member of this group. (2) Liberal flexibilisation regimes are characterised by deregulated labour markets, a laissez-faire approach to workplace policies and low gender equity. This results in a gender-segregated job market featuring low-paid and part-time work, on the one hand, and overtime work, on the other. Both the US and the UK belong in this category. (3) The male-breadwinner work time regime is low in both flexibility and gender equity – while men work long hours, mothers have a low LFP and do most of the care work. Italy represents this group. (4) The transitional work time regimes feature a mixture of inconsistent levels of gender equity and flexibility because of recent policy shifts. Women have high part-time employment rates and collective bargaining has protected men from working long hours. Germany is an example of this cluster. In addition, because Slovenia has features of both the solidaristic gender-equity regime (high female full-time LFP) and of the liberal flexibilisation regime (long hours for men and less job protections), it is also in the transitional category.

Another dimension of work culture is the degree to which organisations provide support for the integration of work and family responsibilities. Den Dulk, Groeneveld and Peper (2014) consider the context in which working parents have higher capabilities to combine work and family (flexibility of work hours, entitlements, workplace infrastructure for family support). The authors use a large international data set of European workplace policies in 21 countries to classify organisations by the overall level of capabilities provided to working parents as low, medium or high: 'Within the high capabilities cluster, organizations had (on average) two flexible work arrangements and almost three leave/child care policies' (Den Dulk et al, 2014: 165). The percentage of organisations in the high-capabilities cluster ranged from less than 10% (Cyprus) to greater than 95% (Sweden). Among the countries of interest here, only Finland is in the high range, Germany is moderate and all others are below 50%. While the US is not included in this data set, the average for the European liberal welfare states (43%) can be used as an estimate.

As a subjective indicator of workplace culture and the 'new male mystique' (Aumann et al, 2011), perceived work–family conflict is included based on Ruppaner and Huffman (2014). Using the 2005 International Social Survey Programme (ISSP) data, the authors present the percentage of men reporting work–non-work interference for 31 countries. Unfortunately, Italy was not included and, thus, ISTAT survey data are substituted as an estimate.

The concept of 'fatherhood regime' is modified here to include not only indicators of fathers' rights and claims (Hobson and Morgan, 2002), as well as capabilities (Hobson and Fahlén, 2012), but also the level of father involvement based on Table 3 in order to estimate fathers' agency gap (Fahlén, 2014; Hobson, 2014). The resulting fatherhood regime concept represents the degree of supportiveness of active fatherhood present in a country.

As the comparison in Table 4 suggests, the relationships among gender regime, family policy factors, workplace culture and support for active fatherhood are not clear-cut. However, despite the inconsistencies in specific indicators, some general 'pairings' can be observed among the six countries. Both the Finnish and Slovenian welfare states, operating under dual-breadwinner regime assumptions, rank low on maternalism and feature supported/optional de-familist policies, which encourage dual-earner families with publicly funded childcare. They also support mothers and children disregarding marital status and, thus, fathers' mandatory provider function is relatively lower. At the same time, Finland's gender-egalitarian policy principles have resulted in one of the most generous paternal leave and pro-father custody systems. Slovenia has a socialist tradition with high maternal employment and is modelling some of its policies on the Nordic countries. It has become a forerunner among former socialist countries in providing paternity leave and encouraging fathers' rights. Nevertheless, an important difference between Slovenia and Finland relates to their national workplace culture. While Finland clearly falls into the solidaristic gender-equity work time regime, Slovenia features the low job security and high working hours more characteristic of the liberal flexibilisation work time regime (Mutari and Figart, 2001). This high level of commodification, combined with a low percentage of organisations in the high-capabilities cluster (Den Dulk et al, 2014) and no direct incentives to take leave (as the highly compensated bonuses in Finland) for working fathers, creates a high agency gap in Slovenia. In contrast, Finland's higher job security, combined with more social rights, claims and organisational support, reflects a comparatively lower agency gap. Hence, Finnish fathers have the capability to use their entitlements even though their uptake of leave is not as high as expected. As a result, the Finnish fatherhood regime is more supportive of active fatherhood than the Slovenian one.

While the liberal UK state has a more developed family support system than the liberal US state and features a one-and-a-half-breadwinner model, the liberal US state subscribes to a market-driven model of family responsibility where both parents are expected to engage in market work full-time. Even lone mothers are encouraged to work and fathers are encouraged to financially support their children. The UK and US share implicit familism and moderate levels of maternalism, but while the UK's policies are non-egalitarian, the absence of paid leave for either gender in the US does not improve the US rank (see Ray et al, 2010). In the liberal flexibilisation work time regimes of both countries, low job security and low institutional support for fathers' capabilities persist. In combination with lower social rights and claims, increased father involvement happens by necessity. Hence, there is a large agency gap for fathers in both countries.

Germany's social-conservative state, like the Italian familist state, also still has policies reinforcing male-breadwinner families and a culture that remains strongly influenced by maternalism. Unlike Italy, however, Germany is pursuing increasing efforts to make childcare-related policies more egalitarian. East Germany's socialist past has left a legacy of the double burden for employed mothers and somewhat more engaged fathers by necessity. West German fathers have a tradition of being 'weekend fathers' and leaving childcare to mothers, who tend to be employed at very low levels. Germany and Italy both practise explicit familism and high maternalism (again, less so in East Germany), but have also recently incentivised taking leave for fathers with bonus leaves. However, while Italy's family policies are generally still quite non-egalitarian, those in Germany strive to be egalitarian, but remain contradictory. Whereas Italy also has a high agency gap, this is due

Table 4: Gender regime, family policy and culture of care, workplace culture, and fatherhood regime in six countries

Country	Gender regime	Family policy (leave and childcare) and culture of care (degree of familism and maternalism[a])	Workplace culture (work time regime,[b] work–family conflict,[c] work hours/week,[d] % organisations in high-capabilities cluster[e])	Fatherhood regime (rights, claims, involvement, agency gap)
Finland	Dual full-time earners	Optional or supported de-familism Lower maternalism	solidaristic gender-equity work time regime High % organisations in high-capabilities cluster (95%) 52% work > 40 hrs in usual work 55% experience work–non-work conflict	Supportive of active fathers: higher social rights higher claims higher father involvement level (childcare participation, % active fathers) lower agency gap
Germany	Modified breadwinner Western states: one-and-a-half earners Eastern states: dual full-time earners	Explicit familism Higher maternalism	Transitional work time regime Moderate % organisations in high-capabilities cluster (58%) 66% work > 40 hrs 59% experience work–non-work conflict	Semi-supportive of active fathers: higher social rights moderate claims lower father involvement moderate agency gap
Italy	Traditional breadwinner (one-and-a- half earners)	Explicit familism Higher maternalism	Male-breadwinner work time regime Low % organisations in high-capabilities cluster (44%) 69% work > 40 hrs 29% experience work–family conflict[f]	Semi-supportive of active fathers: moderate social rights lower claims lower father involvement higher agency gap

Country	Gender regime	Family policy (leave and childcare) and culture of care (degree of familism and maternalism[a])	Workplace culture (work time regime,[b] work–family conflict,[c] work hours/week,[d] % organisations in high-capabilities cluster[e])	Fatherhood regime (rights, claims, involvement, agency gap)
Slovenia	Egalitarian employment (dual full-time earners)	Supported de-familism Lower maternalism	Transitional gender equity work time regime Low % organisations in high-capabilities cluster (48%) 94% work > 40 hrs 64% experience work–non-work conflict	Semi-supportive of active fathers: moderate social rights lower claims lower father involvement higher agency gap
UK	Modified breadwinner (one-and-a-half earners)	Implicit familism Moderate maternalism	Liberal flexibilisation work time regime Low % organisations in high-capabilities cluster (42%) 61% work > 40 hrs 66% experience work–non-work conflict	Unsupportive of active fatherhood: lower social rights lower claims higher father involvement higher agency gap
US	Dual full-time earners	Implicit familism Moderate maternalism	Liberal flexibilisation work time regime Low % organisations in high-capabilities cluster (~43%) 83% work > 40 hrs 54% experience work–non-work conflict	Unsupportive of active fathers: lower social rights lower claims higher father involvement higher agency gap

Notes: [a] Leitner (2003) and Javornik (2014). [b] Mutari and Figart (2001); Hobson and Fahlén (2012) refer to this as the working time regime. [c] Ruppanner and Huffman (2014) 2005–13 ISSP data. [d] OECD (2012) data. [e] Den Dulk, Groeneveld and Peper (2014: 166): high is over 75%, moderate is 50–75%, low is under 50%; for the US, we took the % of all liberal regimes. [f] ISTAT (2010).

to the male-breadwinner work time regime and lower institutional support for working fathers. Germany, however, has higher job security combined with a transitional work time regime and a moderate level of organisational support. Given this constellation of factors and recently increased social rights for fathers, only a moderate agency gap results in Germany.

A conceptual model of father involvement

Based on the insights gained so far, this section provides a conceptual model that reflects modifications of the fatherhood regime concept in an attempt to link structural context to agency and practice. In Figure 1, the relationship among the key concepts and indicators shown in Table 4 are presented. This model of father involvement combines Hobson and Fahlén's (2012; Fahlén, 2014; Hobson, 2014) ideas about capabilities and agency gaps, and adds work time regimes (Mutari and Figart, 2001) and organisational capabilities clusters (Den Dulk et al, 2014) to Hobson and Morgan's (2002) original fatherhood regime conceptualisation. Agency is specified in terms of father involvement in everyday practice. The model depicts the fatherhood regime as composed of fathers' social rights to care, their obligations regarding their children, their claims to entitlements, their agency in spending time with childcare and doing everyday routine care activities, and the existing capability–agency gap. These components are the product of the interplay of the gender regime, family policy and the workplace culture. Depending on the constellation of these factors in a country, fathers will be empowered to be more- or less-involved fathers. In other words, the agency gap increases when fathers' capabilities to be active fathers and their ability to claim their entitlements are inhibited by contradictions among these underlying structures. The resulting fatherhood regime can range from being supportive of active fatherhood and father-friendly by reducing the agency gap, to being unsupportive and creating a hostile climate for fathers by increasing the agency gap. In-between, there are various combinations of inconsistent patterns.

Based on this continuum, Finland has the most consistently supportive fatherhood regime and the US and the UK have the least supportive one. However, while the other countries reveal mixed patterns, almost all of them reflect a relatively high agency gap for fathers, albeit for different reasons. Herein lies a major lesson – whether the agency gap is due to a maternalist culture, a lack of father-friendly policies, imbalanced gender arrangements or a father-hostile work culture, this real and/or perceived agency gap prevents fathers from being more involved with their children. If one believes the surveys showing consistently and in all countries that the majority of fathers want to be 'active fathers' (by whatever definition), all these factors have to be addressed with a view towards increasing men's confidence and competencies to 'do fathering'.

Figure 1: Conceptual model of father involvement

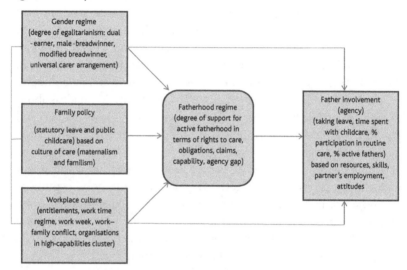

Overall patterns regarding father involvement in the six countries

There are a number of consistencies in the information regarding father involvement found in the six countries, which can inform policymakers and practitioners. First, active fatherhood has, indeed, become a guiding cultural mandate, which means that, disregarding national context, fathers are expected to be both providers and carers for their young children. In every country covered in this book, surveys show that most contemporary fathers report wanting to be more engaged with their children. While the exact nature of this aspiration varies by gender culture, each country features a significant minority of fathers who make being an engaged father a life priority and thus fall into the category of 'active father'. In most countries, this appears to be the result of 'new circumstances' related to shifts in economic and workplace pressures rather than a quick transformation in masculine identity towards nurturing fatherhood. Hence, father-related policy and programming needs to focus more on how to reduce these pressures and provide fathers with more capabilities to be involved. Disregarding government policies, employers need to recognise fatherhood as a major life transition similar to motherhood. A good example of how to make fatherhood more visible in the workplace in order to reduce the agency gap for working fathers are the German father representatives and father advisory boards. These promote networking and advocacy among fathers at work so that fathers feel entitled to care for their children. At the national level, several countries have enacted certification processes to reward care-sensitive organisations that meet family-friendly policy expectations that include fathers.

Second, when countries provide well-compensated leave for fathers, they are more likely to take it. However, there appears to be a preferred time range for leave – between three weeks and two months. The information presented on the six countries confirms previous research (Nepomnyaschy and Waldfogel, 2007; Tanaka and Waldfogel, 2007; Haas and Hwang, 2008, 2009; Huerta et al, 2013; Bünning, 2014) showing that when fathers take leave for at least two weeks early on, they are more involved in childcare, even in the longer term. In addition, the longer the leave, the longer the fathers remain involved. In all countries, the gender division of labour appears traditionalised after the birth of a child, and when women are on leave or both parents are on leave simultaneously, men do less childcare. In addition, when mothers are employed, fathers are more likely to take leave and to be involved in childcare. Hence, policymakers need to focus on how to optimise leave provisions and increase mothers' employment so that men are encouraged to take the leave alone.

At the forefront of the investigation of optimal leave combinations is the small Nordic country of Iceland. According to Arnalds, Eydal and Gíslason (2013), Iceland may be a good 'best practices' model to follow in terms of changing the culture, policy and practice interplay related to father involvement. According to the authors, Iceland was relatively late in adopting the Nordic model of family policy, but became the first nation to grant fathers and mothers the same rights to three months non-transferable leave with high income replacement. This 3/3/3 parental leave package provides each parent with three months and adds another three months of shared leave, with a compensation of 80% of regular pay. This scheme rapidly achieved an increase in fathers' uptake of leave: in 2007, the average number of days taken by fathers was 101 and 21% of fathers used more than the official quota. However, during the economic crisis of 2008/09, the ceiling amount of the compensation was lowered, and in 2011, fathers took an average of 84 days and 14% of fathers used more than the official quota. Hence, high compensation is a major requirement for increasing fathers' leave uptake. Arnalds, Eydal and Gíslason's (2013) research also shows that the 3/3/3 scheme has led to a more equal distribution of childcare between parents, and the length of leave was correlated with increased father involvement in childcare in the long term. The authors conclude that the 'fathers who make use of their right to paid parental leave are the ones most likely to be equally involved in caring for their children as the mothers' (Arnalds et al, 2013: 341).

Third, disregarding what policies are in place, in all countries, highly educated, high-earning, professionally employed fathers are privileged in terms of their capability to care. They have more access to leave options and compensation (statutory and workplace) related to father involvement. Conversely, minority ethnic, unmarried and lower-earning fathers are often disadvantaged due to less secure employment conditions and fewer family benefits. Thus, even when there are entitlements, these fathers may not claim them due to job insecurity or economic pressures. These inequalities should be the focus for both compensatory policies and father-related programming. That means not only that all fathers should be able to have access to highly compensated leave and to reduce work hours, but also that special efforts are necessary in non-professional workplaces to empower working fathers to make use of these entitlements. In addition, part of recognising that all fathers, like mothers, should be able to care for their children requires offering fathers the opportunity to develop parenting skills, preferably starting before birth. Thus, father-focused programmes for all fathers should be offered in father-friendly environments based on father input. The Berlin *Väterzentrum* may be a good model to implement.

Fourth, a more maternalist culture and familism are barriers to father involvement, disregarding policies and rights. In a number of countries, authors mentioned that fathers take on the role of 'apprentices', 'helpers' or 'supporters' of the mothers. Maternal gatekeeping causes fathers to be relegated to the 'secondary' parent role in a similar way as women are often 'secondary' earners. This is related to fathers' care work being considered 'optional' rather than necessary. It also explains why fathers are rarely caring for their children on their own. This issue can be targeted by media campaigns that show fathers as competent parents and by programmes in high schools that prepare young men and women for egalitarian parenthood.

Fifth, fathers of young children often work more hours in employment, and in dual-earner couples, they work more combined hours in care and employment. Fathers in all countries report experiencing significant work–family conflict, which supports the emergence of the 'new male mystique' on an international level. The gender culture and workplace culture should allow men to fit working into the life of a father rather than fitting fatherhood into the life of a worker. This means that work organisations need to educate fathers about their rights and encourage them to use their entitlements.

Lessons learned and recommendations

Overall, it appears that the fatherhood regimes in all countries are in transition. While the model of the father as sole provider, disciplinarian and distant parent is eroding, the new model of the 'active father' is only slowly emerging in practice. The patterns found in this collection of countries point to an agency gap (Hobson and Fahlén, 2012) among fathers between relatively high aspirations to fulfil the cultural mandate of being an active father and their actual practice in leave uptake, time spent with young children and participation in direct care activities. Most contemporary fathers state that they want to be providers and nurturers, but they experience problems due to economic pressures, time pressures from the demanding work culture in the new economy and maternal gatekeeping. The degree of mismatch between cultural expectations of active father involvement, fathers' intentions to be both providers and nurturers, and fathers' capabilities in terms of entitlement and agency is different in the countries covered. Nevertheless, even in egalitarian Finland, only between one third and one half of fathers can be classified as active fathers.

This is mainly due to gaps between values, entitlements and agency, as well as a lag in institutional support for fathers from policy and workplaces. Tamilina and Tamilina (2014) show that there is a gap between egalitarian values (ideological component) and individual compliance with them (behavioural component), and that both the values and the practice can be targeted by policies. When applying the authors' logic to men, fathers' compliance with normative expectations to be involved fathers depends on their motivation (education and aspirations) and their opportunities to act (capabilities). Policies can serve to empower fathers via incentives (such as highly compensated, exclusive and lengthy paternity leave) to perform more care work, thereby motivating them to live up to egalitarian values. Policies can also provide opportunities for men to leave employment or reduce work hours in order to engage in care work (flexitime, part-time work).

However, as shown in this analysis, policies only go so far in enabling fathers to meet the new cultural mandate. Competing cultural ideas rooted in familism and maternalism, as well as organisational barriers related to high workplace demands, can significantly impede the success of policies in affecting individual behaviour. Policies are of limited usefulness if the gendered culture of care works against them and workplaces are insecure and demand all available time. In addition to problematic policies, the main barriers to more father involvement are related to: (1) economics and the workplace; and (2) the gender culture. Hence, it is recommended that additional efforts at cultural and institutional transformation target the 24/7 work culture and maternal gatekeeping. Economic pressures and gender norms encourage men to keep working long hours when they are fathers because they earn more than mothers and the provider norm remains more important than the nurturer expectation. Maternalist values (particularly in Italy and West Germany) discourage fathers from care work and make them feel less capable. In countries with extended paid maternity leave, mothers want to take as much leave as they can and thereby establish a 'monopoly' on infant care (maternal gatekeeping).

In general, statutory parent-care-sensitive leave policies are a necessity and father-friendliness would mean well-compensated lengthy paid leave, opportunities to take leave while the mother works, opportunities for flexitime, reduced hours, job sharing, and working from home. In general, it means more job security and living wages for both parents. This may require a more balanced distribution of leave between fathers and mothers. Clearly, this process needs to include mothers so that they are willing to empower men to be carers. Fathers not only need to feel a sense of entitlement in order to ask for leave, but also must feel competent in performing childcare. The question for policymakers is: how can fatherhood be made more visible as a major life-changing event? In order to mainstream care work, men have to be prevented from avoiding care and women have be encouraged to give up their 'domain' (Jurczyk, 2014).

Clearly, the cases of the UK and US show that the privatisation of childcare and leaving policy to employers is not the answer when it comes to family support. This strategy reinforces existing inequalities by class and creates a 'chilly climate' for parents in general, and fathers in particular. Also, the exclusive focus of providing 'choice' to parents may reinforce gender inequality if non-egalitarian gender cultures and the gender pay gap are not addressed. In fact, freedom of choice usually means a re-traditionalisation of the gender division of labour because women 'choose' to stay at home to care for the child because their income is lower. Hence, women either have no real choice or have to choose between a career and motherhood. In none of the countries do men have to make that choice, but they are beginning to feel the work–family conflict that working mothers have known for a long time. Raising children is a collective responsibility for both parents and for society as a whole rather than a private or individual endeavour.

A crucial issue to be addressed, then, is the gendered nature of parenting in the current cultural contexts. However, does de-gendering care mean that fathers have to do fathering in the same way as mothers do mothering? Do we have the same expectations of approaches to childcare for fathers as mothers? It appears that de-gendered childcare would allow fathers to develop their own style of parenting rather than having to imitate or assist mothers in their manner of childcare. Clearly, this message should guide parenting classes to be tailored to fathers' needs and also be part of parenting programmes that include both parents.

In addition, internationally comparative data collection is needed in order to examine the importance of policy versus gender culture as they affect father involvement. In particular, the quantity of time spent in childcare and the percentage of all childcare performed by each parent, as well as the specific kinds and frequency of tasks performed, have to be assessed. For example, disregarding the time a child spends in external care or is sleeping, on average, how many times must parents change the nappies of, dress, feed, bathe and generally interact with the child per day to ensure well-being? How long, on average, do each of these necessary care activities take? This would allow an estimate of essential task performance and time requirements per day by age of the child. In addition, a list of other tasks that are less hands-on and their estimates can be assessed. Examples include time alone at home when the child sleeps, planning activities, buying items for the child and attending meetings related to the child. An examination of father involvement in essential and less hands-on tasks at each age can lead to a better understanding of involved father engagement.

If, indeed, as Coltrane (1998: 106) claims, 'the move is towards uncoupling gender from caring', then efforts to 'mainstream' care should focus on increasing the value of care vis-a-vis employment, on preventing men from avoiding care and on encouraging women to let it go (Oechsle, 2014). It appears that in order to become truly gender-egalitarian, societies must encourage women to become involved outside the family, and must become 'father-friendly' at multiple levels, and focus on encouraging men to be more involved inside the family. This will clearly benefit children, women and men.

References

Arnalds, Á.A., Eydal, G.B. and Gíslason, I.V. (2013) 'Equal rights to paid parental leave and caring fathers – the case of Iceland', *Icelandic Review on Politics & Administration*, 9(2): 323–44.

Aumann, K., Galinsky, E. and Matos, K. (2011) *The new male mystique*, National Study of the Changing Workforce, New York, NY: Families and Work Institute.

Bünning, M. (2014) 'What remains after the "daddy months"? The impact of taking parental leave on fathers' subsequent participation in paid work, child care and domestic work in Germany', paper presented at the 'Workshop Practices and Policies around Parenthood: Towards New Models of Fatherhood?', Torino (Italy), 8 May.

Coltrane, S. (1998) *Gender and families*, Thousand Oaks, CA: Pine Forge Press.

Den Dulk, L., Groeneveld, S. and Peper, B. (2014) 'Workplace worklife balance support from a capabilities perspective', in B. Hobson (ed) *Worklife balance: the agency and capabilities gap*, Oxford: Oxford University Press, pp 153–73.

Fahlén, S. (2014) 'The agency gap: policies, norms, and working time capabilities across welfare states', in B. Hobson (ed) *Worklife balance: the agency and capabilities gap*, Oxford: Oxford University Press, pp 35–56.

Gregory, A. and Milner, S. (2008) 'Fatherhood regimes and father involvement in France and the UK', *Community, Work & Family*, 11(1): 61–84.

Gregory, A. and Milner, S. (2011) 'What is "new" about fatherhood? The social construction of fatherhood in France and the UK', *Men & Masculinities*, 14(5): 588–606.

Haas, L. and Hwang, C.P. (2008) 'The impact of taking parental leave on fathers' participation in child care and relationships with children: lessons from Sweden', *Community, Work & Family*, 11(1): 85–104.

Haas, L. and Hwang, C.P. (2009) 'Is fatherhood becoming more visible at work? Trends in corporate support for fathers taking parental leave in Sweden', *Fathering: A Journal of Theory, Research, & Practice about Men as Fathers*, 7(3): 303–21.

Hobson, B. (2014) 'Introduction: capabilities and agency for worklife balance – a multidimensional framework', in B. Hobson (ed) *Worklife balance: the agency and capabilities gap*, Oxford: Oxford University Press, pp 1–31.

Hobson, B. and Fahlén, S. (2009) 'Competing scenarios for European fathers: applying Sen's capabilities and agency framework to work–family balance', *The Annals of the American Academy of Political & Social Sciences*, 624: 214–33.

Hobson, B. and Fahlén, S. (2012) 'Father's capabilities for care: a European perspective. Family, ties and care', in H. Bertram and N. Ehlert (eds) *Family transformation in a plural modernity; the Freiburger survey about family transformation in an international comparison*, Obladen: Budrich, pp 99–116.

Hobson, B. and Morgan, D. (2002) 'Introduction', in B. Hobson (ed) *Making men into fathers. Men, masculinities and the social politics of fatherhood*, Cambridge: Cambridge University Press, pp 1–21.

Huerta, M.C., Adema, W., Baxter, J., Han, W.-J., Lausten, M., Lee, R. and Waldfogel, J. (2013) 'Fathers' leave, fathers' involvement and child development: are they related? Evidence from four OECD countries', OECD Social, Employment and Migration Working Papers No 140.

ISTAT-National Institute of Statistics (2010) *Employment rate (20–64 years)*, Roma: ISTAT. Available at: http://noi-italia2012en.istat.it/index.php?id=7&user_100ind_pi1%5Bid_pagina%5D=98&cHash=7410b059e61cae3bff4f10f6b61eaa6a

Javornik, J. (2014) 'Measuring state de-familialism: contesting post-socialist exceptionalism', *Journal of European Social Policy*, 24(3): 240–57.

Jurczyk, K. (2014) 'Fathers: doing work and family', paper presented at the WFRN Conference, New York, June.

Kaufman, G. (2013) *Superdads. How fathers balance work and family in the 21st century*, New York, NY: NYU Press.

Koslowski Smith, A. (2007) 'Working fathers in Europe. Earning and caring?', CRFR Research Briefing 30, Centre for Research on Families and Relationships, The University of Edinburgh. Available at: http://www.socialpolicy.ed.ac.uk/__data/assets/pdf_file/0004/6538/rb30.pdf

Leitner, S. (2003) 'Varieties of familialism. The caring function of the family in comparative perspective', *European Societies*, 5(4): 353–75.

Mutari, E. and Figart, D.M. (2001) 'Europe at a crossroads: harmonization, liberalization, and the gender of work time', *Social Politics*, 8(1): 36–64.

Nepomnyaschy, L. and Waldfogel, J. (2007) 'Paternity leave and fathers' involvement with their young children. Evidence from the American ECLS-B', *Community, Work & Family*, 10: 427–53.

OECD (Organisation for Economic Co-operation and Development) (2012) *OECD family database*, Paris: OECD. Available at: http://www.oecd.org/els/family/database.htm

Oechsle, M. (2014) 'Hidden rules and sense of entitlement – working fathers within organizations', paper presented at the 'Work and Family Researchers Network Conference', New York City, 21 June.

Pfahl, S. and Reuyß, S. (2009) Das neue Elterngeld. Erfahrungen und betriebliche Nutzungsbedingungen von Vätern, Düsseldorf: Hans-Böckler-Stiftung.

Ray, R., Gornick, J.C. and Schmitt, J. (2010) 'Who cares? Assessing generosity and gender inequality in parental leave policy designs in 21 countries', *Journal of European Social Policy*, 20: 196–218.

Ruppaner, L. and Huffman, M.L. (2014) 'Blurred boundaries: gender and work–family interference in cross-national context', *Work & Occupations*, 41(2): 210–36.

Tamilina, L. and Tamilina, N. (2014) 'The impact of welfare states on the division of housework in the family. A new comprehensive theoretical and empirical framework of analysis', *Journal of Family Issues*, 35(6): 825–50.

Tanaka, S. and Waldfogel, J. (2007) 'Effects of parental leave and work hours on fathers' involvement with their babies: evidence from the Millennium Cohort Study', *Community, Work & Family*, 10: 409–26.

Index

Note: Page numbers in *italics* indicate tables. Page numbers followed by the letter "f" indicate footnotes.